DEMOCRACY REMIXED

TRANSGRESSING BOUNDARIES

Studies in Black Politics and Black Communities

Cathy J. Cohen and Fredrick Harris, Series Editors

DEMOCRACY REMIXED

CATHY J. COHEN

OXFORD
UNIVERSITY PRESS

2010

OXFORD
UNIVERSITY PRESS

Oxford University Press, Inc., publishes works that further
Oxford University's objective of excellence
in research, scholarship, and education.

Oxford   New York
Auckland   Cape Town   Dar es Salaam   Hong Kong   Karachi
Kuala Lumpur   Madrid   Melbourne   Mexico City   Nairobi
New Delhi   Shanghai   Taipei   Toronto

With offices in
Argentina   Austria   Brazil   Chile   Czech Republic   France   Greece
Guatemala   Hungary   Italy   Japan   Poland   Portugal   Singapore
South Korea   Switzerland   Thailand   Turkey   Ukraine   Vietnam

Copyright © 2010 by Cathy J. Cohen

Published by Oxford University Press, Inc.
198 Madison Avenue, New York, New York 10016

www.oup.com

Oxford is a registered trademark of Oxford University Press.

Library of Congress Cataloging-in-Publication Data
Cohen, Cathy J., 1961–
Democracy remixed : black youth and the future of American politics / by Cathy J. Cohen.
p.   cm.
Includes bibliographical references and index.
ISBN 978-0-19-537800-9
1. African American youth–Social conditions.   2. African American
youth–Political activity.   3. United States–Race relations.
4. United States–Politics and government.   I. Title.
E185.86.C5815 2010
305.23'508996073—dc22   2010000428

1   3   5   7   9   8   6   4   2

Printed in the United States of America
on acid-free paper

For Ella

Acknowledgments

It has been written a million times that no one is able to write a book alone. The support necessary to identify interesting questions, engage in research, and finally write and review the text of what you hope will be a compelling and well-thought-out manuscript is provided by many colleagues, friends, and family. This book is no different. I owe many, many people a very deep debt of gratitude for their support, especially all of the young people across the country who took time to answer our survey and talk directly to me and the other researchers associated with this project. Thank you!

I have been told that attempting to name anyone is a mistake because undoubtedly I will forget some person or group critical to the process of producing *Democracy Remixed*. I understand the risk but still want to highlight at least a few people for a more public thank you and hope that others who are not mentioned here, but who contributed greatly to this text, will forgive me for issuing a private thank you the next time I communicate with you.

I want to thank all the students, young professionals, and gifted people 30 and under who took time out of their schedules and lives to help with this book and the creation of the Black Youth Project website (www.blackyouthproject.com). Thank you Alexandra Bell, Jamie Bharath, Paula Nicole Booke, Annette Burkeen, Jamilia Celestine-Michener, Aron Cobbs, Nate Cook, Andrew Dilts, Amir Fairdosi, Samuel Galloway, Tanji Gilliam, Marissa Guerrero, Justin Hill, Crystal Holmes, Marcus Hunter, Mosi Ifatunji, Edward James, Ainsley LeSure, Tehama Lopez, Jonathan Lykes, Jerusalem Melke, Julie Merseth, Charles Miniger, Alexandra Moffett-Bateau, Leigh Richie,

Laurence Ralph, Michael Ralph, Scott Roberts, Jonathan Rosa, Theo Rose, Claudia Sandoval, Fallon Wilson, and Deva Woodly.

I also want to extend my thanks to Michael Dawson, Martha Biondi, John Brehm, Fione Dukes, Mary Ann Esquivel, Richard Iton, Diana Jergovic, Waldo Johnson, Bakari Kitwana, Melissa Harris Lacewell, Taeku Lee, Beth Niestat, Eric Oliver, Mary Pattillo, Mario Small, Rolisa Tutwyler, Celesete Watkins-Hayes, and Lisa Wedeen for their intellectual insights and day-to-day support as I labored to finish this book.

The only way this research could have been conducted was with the support of funding agencies. For such assistance, I want to thank The Ford Foundation and specifically Thomasina Williams and Sarah Costa for their generous intellectual and financial support for this work. I also want to express my gratitude to The Robert Wood Johnson Foundation and the Division of the Social Sciences, the Office of the Provost and the Center for the Study of Race, Politics, and Culture at the University of Chicago for providing time, research support, and space for the Black Youth Project. Similarly, a special thank you must be extended to David McBride, Alexandra Dauler, and Jessica Ryan at Oxford University Press and my co-editor Fred Harris for their patience and good will.

When everyone else is gone or are otherwise occupied, the people I know I can depend on for unconditional support are family and friends. Thank you to Charles and Quinters Cohen, Charlene, Henry, Charles Jr. Terry, Tamara, Charles III, Tony, Milton, Milyon, Malaiya, Mikayla, Da'Washa, Ti'Erica, Tiana, Kamontae, Tyshonn, Terryon, Harmony, Peyton, Barbara, Peter, Jason, Asha, Tracye, Amir, Kim, Michelle, Jocelyn, Robert, Thomas, Winston and Beatrice Richie, Winston Jr, Charlotte, Kara, Laurel, Anne, Alex, Camille, Louis, Janet, Doug, Katherine, Len, Jackson, Acey, Mary, Willa, Catlin, Sansi, Laura, Jill, and Nate.

Finally, if any two people have left their imprint on this book and my heart it is Beth Richie and Ella Carmen Cohen-Richie. Beth did lots of heavy-lifting around this book, including reading and commenting on every chapter at least twice. Both of them were extraordinary in the time they afforded me away from our family to work on this book. Most importantly, they both provided me with needed distractions from the book as a reminder of what really is important in life. I cannot imagine my life without them and the book and I are better because of them.

Contents

DEMOCRACY REMIXED

CHAPTER I

"My Petition"

Black Youth and the Promise of Democratic Citizenship

MY INITIAL INSPIRATION for this book was my nephew Terrance, or Terry as our family calls him. Terry was the first grandchild, which meant that all the hopes and dreams of earlier generations were entrusted to him. Yet, despite the best efforts of his mother, his stepfather, and the rest of his family, Terry's life trajectory was different from what we'd hoped. Terry never graduated from high school, and by the time he was 25 he had seen two of his best friends killed by other young black men. Terry spent time in prison and fathered a number of children, while having difficulty finding and holding a job. To an unsympathetic reader, Terry might be the stereotypical black youth, without direction and doing harm to responsible black people trying to get ahead. For many who do not know him, Terry might seem like the young black men and women who appear briefly on the evening news: those young black people who many believe have chosen a "deviant" lifestyle immersed in a culture of poverty, sex, violence, and consumerism.

While researching and writing this book, I came to realize that Terry's story, while special to me, in many ways epitomizes the experiences of many young black people who are living lives of alienation, marginality, and confusion. The idea of young black Americans as marginal subjects is no doubt a familiar theme. The literature on the "underclass" is filled with theories and qualitative accounts of a "sub-population" of black people presumably operating on the normative outskirts of society with little hope of mobility. The irony of Terry's story, however, is that all in all, he did not grow up impoverished with severely limited resources and opportunities. For most of his life, Terry grew up in a two-parent household with each of his parents working at least one job. He did not live in public housing or "the projects," but in a single-family home outside of what might be designated the inner city. He attended what seemed to be a decent public school where his parents were involved and monitored his education.

Terry's story, like those of so many other young black men and women, is much more complicated than the one told by the media, academics, and now celebrities. He is not just another young black person who is culturally deprived and intent on making bad decisions that could end his life prematurely. His life, like the lives of many at the center of this book, is one of contradictions. Terry is someone who believes in the importance of family, but has only recently begun to figure out how to fulfill his parental duties. He works hard daily, but not always in the state-certified economy, where his work ethic would be acknowledged. He is polite, has good manners, and is respectful to adults, but he lives in a context where violence is present and the use of violence is a means to gain respect. He is part of a generation that has been told that their life is much better than that of their elders, yet he and his peers have inherited an economy from which most of the "good" manufacturing jobs are gone, and they face a life in which they are more likely to spend time in prison than to receive a college degree.

Terry's story highlights the collateral damages that result from the absence of low-skilled, living-wage jobs; educational systems that are uncommitted and underresourced to teach and meet the needs of young black people; the transformation of what was once our limited welfare state into a neoliberal project with an emphasis on privatization and personal responsibility; the move toward incarceration in place of employment; the explosion of technology and its adjoining hypercon-sumerism; and the emergence of a dominant rhetoric of a supposedly color-blind society, which asserts that talk of system or institutuional racism is the purview of "victims." And while these largely structural influences explain much of Terry's difficulties, they do not tell the entire story. A central component of his life history also has to do with bad personal decisions, by his own admission.

This is what is interesting about Terry and the young black people who are the subject of this book: their willingness to provide a complex analysis of their lives and this society, even when others do not, and their willingness to highlight both structure and agency in their lives. Terry and I talk a lot about the difficulties he has encountered; his is a balanced account, noting structural barriers such as the lack of jobs one can find with a criminal record but also detailing how he has contributed to his own struggles by, for example, having children without being able to fully care for them, emotionally and materially. While Terry is willing to discuss the impact of being tracked at an early age into special education classes largely because the teachers in his school were unable or unwilling to deal with the learning challenges and energy of young black boys and girls, he also is quick to point out that he did not take advantage of the educational opportunities presented to him.

The complicated story of being young and black in the United States today, I believe, continues to deserve exploration and detail. While others have written important and insightful books about the structural challenges that black youth face as well as their "culture," this book is about the uncertain place of young black people in our political communities.[1] I focus on the political lives of young black people because the political domain is a critical area that shapes many of the opportunities and barriers young blacks will face in other parts of their lives. Politics and policies help determine the quality of economic and educational systems, chances for civic and political participation, even how standards of morality will be used to influence someone's status in society. In the pages that follow, I take a look at the political consequences of being black and young in our society. I explore what black youth think about the government, black communities, and their futures. How do they make political sense of an environment in which more black youth than ever before are in college at the same time that more black youth than ever before are in prison? What is the impact on the political attitudes and actions of young black people living during a time when the first black president has been elected at the same time that there is record unemployment in black communities and among black youth? The young black people at the center of this book will answer these questions.

Although this book is about the political lives of young black people, the boundaries of what counts as politics is always in dispute (or at least should be). So while one obvious political dimension—the relationship between black youth and the state or, more narrowly, the government—will be a constant theme in the pages of this book,

I also delve into the broader political world of young black people. For example, the politics of values, morals, and norms exhibited by and presented to black youth by their peers, by members of black communities, and by the larger society will receive critical attention throughout the book. Given the power of moral argument to frame political debates, early in the book I explore questions surrounding morality and respectability, especially as these concepts inform black community-based discussions about the lives and choices of black youth.

In fact, the question of moral panics in black communities and their impact on black youth is the center of chapter 2. For instance, I take up the question of how black communities engage in a politics of respectability, attempting to win acceptance into the mainstream white society by demonstrating their worth and adherence to dominant norms. At odds with such a political strategy is what many black people believe to be the immoral behavior of significant numbers of black youth. Using the repeated attacks on the black poor and black youth coming from celebrities such as Bill Cosby and Don Imus as a jumping-off point, I explore the questions of whether the black community is engaged in a moral panic targeting black youth and what effect such actions are having on how black youth think about themselves. Are some black leaders contributing to the continued pathologizing and exclusion of young black people, lessening their political status? Have such messages been internalized by black youth, promoting a disparaging view of themselves and other young black people?

Having explored the perceived immorality of black youth by those in black communities, in chapter 3 I turn the tables and ask black youth themselves about the moral politics they adhere to and embrace. Specifically using data from three different approaches—surveys, focus groups, and in-depth interviews—I detail what young people say they are doing sexually. Possibly more important, I explore the sexual attitudes of young people and how they talk about and explain their sexual choices. I am especially interested in how they understand their own moral politics and that of their peers. In contrast to many of the published reports about black youth, they seem ready and willing to take on the responsibility for making unwise choices in the domain of intimacy. I was struck in talking to young blacks with how often they articulated disapproval of the behavior of other young black people, especially when it came to decisions surrounding sex and relationships. Not surprisingly, the same young people expressed more conservative attitudes when asked about topics such as abortion and same-sex marriage—attitudes that were at odds not only with those expressed by white and Latino youth but also with their own reported behaviors.[2] Trying to understand the disjuncture between the articulated and practiced politics of morality among black youth is a key focus of chapter 3.

In chapter 4, I begin to narrow my investigation of the politics that define the lives of black youth, focusing on more traditional subjects like the government. I take on the topic of political alienation among black youth, investigating whether their views toward the government have changed since the election of President Barack Obama. Prior to Obama's election, black youth exhibited greater skepticism than other young people, not only toward elected officials but also to the idea that they were full members of the larger political community. One question I pursue is whether black youth continue to register higher levels of political alienation than young people from other racial and ethnic groups. Do significant numbers of black youth still believe themselves to be second-class citizens who are treated worse than recent immigrants to the United States? Moreover, what must we do as a nation to ensure the participation of black youth in civic and political life, so that they can help shape our priorities and principles?

Having established higher levels of some forms of alienation among black youth, in chapter 5 I explore to what degree such alienation might be related to whether and how black youth engage in the public sphere attempting to voice their own political agenda. I detail the political and civic participation of black youth, looking at 2004 and 2008. In 2008, record numbers of young black adults turned up to the polls to vote for Obama. Should we expect young black people to remain politically and civically engaged in the years to come? Beyond voting, are there ways the politics of black youth differs from that of their white and Latino counterparts? And how do we account for the significant numbers of black youth who refrain from participating in any form of political action? I discuss what I label the politics of invisibility among black youth: a politics of absence that mutes their voices and needs from the government. While some young blacks believe invisibility to be a successful survival strategy, I explore the negative ramifications of removing oneself from the political process.

Finally, in chapter 6 I focus on the racial politics that young black people face and embrace in light of the election of the country's first black president. Does the election of Obama signal both the end of black politics and the beginning of a postracial society? Or do young black people still find themselves at the bottom of America's racial order? The data I discuss suggest that a wide gap still exists between young whites and blacks when it comes to assessing the racial landscape of the country. What will it take to bridge such a divide? Similarly, while President Obama seems willing to gesture, more often than not, to a time in the not-so-distant future when race will be much less of a problem for young people of color, black youth seem much less optimistic that such a day will arrive anytime soon. What does the distance in racial optimism between the president and many black youth mean for the future of black politics and the politics that will guide the country—that is, what others have called broadly American politics?

This book contributes to a critical dialogue about the lives of black youth and their role in the future of American politics. At the heart of this project is an attempt to open up discussions about how to transform the lives of some of our most marginal citizens while continuing to support the advancement of some of our most socially mobile citizens— both young black Americans. There is a fundamental question that has to be addressed: can our current configuration of politics address the substantial inequality that defines the lives of many black youth and other marginalized young people or must we imagine and implement a more radical response to the status of some of our most vulnerable citizens—black youth? Ironically, missing from much of the debate over the lives of black youth and the political course of the country has been the sustained and detailed presentation of the voices, opinions, and attitudes of black youth. This book fills that void by asking young black people directly what they think about race and racism, the impact of having a child before you are married, the election of President Obama, and what must be done to improve their lives, among other topics.

Driving every chapter are the voices of young black people as they define for themselves and in their own words their hopes, fears, and dreams as detailed through surveys, focus groups, and in-depth interviews. Throughout the book three sources of data figure prominently in my discussions of black youth. The first is data from the Black Youth Project, a research effort centered on exploring and highlighting the attitudes and actions of young black people. The first stage of this work included the mounting of a nationally representative survey of black, white, and Latino young people aged 15–25. The sample included an oversample, or the inclusion of larger numbers, of black youth and a small oversample of Latino youth for greater statistical accuracy of these two groups in our analysis. The survey was constructed using the lives of young black people as the normative experience, so the survey instrument includes questions about rap music, race and racism, and feelings toward the government.[3] The survey was then followed in 2006 by a series of 40 in-depth interviews, primarily with black youth from the Midwest who answered the survey. Responses to some of the questions from the in-depth interviews will also be featured throughout the book.

The second major data source used in the book is the Mobilization, Change, and Political and Civic Engagement Study (MCPCE), which investigated whether and how the heightened political environment surrounding the 2008 presidential election would impact the political attitudes and behaviors of individuals in the United States. The data came from a nationally representative sample and were collected in three waves or parts by Knowledge Networks using an online computer methodology. The first wave of data was collected between October 18 and November 2, 2008. These data reflect the attitudes of respondents just days before the 2008 presidential election. The second wave was collected in May 2009, about six months after the election. The final, third wave was collected during November and December 2009, just a year after the election of Obama. There were over 3,181 respondents in the first wave of data of which one-third were aged 18–35 and two-thirds were people of color.[4]

Third, throughout the book I refer to comments from a series of focus groups with black youth aged 18–24 in Chicago in 2004 and then again in 2009. I held three focus groups in 2004. One group consisted of only young women who identified as heterosexual; another group was comprised of heterosexual males; and a third group included young people who were gay, lesbian, or bisexual. In 2009, only weeks after the inauguration of President Obama, I held one final focus group with a diverse group of young blacks. In all four groups, I wanted to hear in greater detail how these young people thought about their lives, the government, and the country. Finally, I will mention a few other data sources throughout, in the hope of rooting my analysis in more substantial evidence than is generally found in anecdotal accounts of black youth. While data will figure prominently in chapters 3, 4, and 5, the reader will always find an accessible discussion of the findings from our data analysis in every chapter.

Ironically, the ideas and words of my nephew Terry will not be featured in this book. He is now too old to be included. When I started thinking about this book over 10 years ago, Terry was in his midtwenties; he is now 35. The empirical research in which this book is rooted focuses on young black Americans aged 15–25. While Terry was the initial inspiration for this work, his story is a familiar theme in the lives of middle-class, working-class, and poor black youth across the country. It is a troubling fact that elements of Terry's story have now become customary parts of the coming-of-age process for substantial numbers of young black men and women, boys and girls. I had hoped that the dilemmas Terry faced throughout his life would no longer exist for the generation of young people that came after him, but the data I have gathered suggests that these issues are alive and well.

Some might still wonder: why write a book on the political lives of black youth when the country has arrived at a point when we have elected our first black president? To many, this incredible milestone marks a radical turning point in the country's history of using race and racism to separate, divide, and marginalize. For example, the majority of young whites, as the data detail in the final chapter, believe that racism is no longer a major problem in the United States. Thus, for these individuals the mere mention of race and surely a book focused on black youth that discusses, in part, their racial attitudes, is a step in the wrong direction. Similarly, black leaders such as congressional majority whip James Clyburn has argued that with the election of Barack Obama "every child has lost every excuse."[5]

It is my belief that racism, as it does for the majority of black youth in this country, continues to be a major problem for the nation, even with President Obama at the helm. Far from relying on excuses to explain their lack of progress, one need only survey the structural environment many young blacks inhabit to gain a greater sense of the challenges they continue to face. For example, as I finish this book the unemployment rate for black youth is 30.5 percent, three times that for the general population. The October 2009 unemployment rate of 34.5 percent for black men aged 16–24 has been said to rival unemployment rates witnessed during the Great Depression. Month after month, the numbers indicate that African-American youth are the group hit hardest by the economic recession that started in 2008.[6] Given the negative structural environment that many black youth face, it seems only appropriate to briefly explore just some of these conditions before launching into the rest of the book.

STRUCTURE (AND AGENCY)

By now, the discussion of structural conditions facing black youth has been rehearsed with regularity. Many people know that black youth suffer disproportionately from poverty, HIV/AIDS, childhood obesity, incarceration, and unemployment, and the list could go on. One particular area that has garnered significant attention is the disproportionate incarceration of young black people. For example, the work of the Sentencing Project has brought to light many of the racial disparities that exist in our criminal justice system. Research has shown, for example, that one in six black men was incarcerated by 2001; that of black males born today it is expected that one in three will spend time in prison at some point in their lives; that on any given day one in eight black men in their twenties is in jail.[7] Incarceration is not an issue that threatens only black men. Black women are three times as likely as white women to be in jail or in prison, and 30 percent of the women incarcerated under state or federal jurisdiction are black.[8] More generally, while the United States has only 5 percent of the world's population, 25 percent of all the world's prisoners are behind bars in the United States. Currently, we incarcerate 2.3 million Americans. As a nation, we incarcerate a higher percentage of our population than any other country, a disproportionate number of them black and young.[9]

Similarly disturbing are data outlining disparities in high school graduation rates between white and black youth. An article in the *Journal of Blacks in Higher Education* observes that across the country there are significant differences in the overall high school graduation rate between blacks and whites. Nationally in 2005, 55.3 percent of black students graduated from high school, compared to 77.6 percent of white students. An even greater trend of such disparities can be found at the state level, with a gap of 38 percentage points between the white and black graduation rates in Michigan, for example. The article also notes that "nationwide, about 69 percent of all students graduate from high school on time. But in graduation rates there are major differences between blacks and whites. In the United States, 76.1 percent of white students graduate from high school on time. For blacks, only 51.2 percent of all students graduate from high school on schedule."[10]

Beyond incarceration and education, we have to explain how we as a nation allow so many black children to live in poverty. While approximately 11 percent of non-Hispanic white children lived in poverty in 2008, the poverty rate for black children was 35 percent.[11] Furthermore, when we ask about the number of children living in low-income families, we find that a majority of black children live under such conditions—61 percent—compared to 27 percent of white children.[12] Black youth and their families have also been hit especially hard by the recession. Back in August 2003, 30 percent of African-American youth aged 16–19 were unemployed, compared to only 15 percent of white youth in the same age range.[13] The seasonally adjusted unemployment rate for black youth aged 16–19 in October 2009 was 41.3 percent, compared to 25.3 percent for 16- to 19-year-old whites.[14] More specifically, a 2008 *Demos* report stated that "young African-American men have the highest rate of unemployment among young people and the lowest percentage of individuals participating in the workforce.... Between 1979 and 2000, the labor participation rate among non-college-educated young men declined for all racial groups, though African-American men experienced the steepest declines."[15] As others have noted, the combination of the loss of manufacturing jobs, the use of predatory lending practices, an unparalleled number of foreclosures, a shocking drop in property values, and the continued use of discriminatory hiring practices in a jobless recovery has meant that black youth and their families face not a recession but a "silent depression" and the loss of any generational progress for young blacks.[16]

Unfortunately, I could fill this chapter with similar disturbing statistics that point to the dangerous and defeating lived conditions that black youth face. I recognize that the mere presentation of statistics can be overwhelming and not very helpful in trying to map out how these numbers correspond to daily challenges and choices faced by black youth across the country. In fact, some might challenge my focus and suggest that we should pay less attention to the structural barriers black youth face, and instead concentrate on the significant numbers of young blacks who have found a way to at least persist and succeed in the midst of such crushing conditions. It is right to applaud those young people, but we must also face the fact that morally the country has failed many young black people who are more likely to live in poverty, who are at risk when they go to school because of uncontrolled violence in their neighborhoods, who when they show up at school are less likely to graduate than their white counterparts, and who, if they graduate, will face higher rates of unemployment, even with a college degree.

Another way to think about the structure many black youth face is to question what these statistics—that repeatedly indicate that black youth receive less support yet have more burden than other young people—tell us about how the country values black children and young adults, as well as what progress we are willing to forego in order to ignore, and thus maintain, such racial disparities? While I strongly believe that the nation's commitment to the progress of black youth is a moral obligation, others may be convinced of our responsibility by understanding that by ignoring the basic needs of far too many black youth, we have created a crisis not only for these young people but also for our nation.

A recent study by McKinsey & Company details the economic cost to the country of allowing such disparities to continue.

> If the gap between black and Latino student performance and white student performance had been similarly narrowed, GDP in 2008 would have been between $310 billion and $525 billion higher, or 2 to 4 percent of GDP. The magnitude of this impact will rise in the years ahead as demographic shifts result in blacks and Latinos becoming a larger proportion of the population and workforce.[17]

Again, it is one thing to acknowledge that black young people have a far tougher road to travel toward success than other young people; it is another thing to acknowledge the role of government policies in helping to construct the uneven terrain black youth must navigate. Many have commented on the changing political and economic priorities of the country as its presidents since Nixon, in particular Reagan, have adopted a more neoliberal approach to governing.[18] By "neoliberalism" I mean, as many other scholars have previously written, a governing agenda that includes the increased privatization of government programs and institutions like public schools or even prisons; the scaling back and in some cases elimination of the welfare state, that is, government assistance to the poor, low-income, and elderly; a move toward fewer economic regulations and more trade that is free of constraints that would protect jobs, the environment, and entities such as unions, in order to produce greater profits for companies that, some would argue, will lead to more jobs. Neoliberalism also involves an intensifying rhetoric that is grounded in the belief that markets, in and of themselves, are better able than governments to produce, in particular, economic outcomes that are fair, sensible, and good for all. This rhetoric is bolstered by a discourse that is more familiar to the larger public, one that emphasizes personal responsibility and the role of individual agency or choice in determining one's success.

The problem with neoliberalism, for those invested in the future of black youth, is that it has meant that many of the resources and beliefs that blacks struggled to win are now being lost, such as the idea that the government should be an active, if not "the" active, player in guaranteeing equality and providing for the basic needs of its citizens. This change in the governing agenda leaves current generations of black youth with fewer options and fewer supports. As noted, the loss of much of the manufacturing industry, and with it relatively high-paying, low-skill jobs that once helped to expand the black middle class has meant that black youth who are less likely to finish high school or college will have greater difficulty landing a decent paying job with which they can support their families. Further, the privatization of important and public institutions like schools suggests that profit, not societal responsibility, will strongly influence the decision-making of institutions that are critically important to the well-being and progress of young black people and their communities.

The importance of government policies that shape the environment in which many young black people exist has to be recognized and accepted, especially in a book on the political lives of young black Americans. And while I believe that most individuals would acknowledge that the conditions evidenced by the statistics listed earlier make it difficult for young black people to get ahead, many would again point to the majority of black youth, who despite such circumstances never engage in violence, attend school daily, and do what they must to make a better life for themselves. From this perspective, what is thought most important to improve the lives of black youth is not more government involvement but individual will and better decision-making by black youth and their parents. Here the focus is on their agency and that of their parents.

Increasingly, this focus on the agency of black youth and black parents to make better decisions has come to dominate the range of solutions offered to address the challenges faced by black youth. In the words of individuals such as Bill Cosby and even, at times, President Obama, one can hear them discounting structural explanations for problems black youth suffer and instead emphasizing their personal agency. While telling black parents and children that they need to turn off the television and read a book makes for a nice sound bite, especially when the intended audience is as much those outside of black communities as those inside them, it ignores the reality that structure or environment limits agency and choice. The evolving literature on agency suggests that one cannot understand personal choice without attention to the surrounding conditions in which a person exists. For example, Nobel Prize–winner Amartya Sen writes: "Indeed, individual agency is, ultimately, central to addressing these deprivations. On the other hand, the freedom of agency that we individually have is inescapably qualified and constrained by the social, political and economic opportunities that are available to us. There is a deep complementarity between individual agency and social arrangements."[19]

It was this sense of the complexity of agency and structure that I heard voiced most often when talking to black youth about their lives. The importance of structure in shaping their lives was undeniable, but they never allowed me to discount the control they had over their own lives, however limited. To do so would be an insult to these strong and insightful young people. However, even after acknowledging the intersection of structure and agency in the political lives of black youth, we still have to ask why they hold such a precarious position in our nation. I am talking about our lack of will not only to change the underperforming and failed schools that many attend or to create meaningful avenues of employment for them, but at a very basic level to provide for their very survival. Are they not full members of our political community?

CITIZEN OUTSIDER—THE PRECARIOUS POSITION OF BLACK YOUTH

In Chicago where I live and work, over the last three years, there has been a killing spree, an epidemic of violence, with young black people the targets. The *Huffington Post* reports that "before 2006, an average of 10–15 students were fatally shot each year [in Chicago]. That climbed to 24 fatal shootings in the 2006–7 school year, 23 deaths and 211 shootings in the 2007–8 school year and 34 deaths and 290 shootings last school year."[20] Another article indicates that "more than 40 children younger than 18 have been murdered in Chicago this year [2009], and at least 298 students enrolled in Chicago public schools have been shot since September 2008."[21] Phillip Jackson, of the Black Star Project, a local program working to, among other things, stop the violence directed at black youth, has asserted that "605 children [were] shot—wounded or killed—in the city over the last year.[22]

In July 2007, then senator Obama, in a speech on the spate of violence in Chicago, noted that "during the course of this past school year, the number of public school students who were killed in this city was higher than the number of soldiers from this whole state [Illinois] who were killed in Iraq. Think about that. At a time when we're spending $275 million a day on a war overseas, we're neglecting the war that's being fought in our own streets."[23] Unfortunately, we can now amend President Obama's remarks, noting that more young people were killed in Chicago last year than soldiers from Illinois were killed in both Iraq and Afghanistan. And while the number of young blacks killed in Chicago varies from report to report, or speech to speech, depending on when one starts counting, in all such accounts the numbers are unbelievable and should be unacceptable.

What makes the killing of black youth in Chicago even more poignant today, if something besides their deaths was needed, is that many of these murders are taking place within walking distance or a bus ride from the Chicago home of the president of the United States. Journalist Ed Pilkington of the *Guardian* notes that all of the deaths are taking place in black communities, with white neighborhoods in Chicago escaping the deadly violence that threatens the young. "The centre of the blood-letting is the city's poor and overwhelmingly black South Side, precisely the spot where Michelle grew up and Barack set out on his self-proclaimed 'improbable journey' as a community organizer in his 20s.... It is as if there are two Chicagos, two Americas."[24] The topic of whether there are two Americas is a question repeated often in Chicago and black communities across the country by frustrated parents and scared young people: Why is this country willing to spend billions of dollars to fight wars in Iraq and Afghanistan and not protect young black people at home?

The question of the political status of black youth was raised again, just as I was submitting this manuscript, when the killing of Derrion Albert was reported on the news. Albert, a 16-year-old black honor-roll student in Chicago, was beaten to death on his way home from school on September 24, 2009. We know the specifics of Derrion's brutal murder because it was caught on a cell phone camera in a video that was seen around the world, as it was both shown by broadcast media and posted on Internet sites such as YouTube. As can be seen on the video, Derrion was hit repeatedly with a board and then stomped while on the ground by a group of boys and young men. He was pronounced dead on the same day at 6:17 P.M. at Advocate Christ Medical Center.

All reports of his murder underscore the fact that Derrion was an innocent victim. He was described as a "Grandmomma's boy" who "loved wrestling, basketball, and shopping." His mother said, "He was a great kid, a good student." She recounts that she and Derrion "were getting ready to start a plan for college. That's all we would stay focused on.... [We were] moving to the next stage."[25] Derrion was not a part of a gang and seemed to have no connection to the young men who were fighting with fists and boards other than the fact that some attended the same school he did—Christian Fenger Academy High School—and that on that day they were fighting on the path he used to travel home from school. Articles indicate that a shooting earlier in the day that involved two groups of students from different neighborhoods, both of whom attended Fenger, was the catalyst for the fight.

Bystanders said the entire fight took less than five minutes. But in that short gap of time, many young lives would be lost forever.

There are many things that are horrifying and revolting on the footage documenting the killing of Derrion Albert. First and foremost is the brutality of Derrion's death. It is sickening to watch this young man being struck by a splintered wooden plank in what appears to be the back of his head, knocking him unconscious; to watch him fall to the ground where his body hits the hard concrete, forcing him to endure yet another blow; to watch him gain consciousness and try to get up, only to be punched in the face and then hit again with another wooden board; and then to watch his limp body sink for the last time to the ground where his attackers surround him, kicking and stomping him. It is hard to watch this video, imagining the physical and emotional pain Derrion endured, blindsided and confused, as he merely tried to walk home from school, the target of such violence by individuals with whom he had no fundamental tie.

If while watching this video one is able to take one's eyes away from what is happening to Derrion, one will also see images that fill out the desperate nature of this event. For example, one sees and hears cars blowing their horns at the kids fighting in the street, as the drivers, either too scared or unconcerned, refuse to stop and instead try desperately to make their way through this conflict. In addition, one sees young black men, some without shirts, fighting each other with fists and boards, intent on hurting those they perceive as enemies. Finally, at the end of the short but devastating video, one hears the cries of other young black people trying to help their friend Derrion. They beg him to get up, shouting, "Derrion get up please!" Recognizing that he cannot help himself, they, and staff from the Agape Community Center, drag Derrion into the building, hoping that someone there can bring this young man back to life. Unfortunately, their attempts to help Derrion come too late.

In the screams and efforts of these young black people to save one of their own, we are confronted with, at least, part of the reality of their lives. While the young people who try to save Derrion were not killed or beaten this time, they have to wonder when they will be the target of unexpected violence. When will a bus ride or walk home from school be their last, as they are killed by a stray bullet or a board to the back of their head? And why is no one, anyone, willing to protect them? Are their lives not worthy of protection? Are they not full members of our political community? Does no one care about them?

It is the question of the perceived worth of young black people by the larger society, specifically the government, by black people and by other young black people that is at the heart of this book. Again, how do young black people, who often rightly perceive themselves as tangential to American democracy, create and understand their political lives? While the death of Derrion Albert may seem an extreme case, it underscores the question of the tenuous position of black youth in the political sphere. Derrion Albert did everything we asked of him. He went to school, avoided any gang affiliation, involved himself in productive activities like wrestling, and thought about how to better his life by going to college. Derrion deserves our sympathy and the outrage that accompanies his death. However, if our concern and this book only focused on the political status of young black people who seem to be good and productive, the innocent victims in black communities, those who have used the opportunities provided to better their lot, we would do little to clarify the complicated and contradictory experience of being young and black in the United States today. We must pay attention to the challenges facing *all* young black people, whose lives are filled with contradiction as they struggle to do better than the generations who came before them.

As the video of Derrion Albert's murder makes clear, there is no monolithic experience of young black people today. Albert was killed by other young black men who may have internalized both dominant and community-based messages that suggest that the lives of black youth, in particular poor black youth, are worth less than others in society. However, if we seek to explain the murder of Albert by focusing only on the actions of Silvonus Shannon, 19, Eugene Riley, 18, and Eric Carson, 16, the three black youth charged with first-degree murder in his death, we miss an opportunity to address the numerous factors that created an environment in which the life of another young black person is made irrelevant in the middle of mindless rage. What is commonly deemed "black-on-black crime" may be facilitated in part by the discourse and practice of neoliberalism and the ensuing moral panics in black communities which signal the secondary or even superfluous status of black youth. This is not an attempt to excuse those accused of killing Derrion Albert, but to understand the reality they encounter daily—one that could produce such reckless disregard for human life, even momentarily.

It is the totality of black youth's experiences, attitudes, and actions that this book interrogates and discusses. That means that we must ask not only how the deaths of young people like Derrion Albert could happen but also where the three young men accused of killing Derrion Albert fit into our political community. How do we discuss the difficulties faced by many young black people who come not from extreme poverty but middle- and working-class communities, whose families thought their trajectory would be higher? Similarly, how do we understand and promote the success of many young blacks who are graduating at higher rates from colleges and universities than their parents' generation, are moving up the employment ladder and holding prestigious positions of political and economic power at ever growing rates, and are living what is thought to be the American dream of opportunity and mobility? Given the varied and sometimes desperate reality faced by black youth, how do all black youth make sense of their political lives—lives that for some include intolerable levels of violence and for others unprecedented opportunities? What does it mean to be a young black American today and how will their views, opinions, and lives shape the future of American politics?

This book is a plea that we as individuals and as a country do something radical and significant to change the life trajectory (and increase the life span) of black youth. It is also a challenge to black youth and all those who care about them to acknowledge the things they can change through their own agency, while also recognizing the ways their structural environment both limits their power to make real choices—their agency—and imposes high costs on their lives. Throughout the pages of this book I struggle to understand our societal, communal, and human responsibility to black youth, and theirs to each other and to society at large. How do the political, economic, and social realities of young black Americans that are detailed in the following pages reflect or contradict our national, communal, and individual commitments to equality, respect, and community? Hopefully, in the pages that follow we can gain clarity on what must be done to fulfill the promise of full democratic citizenship for black youth.

CHAPTER 2

"Gangsta Rap Made Me Do It"

Bill Cosby, Don Imus, and
Black Moral Panics

O N JULY 9, 2007, in Detroit, delegates from the NAACP's ninety-eighth annual convention held a public burial for the N-word. Delegates from across the country marched through downtown Detroit as part of a ceremonial funeral that included a horse-drawn carriage pulling a pine-box coffin with the N-word inside. Atop the coffin was a black wreath. Like the symbolic burial that the NAACP held for Jim Crow sixty-three years earlier in the same city, this coffin was buried and marked with a headstone in a historically black cemetery. Speaking at the funeral, Detroit mayor Kwame Kilpatrick, who was labeled "the hip-hop mayor," said, "Today we're not just burying the N-word, we're taking it out of our spirit, we are taking it out of our minds. To bury the N-word, we gotta bury the pimps and the hos and the hustlers. Let's bury all the nonsense that comes with this." He continued, "Die, N-word, and we don't want to see you 'round here no more!"[1] His comments were greeted by cheers and applause from the thousands who had congregated at Hart Plaza to hear the speeches of dignitaries and the music of a gospel choir.[2] As we now know, Kilpatrick would fill his remaining time as mayor fighting more than the N-word. He was forced to resign on September 4, 2008, when he pled guilty to two felony charges for obstruction of justice relating to an affair he had with his chief of staff. Ironically, it was Kilpatrick who used the N-word in his 2008 Detroit State of the City address as he attacked the media and his opponents for their demonization of him and his family.[3]

Two rap innovators, Kurtis Blow and Eric B., were also on hand for the funeral. Both artists encouraged young people not to buy rap music they really didn't want—specifically, songs full of profanity and those that are degrading to black people. And while the Reverend Wendall Anthony, a member of the board of directors of the NAACP, stated that the funeral was not an attack on young people or hip-hop, the presence of these two rap stars, the public announcement that the event had been initiated by the youth and college division of the organization, and the growing public outcry against rap artists who use such words as "nigga," "bitch," and "ho," made the reverend's declaration hard to believe.[4] The funeral also seemed to have another motivation, namely, to show the public that the black community could be just as critical of black people, in particular young black rap artists, as it was of Don Imus.[5] Julian Bond, chairman of the NAACP, explained that "while we are happy to have sent a certain radio cowboy back to his ranch, we ought to hold ourselves to the same standard.... If he can't refer to our women as 'hos,' then we shouldn't either."[6]

Not surprisingly, some critics have suggested that the funeral proved, once and for all, that the NAACP at worst is completely out of touch with the issues of importance to black people or at best has the wrong priorities. They argue that structural conditions, including massive incarceration, failing educational systems, and a lack of living-wage jobs, not the symbolic burial of the N-word, should garner the NAACP's immediate attention and energy. Professor of race and popular culture Todd Boyd said the funeral was an "incredible waste of time." He added, "They are putting a Band-Aid on a bullet wound. The issues that plague black America far transcend the usage of a word."[7]

At the center of such debates about the NAACP's priorities, and black politics in general, are young black Americans. This group is thought by many to have more opportunities and agency than any other generation of black Americans in the history of this country. It is also a group that is increasingly vilified, not only by the media but—possibly more important—by black leaders and celebrities. Whether it is Bill Cosby, Oprah Winfrey, or Julian Bond, it seems that the civil rights generation has seen enough of what they consider to be the bad behavior and self-destructive culture of too many young black Americans.

They are tired and they aren't going to take it anymore, so they have made up their minds to go public with their disgust.

The idea of holding young people accountable for their actions is not a new one for black communities. This principle, which is central to the assertion "It takes a village to raise a child," is widely accepted among black people. However, focusing on individual accountability does raise a question of balance. Specifically, how do we parse out responsibility for the marginal status and lived conditions of many young black Americans? What responsibility do parents, communities, governments, and corporations have in shaping the life trajectory of black youth? Moreover, how do we resist the instinct to panic and demonize every aspect of black youth culture that is perceived as deviating from mainstream norms? It is, in fact, the multiple perspectives of black people about what constitutes communal priorities and responsibilities that continue to make vibrant black politics today.

A simple outline of the structural difficulties facing black youth today, like the one presented in chapter 1, is all that many people need to fully ascertain the challenges that exist in our post-civil-rights-movement era. This generation of young blacks may not have experienced the hardened system of Jim Crow, but they still must negotiate, on a daily basis, the absence of low-skill, living-wage jobs, a dysfunctional public education system, a crumbling neoliberal state that is short on social support and high on privatization and corporate control, and an incarceration system that negatively affects nearly every black family in some way. This is not to suggest that all young black people face dire circumstances. For some, the structural readjustment that took place during the last thirty years, as well as policies such as affirmative action, have created new opportunities, especially in higher education and employment. But for far too many young blacks, the structural landscape of their lives is still rife with racism, limited opportunities, and threatening social conditions. As one 21-year-old black male explained, "What concerns me is having a job and *living*. Will I be alive?...It's a very tough struggle because the United States isn't a fair country."[8]

And while structural conditions are still cause for concern, as I discussed in chapter 1, they do not tell the entire story of young black Americans' lives and the many obstacles they face. Certainly, the rhetoric that surrounds black youth is another important issue. Specifically, how has the public come to characterize and imagine young black people? In chapter 1, which explored how factors outside of black communities shape the lived experience of black youth, I asked how young black Americans, especially those most marginal, understand the political world that confronts them. How do they deal with violence, incarceration, and even different levels of opportunity at the beginning of the twenty-first century? In this chapter, I will focus internally, turning my attention to the ways members of black communities, especially some black elites, depict and evaluate our young people.

When we asked black youth on surveys, through in-depth interviews and in focus groups, how they believe older black Americans view them, there was almost unanimity in their reports that older blacks are afraid of, are disgusted with, and generally disrespect black youth. In one of our in-depth interviews with black youth, a 21-year-old young woman from Chicago said that older blacks "think we're disrespectful and we're lazy." A 17-year-old male from Milwaukee reported that older blacks "look down on us, frown on us." A 19-year-old young woman from Chicago said that when she talks with older blacks at her job at a nursing home they tell her, "You know what? It's so many ignorant black little kids out there and they're not grateful for what we had to do to get them where they are now." Finally, a 22-year-old male from Chicago talked about what happens when he walks down the street in black neighborhoods. "If I'm walking down the street an old black lady will clutch her purse like I'm about to take it. You know it's kind of sad, but that's just how it is. They, they don't give us the same respect. They don't feel we're superior. It's like we all doing bad things."[9]

Ironically, the voices *inside* black communities may be the most effective at both publicly and internally demonizing young blacks. When Bill Cosby, Oprah Winfrey, or even President Obama depict young blacks as having lost their way, they point to self-destructive decisions, behavior, and culture. They rarely mention with equal verve the structural difficulties this generation faces. These leaders legitimize an analysis of the condition of young blacks that reduces—if not negates—the responsibility of the state and the public to improve the life trajectory of these young Americans. When "black crusaders" such as Cosby and Winfrey neglect to mention racism as an important factor inhibiting the progress of young blacks, their silence conveys to the country that racism is no longer a problem.[10] Moreover, when black elites draw the line between honorable, hardworking, and respectable young blacks, and deviant, drug-selling, and baby-producing ones, they rearticulate a class and culture divide that has existed in black communities for centuries.

It is therefore important to examine the powerful words of black elites such as Bill Cosby, not only because his analysis is incomplete, largely incorrect, and based on at best anecdotal stories, but also because the stories he tells seem to resonate with many in black communities, young and old. In his representations, Cosby has stumbled on some partial truths that instinctively conjure up images of mostly poor, young black people and their parents. These images, though completely void of details about the serious economic and political challenges these individuals face, are hauntingly familiar to many black people (myself included) as they look out their windows, visit relatives, and drive through poor black neighborhoods.

Unfortunately, Cosby is not alone in his ability to create fact from fiction or—more accurately—weave "truths" from familiar and pervasive images. The Don Imus controversy and its evolution into a "high-tech lynching" of all rap artists is a particularly notable example of this phenomenon. The Imus episode injected panic into black communities over what is perceived to be the publicly visible deviant behavior and culture of too many young black Americans in the global cultural form of rap music. Let me state unequivocally that yes, there is cause for concern and action regarding the sexist, violent, and homophobic lyrics and images that some rap artists and their record companies promote. However, the panic over rap music that was fueled by the Imus affair is not only, or mostly, about the denigrating lyrics of rap artists; it also encompasses a broader, urgent concern on the part of many black Americans that the current generation of young black adults, or at least the most visible segments of that group, are engaged in behaviors that not only threaten their very survival but also negatively affect the progress of respectable middle- and working-class black people.

Many have rightly interrogated the words and actions of Don Imus, but I will focus instead on the firestorm about rap music that was heightened by Imus's suggestion that the degrading phrases he used to describe the Rutgers University women's basketball team, including "nappy-headed hos," originated in black communities and his assertion that black men, especially rappers, regularly use such language to denigrate black women. He went on to argue that the same black leaders that were condemning him for such language had, for years, been silent when similar words were used by their brethren in the rap industry. I am especially interested in how black leaders responded to Imus's defense, nearly tripping over each other to be the first in line to condemn rap music. Even Oprah got into the act, dedicating two days of her program to a discussion she labeled "After Imus: Now What?"

Interestingly, that discussion focused exclusively on rap music; not one person on Oprah's panel of experts seemed at all interested in the many other forms of misogyny that black women face each and every day.

The stature, words, and influence of black elites have legitimized a public fear of black youth that must be challenged. Their explanations for the failures of young black people, particularly poor, young black people, while incomplete, resonate not only with many white people but also, and more important, with many black people. And these partial truths have the potential to significantly and negatively influence how young blacks think of themselves and their peers. The 21-year-old black woman from Chicago who earlier suggested that older black people think of black youth as disrespectful and lazy explained that such an assessment of black youth is probably warranted. "Disrespectful and lazy would probably be the two words [I would use to describe black youth]. We don't think we supposed to go to school or work. And if they try to tell us to do it, we so quick to say 'shut up' or 'sit down,' you know, disrespect them. Yeah, we very disrespectful, very." Sadly, similar sentiments highlighting the deficiencies among black youth were routinely heard from black youth when asked to describe their peers. A 19-year-old black woman from Chicago said, "these [black] kids now don't have no respect. None. If you sit...just one day on the bus while kids get out of school and you hear how they talk. You'll be ashamed to be black. I'm ashamed to be black sometimes when I'm on a bus and see a lot of white people that just got out of work on the bus trying to get to the train so they can get home. And I feel ashamed too because it's like wow, you wouldn't believe the stuff like that come out a 12- or a 13-year-old mouth."

Public opinion research indicates that what I am calling partial truths—those familiar images and narratives of young black people engaged in seemingly deviant behavior that are accepted as truth—do not need irrefutable evidence to be effective. Such representations are used to justify the public's instinctive biases about certain groups, in this case that both hip-hop and its putative community of young adherents are pathological. Moreover, these narratives are especially effective in supporting distinctions between those seen as "respectable" black people—the "eloquent" black women on the Rutgers women's basketball team—and those characterized as deviant—the black rappers under attack. Political scientist Martin Gilens, in his work exploring the impact of media distortions on racial representations of the poor, argues that the mass media is a critical information source for most

TABLE 2.1   Rap Music's Perceived Influence on Black Youth

Influence of rap music on black youth	Respondents agreeing (%)
Encourages having sex too early	70
Encourages multiple sexual partners	61
Encourages taking drugs such as marijuana	69
Encourages illegal activity such as selling drugs	65
Encourages taking school less seriously	63
Encourages disrespect of elders	65
Encourages having babies before married	54
Encourages disrespect of police	63
Encourages violent behavior	70
Encourages poor treatment of women	76

Source: The Black Youth Project

Americans and that media "distortions of social conditions are therefore likely to result in public misperceptions that reinforce existing biases and stereotypes."[11]

The truth of Gilens's observation is evident in findings from a national survey I designed to explore the attitudes of black Americans aged 30 and older toward younger black people.[12] When respondents were asked about the influence of rap music on young black Americans, their evaluations of this art form were overwhelmingly negative. For example, 76 percent believed it encouraged them to treat women poorly; 70 percent believed it influenced them to have sex too early; 70 percent believed it encouraged them to engage in violent behavior; and 69 percent believed it encouraged them to use drugs such as marijuana. The list of negative consequences believed to derive from listening to rap music is staggering, as is detailed in table 2.1.

Other data from the same study suggest that black Americans aged 30 and older are also concerned about the behavior of young blacks and the threat it poses to the larger black community. In the same survey, 50 percent of respondents agreed with the statement "The behavior of too many young black Americans threatens the progress of *respectable* black people who are trying to do the right things." It is important to note here that 27 percent neither agreed nor disagreed with that statement; that is, only 23 percent stated that they outright disagreed with the idea that the behavior of young black people threatens the progress of respectable black people. The same general pattern of agreement or ambivalence with lower levels of disagreement

TABLE 2.2 The Behavior of Too Many Young Black Americans Threatens the Progress of Respectable Black People Who Are Trying to Do the Right Things

Income level	Strongly agree (%)	Agree (%)	Neither agree nor disagree (%)	Disagree (%)	Strongly disagree (%)
$1–$14,999	22.6	37.1	23.9	11.3	5.0
$15,000–$29,999	19.0	34.1	31.0	10.3	5.6
$30,000–$49,999	12.4	32.2	32.2	13.2	9.9
$50,000–$74,999	14.0	38.6	24.6	12.3	10.5
$75,000–	22.2	24.4	22.2	22.2	8.9

Source: The Black Youth Project

is found across income levels, as is shown in table 2.2. Support for the statement "The behavior of black youth threatens the progress of respectable black people" was highest among those we might consider the poor, making less than $15,000, and the upper middle class, making between $50,000 and $75,000. The lowest levels of support for the idea that black youth threaten the progress of respectable black people was found among those who might be thought of as middle class—making between $30,000 and $50,000—and those making over $75,000. So while there seems to be no clear linear relationship between income and feelings about the behaviors of black youth, across all income categories less than one-third of respondents disagreed with the statement that the behavior of some young black Americans threatens the progress of black people trying to do the right thing.

Interestingly, when we asked black Americans aged 30 and over to explain why young blacks have a hard time getting ahead, a relationship between income and the favored explanation began to emerge (see table 2.3). For example, when asked why black youth found it hard to get ahead, most respondents making at least $15,000 believed that a combination of bad personal decisions and continuing discrimination were the reasons. Interestingly, the respondents making less than $15,000 were just as likely to answer that most of the problems black youth face arise because of their own bad decisions and behaviors as they were to suggest that it was a combination of bad decisions and discrimination. It was the black poor (among all the class categories listed in table 2.3) who were more likely to suggest that black youth created their own difficulties through their decisions and behaviors. Among those who believed that "Discrimination and a lack of jobs are

TABLE 2.3   Reasons Young Black Americans Find It Hard to Get Ahead

Income level	Most of their problems arise because of their own bad decisions and behaviors (%)	Black youth are making some bad personal decisions, but they also face substantial discrimination (%)	Things like discrimination and a lack of jobs are the real reasons black youth find it hard to get ahead (%)
$1–$14,999	36.3	38.2	25.5
$15,000–$29,999	34.9	50.8	14.3
$30,000–$49,999	27.7	61.3	10.9
$50,000–$74,999	21.1	66.7	12.3
$75,000–	35.6	44.4	20.0

Source: The Black Youth Project

the real reasons black youth find it hard to get ahead," it was both the respondents making less than $15,000 and those making more than $75,000 who were more likely to offer that as their answer. I should note that at most only about a quarter of the respondents in any of the class categories listed in table 2.3 thought discrimination was the primary reason black youth faced a hard time getting ahead.

I am not concerned that people have negative opinions of some rap music and, for that matter, some black youth. My worry, instead, is that with little evidence or proof, large numbers of black Americans, across the class divide, are condemning both black youth and the culture they generate and consume. This could lead to a generational impasse that will affect black communities and black politics for years to come. The scientific evidence that supports the conclusion that rap music has a negative effect on the decision-making and behaviors of young black people is sparse and generally found in studies that have not been widely distributed to the general population. Why, then, do black Americans aged 30 and older, who have little to no knowledge of this literature, hold such a negative view of rap music, believing that this music and these music videos encourage young blacks to engage in what might be considered deviant behavior? Why do half of black Americans aged 30 and older feel that the actions of "too many" young black people threaten the mobility of more "deserving" black people? How do such unsubstantiated positions about rap music on the part of older black Americans influence their opinions regarding policies aimed at improving the lived conditions of young black people? And why does so much of the rage and fear that Cosby embodies regarding young black people seem to resonate with so many members of black communities?

MORAL PANICS

I believe the concept of moral panic can help us explore these questions and begin to understand why older black Americans are so dismissive of rap music and hip-hop culture. Moral panic is a concept typically used by scholars to explain irrational and inflated reactions to lesser events that have been exaggerated by the media. Fundamental to the concept of a moral panic is the idea that the events or actions at the heart of the crisis do not merit the level of concern that has been generated by the public. Using as a starting point both Cosby's rage and the hysteria surrounding rap music in light of the Imus incident, I will explore an alternative conceptualization of moral panics, particularly those emerging in marginal communities. In this case, I am interested in the development of moral panics in black communities, driven by what some have deemed the deviant behavior of other group members.

I am especially concerned with trying to think through how moral panics work differently within marginalized or oppressed communities. The histories of marginalized communities raise a number of critical questions about the moral panic framework. When and how can we judge community panic to be truly irrational and exaggerated? What past experiences and collective memories must be considered when trying to understand the current actions and attitudes of any group? For example, given the past actions of a disapproving state, such as the institutionalization of the Jim Crow racial order, we must factor in how that history and those experiences shape current expectations within black communities about appropriate behavior and what counts as exaggerated or irrational panic in those communities. Moreover, although much of the moral panic literature either explicitly states or implicitly assumes that the targeting, blaming, and shaming of a group comes, in large part, from people external to the targeted group, today we see black leaders publicly policing other blacks whom they perceive as deviant, destructive, and dangerous.[13] To be sure there has always been a practice of self-policing in black communities. What is different today is the access some black elites have to the dominant media, where construction of black pathology by black elites is able to reach a broader public, including various white communities and public officials. This public policing by elites in marginal communities can lead to what I have termed the *secondary marginalization* of those who are most vulnerable in oppressed communities, namely, in this case, the denial of community recognition and resources to those labeled deviant in black communities by indigenous organizations, institutions, and leaders.

As with all moral panics, I believe the attacks on black youth from black leaders derive not only from concerns about their purportedly deviant behavior but also from the understanding that the fortunes of black people are tied together—that they have a "linked fate."[14] Moral panics in black communities are one of the practical and possibly negative consequences of a strong linked fate among black people. If you add to this picture the conservative political environment that dominated our country for eight years under the direction of President George W. Bush, a political and economic climate that produced real losses for the black middle class, it is not surprising that black people in search of real gains, and with a lot to lose in the current economic crisis, are panicked about the behaviors of those thought to be threatening the progress of all black people. But before delving into a discussion of the fragile position of the black middle class and our evolving understanding of moral panics, I will explore two public events that have contributed to an indigenous or internal moral panic in black communities concerning black youth: the ongoing comments and opinions of Bill Cosby and the backlash against rap music resulting from Don Imus's statements about the Rutgers University women's basketball team.

BILL COSBY

It was May 17, 2004, when Bill Cosby, speaking at Constitution Hall in Washington, D.C., at a commemoration of the fiftieth anniversary of *Brown v. Board of Education*, began his attack on poor black people and black youth. Cosby's initial comments were actually focused largely on the issue of faulty parenting among the black poor. As he continued his tirade at numerous speaking events across the country, poor black children and black young people, of whom he clearly believes a significant number are deviants (and no doubt as a consequence of their parents' pathological choices), became the center of his disgust. His running commentary on the subject, which has lasted for more than five years, is too extensive to recount in this chapter; a few excerpts from his initial speech will serve to highlight many of the issues, concerns, and crises that are regularly voiced by some black people about other black people, especially black youth.[15]

On the Black Poor:

"Lower economic people are not holding up their end in this deal. These people are not parenting. They are buying things for kids—$500 sneakers for what? And won't spend $200 for 'Hooked on Phonics.'"

"We as black folks have to do a better job. Someone working at Wal-Mart with seven kids, you are hurting us. We have to start holding each other to a higher standard. We cannot blame white people."

On Black Youth Culture:

"People putting their clothes on backwards: Isn't that a sign of something gone wrong?...People with their hats on backwards, pants down around the crack, isn't that a sign of something, or are you waiting for Jesus to pull his pants up? Isn't it a sign of something when she has her dress all the way up to the crack and got all type of needles [piercings] going through her body? What part of Africa did this come from? Those people are not Africans; they don't know a damn thing about Africa."

On Civil Rights:

"*Brown versus the Board of Education* is no longer the white person's problem. We have got to take the neighborhood back. We have to go in there—forget about telling your child to go into the Peace Corps—it is right around the corner. They are standing on the corner and they can't speak English."

On Literacy:

"Basketball players—multimillionaires—can't write a paragraph. Football players—multimillionaires—can't read. Yes, multimillionaires. Well, *Brown versus Board of Education*: Where are we today? They paved the way, but what did we do with it? That white man, he's laughing. He's got to be laughing: 50 percent drop out, the rest of them are in prison."

On Poor Black Women:

"Five, six children—same woman—eight, ten different husbands or whatever. Pretty soon you are going to have DNA cards to tell who you are making love to. You don't know who this is. It might be your grandmother. I am telling you, they're young enough! Hey, you have a baby when you are twelve; your baby turns thirteen and has a baby. How old are you? Huh? Grandmother! By the time you are twelve you can have sex with your grandmother, you keep those numbers coming. I'm just predicting."

On the Sons and Daughters of Poor, Black, Unmarried Mothers:

"…with names like Shaniqua, Taliqua, and Mohammed [!] and all of that crap, and all of them are in jail."

On Blacks Shot by Police:

"These are not political criminals. These are people going around stealing Coca-Cola. People getting shot in the back of the head over a piece of pound cake, and then we run out and we are outraged, [saying] 'The cops shouldn't have shot him.' What the hell was he doing with the pound cake in his hand?"

While there are many comments one can make after reading this diatribe, one thing that stands out is that his rendition of the failures of the black poor, and especially young black people, is amazingly similar to earlier cultural theories of the "underclass."[16] These theories argue that structural limitations do not dictate the behavior of the black poor; rather, this group is afflicted by nonnormative cultural values and behaviors that replicate intergenerational cycles of poverty and alienation from mainstream society. According to these theories and to Cosby, poor blacks are disreputable people who cannot be helped simply through jobs, government support, or quality education. They need a cultural revolution that starts from within. And just as in many earlier theories of the underclass, sexuality is interwoven throughout Cosby's statements with ideas of criminality and cultural deviance. For Cosby, and many others concerned with deviance in black communities, sexual deviance is an important dimension, but only one dimension of a totalizing deviant lifestyle.

Just as provocative as Cosby's comments are the responses his words garnered throughout black communities. Far from being uniformly reprimanded for his public belittling of black people, and specifically the black poor, Cosby was largely supported and was hailed as a truth-teller among black elites. Black leaders from Jesse Jackson to Cornel West to Kweisi Mfume to Skip Gates all went on record saying that, although it was painful to hear, Cosby had spoken the truth about young black people and far too many poor black parents: a truth, it was claimed, most people in black communities quietly shared.[17] Gates, in his August 1, 2004, *New York Times* op-ed piece on Cosby, wrote: "Any black person who frequents a barbershop or beauty parlor in the inner city knows that Mr. Cosby was only echoing sentiments widely shared in black communities."[18]

It is the joining of forces against black youth and the black poor by those with access to the media and resources and power within black communities that demands our attention here. By now I have grown accustomed to—though I am no less disturbed by it—the constant maligning of black youth by those outside of black communities, whether it is former secretary of education William Bennett's statement that "you could abort every black baby in this country and your crime rate would go down" or Don Imus's description of the Rutgers women's basketball team as "some nappy-headed hos."[19] On a daily basis, one is reminded of the contempt held for young black people across large swaths of American society.[20] But just as alarming is the heightened condemnation of and moral panic about young black people on the part of the black elites that Michael Eric Dyson calls the "Afristocracy."[21]

DON IMUS AND GANGSTA RAP

This time the controversy started on April 4, 2007, with Don Imus engaging in his usual morning banter with his staff on his radio and television show *Imus in the Morning*. The commentary that morning was about the two teams competing in the NCAA women's basketball championship—the University of Tennessee Lady Volunteers and the Rutgers University Scarlet Knights:

> IMUS: So, I watched the basketball game last night between—a little bit of Rutgers and Tennessee, the women's final.
> ROSENBERG: Yeah, Tennessee won last night—seventh championship for [Tennessee coach] Pat Summitt, I-Man. They beat Rutgers by 13 points.
> IMUS: That's some rough girls from Rutgers. Man, they got tattoos and—
> MCGUIRK: Some hard-core hos.

IMUS: That's some nappy-headed hos there. I'm gonna tell you that now, man, that's some—woo. And the girls from Tennessee, they all look cute, you know, so, like—kinda like—I don't know.

McGUIRK: A Spike Lee thing.

IMUS: Yeah.

McGUIRK: The Jigaboos vs. the Wannabes—that movie that he had.

IMUS: Yeah, it was a tough—

McCORD: *Do the Right Thing*.

McGUIRK: Yeah, yeah, yeah.

IMUS: I don't know if I'd have wanted to beat Rutgers or not, but they did, right?

ROSENBERG: It was a tough watch. The more I look at Rutgers, they look exactly like the Toronto Raptors.

IMUS: Well, I guess, yeah.

RUFFINO: Only tougher.

McGUIRK: The [Memphis] Grizzlies would be more appropriate.[22]

Imus was eventually fired from both MSNBC and CBS, when his sponsors with their advertising dollars began to abandon him. He returned to the airwaves approximately six months later in December 2007 on WABC. Independent of his reemergence, it was his attempt to deflect his use of the term "nappy-headed ho" onto black rappers, and the ensuing response of black leaders and community members, that makes visible the existing moral panic surrounding black youth in black communities. On April 10, on both the *Today Show* and his own program, *Imus in the Morning*, Imus introduced his ineffective but contagious defense: if black men can call black women "hos" and get away with it, why shouldn't he be able to? Specifically, he said, "I may be a white man, but I know that...young black women all through *that* society are demeaned and disparaged and disrespected...by their own black men and that they are called that name." Later on his show, Imus attempted to clarify his argument about the term "ho" originating in the black community, stating, "Because this phrase that I used didn't originate—it originated in the black community. That didn't give me a right to use it, but that's where it originated."[23]

Not surprisingly, commentators ran with Imus's second muttering about the "bitch/ho" double standard, in which he called out black leaders for decrying his use of those terms while they said nothing about the black men who daily and publicly call black women bitches and hos. And as the focus of media reports began to shift from Imus's original derogatory comments about the Rutgers players to the so-called double standard in black communities, commentators began confronting every black guest on their news programs with this question: Is it fair to go after Imus if you haven't done anything about "your" black rappers? Black spokesperson after black spokesperson responded by taking the defensive, and perhaps appropriate, position of condemning any and all rappers who called women "bitches" and "hos" and black men "niggers." Those who could do so pointed out that they decided "to take on rap music" long before the current Imus uproar and used this tactic to lend legitimacy to their position on the Imus controversy.

Others reminded the public that multiple, pervasive forms of misogyny and sexism exist in this country that equally demean black women. Still others attempted to broaden the discussion by questioning the assumption that black people have some special responsibility for policing rap music—a genre of music produced and performed by black entertainers but largely controlled by major white-owned record companies. On occasion, smaller subgroups took the time to remind the public that hip-hop is neither confined to nor defined by gangsta rap, and that the majority of young black people also believe that rap music videos are too violent, include too much sex, and are degrading to both black men and women.[24] These arguments were usually summarily dismissed—portrayed as avoiding the real culprit: rap music. No matter how accurate or persuasive the counterarguments were, the conversation always ventured back to the same bottom line: the partial truth that gangsta rap is performed by black men and is demeaning to women—especially, and nearly exclusively, black women.

The complicity of black spokespeople in the framing of rap music as the most important instrument that denigrates black women suggests that most black male leaders do not understand, nor are concerned about, the historic, systematic oppression and denigration that black women have faced and continue to face. Of course, the use of words such as "bitch" and "ho" is reprehensible, as is the commodification of black bodies, in particular black women's bodies, in rap videos. Our society has a long history of using such words and images to dehumanize black women and strip them of their status and rights. Gangsta rap should be viewed as continuing this troubling tradition. There can be no denying the significant impact of the words and images found in too many gangsta rap lyrics and videos.

That said, Imus's implicit suggestion that he would never have referred to the black women on the Rutgers basketball team as "hos" had it not been for the significant role rap music plays in our culture seems ludicrous. The characterization of black women in derogatory, explicitly sexual ways extends back to the arrival of African women in the new colonies.[25] Given the historic tradition of degrading black women, as well as Imus's long pattern of vitriolic attacks on those with less power, it is no great surprise that Imus attacked and degraded these women. It was, in fact, the long (albeit always evolving) history of degrading black women that gave Imus license to partake in this particular American tradition.[26]

We should also note that left unexplored in the Imus uproar was the homophobic nature of his comments. The truth is that not only was Imus degrading the gender presentation of these women, he was also making an intersectional attack that not only questioned their gender conformity but also their sexual identification. While he called the Rutgers women "hos," he could have just as easily called them "nappy-headed bull-daggers" or "dykes," since the conversation between Imus and his underlings was as much about calling into question the sexual nonconformity of the players as it was about their gender presentation.

Of course, the idea that gangsta rap is the primary or most effective messenger of misogyny in demeaning black women is wrong. Black women face larger, systematic forms of degradation daily: the criminal justice system, their lack of access to reproductive rights, their demonization and humiliation in film and on television, and the violence they experience in their homes and communities. Surely rap artists must be held accountable for their lyrics, but they operate with limited agency: to make largely invisible in this discussion the corporations that profit from such language and images—corporations like Viacom and BET—is again to produce partial truths when the complete story is desperately needed.

The double standard is not that black leaders have been silent about the degradation of black women in rap while attacking Imus. Some black leaders, hip-hop "heads," and black feminists have written and spoken about this issue for the last fifteen years.[27] The real double standard is that in both the larger society and black communities, black women's voices and concerns are silenced, while their bodies are put on display. When black women complained about the images and messages being promoted in commercial rap and popular culture in general, most black leaders did nothing. But when a racist and misogynist white man complained about the language and images in rap music, black leaders, many of them male, who had long been silent on this issue, finally felt compelled to act. Ultimately, the double standard is the historic truth that white men have power and black women have little, even in their own communities.

So we might ask, why did most black leaders allow such an incomplete framing of the degradation black women face to evolve into a referendum on rap? Maybe the answer has to do with black people's worries about our public presentation. As one 17-year-old black male from Chicago explained, "If you were just to watch music videos and never have met a black person in your life, you probably would think ill of black people altogether...white people probably think that black people don't care about anything but sex, and selling drugs, and partying all the time. I mean, that's the images you get from rap music videos."[28] Perhaps some black people with some privilege and access are concerned that they (we) will be confused with "too many young black Americans" who they think "threaten the progress of respectable black people who are trying to do the right things." Given such concern, it is possible that many black leaders, trying to distinguish themselves from the "riff raff" better known as gangsta rappers, thought it more prudent to be part of the group throwing stones than the one getting hit. Or maybe less cynically, these leaders believe that gangsta rap is a negative force in black communities and through the auspices of the Imus controversy found a vehicle that would allow them to condemn gangsta rap while also condemning white racism.

On Oprah's programs targeting rap music, the comments of one young woman from Spelman College underscored the role that class and status played in the response of black people to the Imus incident as even young women sought to distinguish themselves from the real "hos" and bitches. She complained, "I've heard a lot of rappers say that they are speaking about the 'hos' from the street and the 'hos' from their experience. But they have to understand that men don't make distinctions between *those hos and us*. When you go to a club, they don't say, 'Let me see your school ID,' and then distinguish whether they are going to call us a ho or not. It affects us globally, and it has informed how people feel about black women."

In response to this revelation, Oprah asked all the young women representing Spelman on the program (via satellite) in a surprised and panicked voice, "So have you all been called hos?" "Yes," they responded in unison. Horrified, Oprah responded, "You have been called hos by whom? Who is calling you hos?" Finally, the young women responded, "At the club, everywhere." The truth in their final response highlights the need to look beyond rap music when considering the degradation black women face in this society. Yes, the Spelman women have been called hos not just at the club or in rap music, but everywhere. It is this pervasive practice of the degradation of black women throughout our society that makes the virtually exclusive focus on rap music so puzzling and troubling. When given the chance to have a broader discussion about the treatment of black women, black leaders have collaborated with the mainstream to constrain the discussion to one that begins and ends with rap music and primarily rap artists.

UNDERSTANDING MORAL PANICS

Many traditional theories of moral panics, such as sociologist Stanley Cohen's canonical work *Folk Devils and Moral Panics*, focus on understanding the construction of a moral panic.[29] These works conceptualize a moral panic as an overreaction by an often vocal minority to rule-breaking by a suspect and relatively powerless group whose actions negatively impact a sympathetic and respectable victim. Researchers in this field argue that the impact of such events and actions is exaggerated, often through media reports and rumor in which the story of the infraction is magnified to suggest that it threatens "our" agreed-on respectable behavior and civilized ways of living. Not only are the facts of the story distorted; more important, its implications are inflated, suggesting that a socially necessary moral code has been broken. As one consequence of such exaggerated reporting and misinformation, the public (or at least a substantial component of it) becomes extremely concerned about the reported activities and demands that an authority such as the state control the group of deviants, or "folk devils." These calls for control often focus on the criminalization of the offenders. The state and its agents, particularly the police, are regarded as an essential part of the solution to the moral crisis.

Moral panics can arise without much warning and subside in the same manner. Behaviors that have been occurring for some time may suddenly be revealed to the public in such a way that their impact is thought to be a serious and immediate threat. History and religious studies professor Philip Jenkins in his work on moral panics reminds us that the facts of a situation do not need to change for a moral panic to emerge.[30] Instead, the framing and consequent public understanding of a situation or phenomenon can be altered without its objective reality having varied. Where once a group may have been viewed as suffering from systems of oppression beyond its control, the public framing of the group's members can change so as to emphasize instead their agency and control. In their discussion of the moral panic surrounding Prohibition, sociology professors Erich Goode and Nachman Ben-Yehuda note the transformation of the public's understanding of those who drank. "In early twentieth-century agitation for national Prohibition, the temperance movement came to define drinking as an unmixed evil, and opponents of Prohibition were seen as 'enemies to be conquered.' Drinkers were seen not as unfortunate wretches to be helped so much as enemies of society who should be punished."[31]

At the heart of any moral panic is what sociologist Howard Becker labels moral entrepreneurs.[32] He distinguishes two forms of these: rule creators and rule enforcers. Rule creators are those individuals, groups, and communities who believe that some folk devils engage in practices that threaten the moral fiber of society; rule creators think it is therefore their responsibility to challenge the nonnormative behavior of these folk devils for the betterment of society. Rule creators are involved in the creation of a moral panic in various ways. They may attempt to frame the issue and shape public opinion through their access to the media or other venues for getting one's message out. Others use preexisting organizations such as churches, schools, or labor unions to mobilize their constituency around a particular event or issue. Still others are involved in developing solutions to the purported crisis: policies, laws, and informal mechanisms of regulation.

There is a debate in the literature as to whether the media should be considered moral entrepreneurs or necessary, but not sufficient, independent agents in the creation of a moral panic. In Cohen's rendition, the media (or some members of the media to be more accurate) are the originators and main culprits in the construction of such panics. He suggests that many factors contribute to such exaggerated reporting, including the need to create news as well as the biases and sensationalism that typically exist in news organizations. For Cohen, then, the fuel for such panics is contagious reporting, wherein multiple news organizations repeat not only the specific story line but also the supposed implications of such actions for the larger society.

The impact of media reports and the ability for a moral panic to develop also lie in the *preexisting* feelings and attitudes toward the group being targeted as folk devils. Cohen talks about a process of "community sensitization," or demonization, whereby once a group is labeled deviant its actions are continuously scrutinized and are more likely to be seen as deviant.[33] Goode and Ben-Yehuda note that "once a class of behavior, and a category of deviants, are identified, extremely small deviations from the norm become noticed, commented on, judged and reacted to."[34] Like the rest of society, the media are predisposed to think of as deviant some groups whose cultures and attitudes differ from the mainstream. Stories that exaggerate the behaviors and the impact of such targeted groups are more likely to be believed by the general public and more likely to be repeated by other news agencies without corroboration.

Whereas rule creators are thought to proceed often with an agenda that is rooted in their ideological commitments, rule enforcers are the individuals who are responsible for implementing solutions to the moral crisis through the auspices of their job. Certainly, the police qualify in many cases of moral panic as rule enforcers; other arms of the state and public entities act in this role as well. For example, in the case of the public concern about gangsta rap, it would not be a leap of faith to imagine that some schools will ban the playing of gangsta rap generally or especially during school events. It wouldn't be surprising if prison officials no longer allowed those incarcerated to watch rap videos. We might even imagine a scenario in which elected officials would outlaw other behaviors thought to be associated with gangsta rap, such as the wearing of sagging pants. In such circumstances, school officials, prison administrators, and legislators all become rule enforcers reacting to a moral panic about gangsta rap music and videos.

The framework of moral panics is useful in helping us understand how a public uproar can develop in response to actions that are relatively mild in their impact, have existed for some time without significant comment, or are unsubstantiated by evidence. However, the framework of moral panics also leaves many questions unanswered. For example, what level of uproar qualifies as a moral panic? How do we know when the response to an event is exaggerated beyond the impact of the issue or act? Answering these questions is especially difficult because there is never consensus around the existence of a moral panic. Individuals from across the political and social spectrum will contest whether society is truly threatened, whether the public is indeed overreacting, and whether the groups targeted as creating the crisis are deserving of the blame. Furthermore, not all voices have equal access to the media and the public agenda. Some empowered groups have a greater ability to generate fear among the public than others—yet another way they can protect their privilege.[35]

Despite the limitations of this theoretical approach, I believe moral panics can help us understand the construction and treatment of black youth in black communities, as well as the decision-making and behaviors of some black youth. Exploring the development of moral panics in marginal communities can also shed new light on how such moral panics are created and who are intimately involved in them as moral entrepreneurs. First, moral panics that develop in marginal communities, especially those relating to the presumed deviant behavior of group members, confound the implicit assumption that moral panics originate in or gain strength from moral entrepreneurs or enemies rooted outside a marginal community. In the case of moral panics concerning the behaviors and culture of young black people, many of the experts and stakeholders fueling what I contend is an exaggerated fear of black youth are other black people. Undoubtedly, the mainstream media plays a central role in emphasizing and disseminating images of black youth that highlight perceived criminality, nonnormative family structure, and deviance in general, but their stories are legitimized by black public figures and black media sources.

Second, moral panics in marginalized communities challenge the frequent presumption of the irrationality of such panics. For example, black people's fear of young community members' alleged nonnormative behavior is not only a validation of dominant norms and values of what constitutes proper conduct; it is also based in the knowledge that the dominant society's labeling of certain behaviors by members of the marginal community as deviant and threatening has historically led to the greater regulation, surveillance, and repression of that community. Historically, when black men have been perceived as threatening to white women, whites' violent attacks against black communities and black men specifically have intensified. When black women have been perceived as deviating from the prescribed dominant family structure and reproductive pattern, black women's reproductive options have been stringently regulated—especially those of black women receiving formal aid from the state. Thus, far from being irrational, a community-based panic, even if due to behaviors considered inconsequential by that community but labeled deviant by the dominant society, might be appropriate and surely not be irrational, if the status and progress of black Americans continues to be tenuous and subject to the actions of the state. Given the dominance of neoliberal policies as a governing framework today, where privatization and not state aid is a priority, it makes sense that black communities would be especially worried and possibly panicked about behaviors that will be used to justify a further retreat of the state from supporting the advancement and progress of black communities through government-sponsored programs.

Third, moral panics in marginalized communities also point to the emergence of a different set of enforcement solutions than that generally associated with moral panics. Cohen suggests that in traditional forms of moral panics, rule creators often seek to criminalize the supposedly deviant behavior and turn to formal moral rule enforcers such as the police and courts to restore social control. In contrast, I contend that moral panics in marginalized communities are less likely to be criminalized in this way, given the history of, in this case, black communities' interaction with the criminal justice system. That is not to suggest that the police and the criminal justice system will not be part of the articulated solution to the problem. Instead, what is likely is that black moral entrepreneurs will make regulatory state intervention a secondary strategy and promote as a primary strategy both improved behaviors among individuals, focusing on personal responsibility, and state assistance in the form of resources and support. For even when marginal communities have accepted and internalized narratives of the "deviant" behavior of certain of their members, lurking in their collective consciousness is an understanding that many live with fewer resources, diminished opportunities, and less access to dominant institutions. Given that knowledge, it should not be surprising that moral panics in marginal communities would run a course to a type of attempted resolution that is somewhat different than has been traditionally theorized.

MORAL PANIC AMONG THE BLACK MIDDLE CLASS

One of the most significant strategies for mobility in black communities has been promoting the respectability of black people. This strategy for advancement is rooted in the belief that if black people can show themselves to be dignified, and as sharing the same values as white Americans, the white public will acknowledge black people's humanity and equal status as citizens.[36] Historian Evelyn Brooks-Higginbotham explains this strategy, noting that "African Americans' claims to respectability invariably held subversive implications...the concept of respectability signified self-esteem, racial pride, and something more. It also signified the search for common ground on which to live as Americans with Americans of other racial and ethnic backgrounds."[37] She continues: "the politics of respectability constituted a deliberate, highly self-conscious concession to hegemonic values."[38]

The idea of acceptance through adherence has influenced the politics and scholarship of black communities for centuries. Scholars from W. E. B. Du Bois to William Julius Wilson have engaged in rigorous research to identify and explain the structural conditions that prohibit some members of black communities from securing the economic and social advancement that might be expected on the basis of experiences of other black Americans and some ethnic groups.[39] These researchers had also focused on detailing differences in class, culture, and status within black communities, subtly gesturing to a divide between those in black communities who are respectable and worthy of assimilation and advancement and those undeserving of such status.

Ironically, a reliance on respectability might be viewed as even more critical for black Americans who have secured some mobility but find it threatened in times like the one we currently inhabit. For example, where once the expansion of the black middle class was routinely touted by the Clinton administration, today the continued expansion of this group seems questionable in the face of massive government debt, a devastating downturn in the economy, and layoffs not only from state and city agencies, which have been an important route to economic advancement for black Americans, but also from car factories and the industries that support them. Similarly, the most recent attack on affirmative action, aided significantly by the administration of former president George W. Bush, threatens access to higher education for black Americans and the job opportunities that result.

In addition to the Bush administration's outright attacks on policies meant to promote the advancement of black Americans, that administration worked to reconfigure the politics of black representation—at least as was manifested through administration appointments such as Condoleezza Rice and Colin Powell. These black appointees were much more likely to emphasize personal responsibility over structure when discussing the lived conditions and politics of black communities. And while President Obama is willing to concede the difficult structural challenges faced by all Americans today, he is quick to remind the public, and especially black people, of the role of culture and agency in determining one's life chances and trajectory. Given this situation, we should not be taken aback that 61 percent of black Americans age 30 and older believed in 2007, before the current economic crisis, that "under the Bush administration it is more difficult for the black middle class to get ahead than under previous administrations."[40]

It is not surprising, therefore, that in our current political and economic environment, black Americans with some access to power, mobility, and status, as well as those aspiring to secure such a position, are feeling especially anxious about what they perceive to be bad or deviant behavior among young black people. Moreover, their concern has been legitimized and amplified through the speeches of Obama as both candidate and president. This seemingly intensified concern about the choices and behaviors of black youth may help explain why 50 percent of black Americans age 30 and older believe that "the behavior of too many young black Americans threatens the progress of respectable black people who are trying to do the right things."[41]

The "deviant" behavior of black youth is especially puzzling to older black Americans when they consider the opportunities that they believe this group enjoys. Specifically, 80 percent of older black people indicated that they believed that young black Americans today had more opportunities than when they were growing up. More than 50 percent believe this generation has *many more* opportunities than they had. Older black Americans seem essentially frustrated by two conflicting perceptions: that young black people's behavior is deviant (indeed, they have been told this repeatedly by black leaders they trust) and that the same youth have better opportunities than they themselves ever had. This contradiction leads to a state of moral panic about young black people who they believe are out of control. As one 23-year-old black male from Chicago explained, older blacks "they look at it as like we have so much going for ourselves and so much we can do. And they just want us to take action with it." It is important to remember that moral panics about black youth in black communities is not a phenomenon experienced only in the United States. Scholars have detailed similar indigenous panics among black people targeting black youth in countries ranging from South Africa to England.[42]

THE CONSEQUENCES OF MORAL PANIC

One consequence of moral panic is the heightened policing and criminalization of those believed to be the cause of the problem. Although the intensified policing resulting from moral panic in black communities may not necessarily involve the official state police, other forms of intensified policing exist. As I have argued previously in other writings, in this postindustrial era we face advanced marginalization wherein members of marginal communities have taken on the daily, face-to-face responsibility of policing the individuals in their group who have less resources and power. The proliferation of black welfare caseworkers meant to regulate and police the actions of those on welfare, disproportionately women of color, is one example of this form of indigenous policing.[43] Of course, there are more informal means of community policing as well. Sociologist Mary Pattillo discusses the policing of black youth by the black middle class who move into poor and working-class black neighborhoods through a process of gentrification.[44] It is not surprising, in such instances, for new middle-class black homeowners to first confront their new neighborhoods over what they presume to be their inappropriate behavior and then to routinely call the police as a means of having an external force control the actions of their working-class and poor black neighbors.[45] In these examples, indigenous moral entrepreneurs use both informal means and formal rule enforcers to regulate the public behaviors of group members, especially those thought to diminish the respectability of the community.

Recently, we have seen an expanded public admonishing of black youth by black elites in part because of the perceived threat to black respectability. Black opinion-shapers have turned their attention from the possible structural causes of "deviance" among black youth to what they consider to be their self-defeating decisions and "immoral" behavior. Bill Cosby's continuous tirade against the black poor and black youth is undoubtedly the easiest and most recognized example of this phenomenon, but he is only one among many. President Obama has also engaged in his share of lecturing to the black poor and black youth on topics ranging from what they feed their children—too much cold Popeye's chicken in the morning—to their attitude about work and how they can be better fathers.

In books by noted black journalists and scholars such as John McWhorter, Stanley Crouch, and Juan Williams, in statements by Spike Lee and Wynton Marsalis, and in the debate over rap music fueled by the Imus firing, concerns like those articulated by Cosby and Obama about the culture and behaviors of the black poor and black youth are raised repeatedly. McWhorter, for example, points to the culture of "victimology" found among black Americans. He concludes that even among black youth who "have never remotely known the world that spawned Victimology," it has, astonishingly, become pervasive.[46] McWhorter writes that "much more often in modern black American life, victimhood is simply called attention to where it barely exists if at all. Most importantly, all too often this is done not with a view toward forging solutions, but to foster and nurture an unfocused brand of resentment and sense of alienation from the mainstream."[47]

He adds that "victimology seduces young black people just like the crack trade seduces inner-city Blacks, virtually irresistible in its offer of an easy road to self-esteem and some cheap thrills on the way."[48]

Other authors take their shot at black youth by targeting what is seen as *the* most destructive force in black youth culture—rap music. In his book *Enough*, NPR correspondent and former *Washington Post* reporter Juan Williams describes the evolution of rap music, writing that

> before long the gritty street reporting [found in rap music] gave way to nihilistic glorifications of the "thug life." . . . Along the same path to corruption, the early hip-hop tradition of young men bragging in their raps about being great, passionate lovers took a wrong turn down a path to degrading women as "whores" and "bitches." Time after time, raising the stakes in rap to get attention from listeners and record companies meant descending to self-hating vulgarity (shout-outs to friends and foes alike meant calling them "nigger" or "motherfucker").[49]

Similarly, music critic, syndicated columnist, and author Stanley Crouch also sets his sights on black youth culture. Targeting rap music videos, he comments on the excessive violence, sexuality, and dehumanization of such commercialized products.

> Images of black youth seen on MTV, BET, or VH1 . . . are not far removed from those D. W. Griffith used in *Birth of a Nation*, where Reconstruction Negroes were depicted as bullying, hedonistic buffoons ever ready to bloody somebody. This is the new minstrelsy. The neo-Sambo is sturdily placed in our contemporary popular iconography. He can be seen, for instance, mugging or scowling in Trick Daddy's "I'm a Thug," where gold teeth, drop-down pants and tasteless jewelry abound. There is the fast-tailed hussy, rolling her rump at the camera or challenging some anonymous man to satisfy her in Missy's latest video. These videos are created primarily for the material enrichment of black entertainers, producers, and directors, not present-day whites, who would be run off the planet if they—like the creators of nineteenth-century minstrelsy—were responsible for the images, the ideas and the content.[50]

In addition to Williams, Crouch, and McWhorter, other black elites have sounded off about rap music. Spike Lee suggested that because of rap music, young black kids now grow up wanting to be pimps or strippers; Wynton Marsalis stated that he does not listen to rap or hip-hop because it is ignorant.[51] All of these commentators appear to have given up on analyses of the structural conditions that might lead to "deviant" behavior among black youth, preferring instead to engage in polemical exchanges devoid of any empirical evidence about the deficiencies of black American youth and the negative influence of rap music. It is the partial and familiar truths and images found in all of their comments that generate support for their position from many in black communities.

Most black communities' members were raised to understand what it takes to exist and survive in a fundamentally racist societal structure. They were told to work hard, be respectful, and always have your superior humanity on display for whites to observe. They then look around at a society that they believe is dramatically less racist than the one they grew up in and see young black people engaging in behaviors that not only seem detrimental to their own personal advancement and happiness, but also threaten the mobility of those blacks thought to be holding up their end of the deal and playing by the rules. This leads many black Americans to instinctively gravitate to the uncomplicated and available narrative that represents these young people as simply out of control. These narratives that emphasize the importance of personal responsibility and the deficiencies of black youth in this area are compatible with a neoliberal governing paradigm that underscores the agency of individuals and problematizes an active state. The repeating of these multiple and complimentary narratives by those inside and outside black communities generates an indigenous moral panic that serves as a catalyst for developing policies and rhetoric meant to eliminate the negative behaviors or designate them as something foreign and unacceptable to respectable black people. Rarely is there an investigation as to whether the narrative is true, or a defense of those who stand accused of such nonnormative actions. Instead the focus is on eliminating the behavior or, at the very least, making it less visible.

Part of the frustration voiced by the black middle class and those on its periphery is motivated by their interest in protecting the class mobility their members have secured through hard work and "good moral fiber" or, more specifically, acceptance and adherence to a dominant normative value structure. However, that is not the only explanation for the black middle class's disgust with the present-day behaviors and values exhibited by some black youth. My aforementioned research among black Americans age 30 and older indicates that 70 percent of them believe that "both young black and young white people suffer from the wrong morals concerning important things like sex and work." Some of the angst of black Americans is rooted in the belief that the entire current generation of young people has lost its moral compass. As one 18-year-old male from Detroit explained, "they [older blacks] probably view us as not having enough God in our lives." And while black Americans may believe that all young people are in trouble, they also know that the consequences for such misguided behavior will be much more severe for black youth.

Most people in black communities know firsthand the difficult conditions that black people face in this society. They are clear about the discrimination and inconsistencies inherent in the criminal justice system. They understand that such problems result in the exponential expansion of incarcerated young black people. Members of black communities experience and hear the statistics regarding the disproportionate impact of HIV and AIDS within their ranks. Black Americans also have firsthand knowledge of the unemployment rates in black communities, which are at least double those among comparable white Americans. They did not need Bill Cosby to tell them about the more than 50 percent high school dropout rate among some black males in public high schools.[52] And while many members of black communities show support for the concerns expressed by Bill Cosby, they also are aware of the structural challenges young blacks face today. In fact, my data indicate that 53 percent of black Americans aged 30 and older believe that "although black youth are making some bad decisions, they also face substantial discrimination that limits their opportunities."[53]

Given that many black Americans continue to understand the role of structure in limiting opportunities for black youth, why is it so difficult to put forth a structural argument that will resonate with black audiences? Part of the answer is that while explanations that focus on structure are recognizable to most black people, narratives that tell a story of either individual accomplishment or failure are much more compelling. We cannot minimize the difficulty of producing an accessible structural analysis that has the same power as the "I pulled myself up by my bootstraps, and so can you" story when trying to explain the popularity of personal-responsibility narratives in black communities. It is not that black people don't understand and recognize the structural conditions that inhibit the choices and possibilities of poor people, especially poor black people. The problem is that a structural analysis has little traction today, especially as it is pitted against the stories of real authorities—the Obama narrative in particular but also other black people—who have "made it" against the odds. In the absence of logical, accessible, and easily communicated structural narratives, it is reasonable that black Americans opt for personal-responsibility explanations when trying to make sense of both their own fragile successes and the so-called failure of the young black people they witness cursing in public, hanging out on the street, seeming not to hold real jobs, having children before they are married, and routinely doing the "perp walk" on their televisions.[54]

In this post-post-civil-rights-movement era, significant segments of black communities, especially those whose members grew up under and struggled against Jim Crow segregation, have been told and have indeed decided for themselves that things are not as bad for this generation as they were in the past. They are also increasingly subject to neoliberal policies that emphasize privatization and the rhetoric of individual responsibility and choice. Therefore, they do not want to hear or promote what they believe is the same old story about a racist structure holding our youth down. And while most black Americans are willing to believe that the combination of limited opportunities and individuals' bad choices has truncated the life trajectory of significant numbers of black youth, this more complicated understanding does not play well on television or in news accounts. It is especially difficult to tell the complete truth when images and stories of black people making bad *individual* decisions about school, work, relationships, sex, and childbearing seem to be everywhere, authenticated by black elites. The nuanced nature of systemic discrimination in a neoliberal order, in which on the surface de jure segregation has been eliminated, is difficult to even notice, let alone consistently point out, when the narrative disseminated again and again by the dominant communication machinery is one of "progress," "culture and personal choice," and "a color-blind society."

There is also a historical understanding of the consequences of deviance that black people carry with them. Black Americans, perhaps more than any other group, have experienced how a white supremacist state will construct a group as deviant so as to justify its continued oppression and secondary status. In the history of black people in America, governments, organizations, vigilante groups, and average citizens have referenced what was construed to be the abnormal and deviant behavior of black people as a reason to deny them full citizenship status and rights, as well as to routinely target them for both physical and cultural violence. Given our understanding of this history, it comes as no surprise that deep concern and feelings of panic emerge among many in black communities when the general public starts to construct the behaviors of some black people as outside the norm.

Instead of mounting a rigorous reply to such accusations, increasing numbers of black community members and opinion-makers have engaged in a strategy of indigenous policing or "truth-telling," agreeing with those outside black communities who say something is fundamentally wrong with the norms and practices of a marginal but significant portion of black Americans. It is this process of internal or community self-policing—motivated in part by a rational group panic—that seems to be the intervention in the lives of black youth that commands the airwaves and internet stories today. Those of us interested in improving the lives of black youth might benefit from differentiating between the irrational moral panic of outsiders and the indigenous and rational panic of insiders conditioned through a history of oppression.

We must remember that the policing of young black people or those most vulnerable in marginal communities has significant consequences for them. Most important, policing "blackness," or community membership, threatens the status of those thought not to conform to some ideal of acceptable blackness. As I have noted, black community members are quite cognizant of how black people are perceived by other groups in the larger society. They are especially aware of how stereotypes of their supposedly deficient norms, culture, and behaviors have been used to legitimize systemic discrimination and racism. In light of this understanding, black community members and public leaders believe it is necessary to police the boundaries of public blackness, declaring what behaviors are authentic and indigenous to black communities, which groups are upstanding and deserving of support, and which subgroups and individuals are deviant.

To be labeled a deviant—someone undeserving of community support, someone engaging in behaviors that are portrayed as antithetical to the norms that black communities, and the larger society, have embraced—is to have one's community standing challenged. These individuals and subgroups are not only seen as a detriment to the progress of black people; they are often denied community support. Ironically, such community self-policing may leave the most vulnerable members of marginal communities without access to dominant institutions and resources and without the support of the organizations and groups of the community either. This leads to what I have labeled previously "secondary marginalization," which is largely legitimized and implemented by members of the demonized's own group.[55]

Given the consequences of secondary marginalization, we should be worried about how the narratives of deviance targeting young black people, and promoted by those in their communities, shape their feelings about themselves, their community, and their country. As I suggested earlier, young black people may be internalizing the message of their failure and deviance. A 20-year-old black female from St. Louis reported that "almost everything that happens in the news, young blacks have done it. Just ruin their entire life at the age of 20, by just doing something stupid trying to get by. Or just being greedy in general." Beyond, however, the answers given by individual black youth to in-depth interview questions, data from the Black Youth Project suggest a similar trend of disrespect for other black youth. For example, when we asked respondents what they thought of the statement that "too many young black Americans had the wrong morals about important things like work and sex," 80 percent of young blacks agreed. Similarly, though not as drastically, nearly 40 percent of black youth believe that "most black people over 40 do not respect young black people."

In the opinions of young black people, we can see that the dialogue about their culture, behaviors, and self-worth currently underway in black communities is very much a part of their consciousness, impacting how they think about themselves as well as how they view older black people. This is why Bill Cosby's partial truths must be addressed if we are to move forward realistically, effectively, and ethically to build movements rooted in black communities that are intent on improving the lives of black youth. The truth is, when Cosby talks about a black woman with eight children from eight different men, I find myself struggling with my own panic and respectability impulse, not only because the topic raises issues of community shame but also because I know what the lived consequences of such images and narratives have been for black people in this society and in our own communities. The question now before us is how will this debate, panic, and public fear about black youth impact them? To get at this question in the next four chapters, I explore what young black people think about the political, social, and economic world they inhabit and what they think of themselves and their futures.

CHAPTER 3

"Baby Mama"

Black Love, Black Deviance, and the Sexual Politics of Morality

A S DISCUSSED IN the last chapter, those who gathered for the NAACP's public burial of the N-word in 2007 were completely unaware that in just over a year Mayor Kilpatrick would face his own public burial of sorts. Ironically and sadly, Kilpatrick was forced to resign as mayor after being convicted of two felony counts of obstruction of justice by committing perjury. The perjury occurred when Kilpatrick lied under oath about an extramarital affair he had with his chief of staff. In September 2008, Kilpatrick was sentenced to four months in jail and five years' probation.[1] The hypocrisy on display in the case of Kilpatrick is part of a long tradition of public officials and elites—but especially for my purposes here, black public officials and elites—making pronouncements about the immorality of the black poor and black youth only to have their own moral indiscretions made public.

The list of offenders is too long to recite, but the case of Bill Cosby is notable, given the media attention he's received in recent years for his comments about the failings of black parents and the black poor. Cosby's extramarital affair with Shawn Thompson and claims by her daughter, Autumn Jackson, that he was her father grabbed the public's attention in the late 1990s.[2] The case was disturbing on many levels, but it serves as a reminder that even those who struggle very publicly with their own moral challenges jump at the chance to reprimand the black poor and black youth for their "deviant" culture and self-destructive behavior. Pointing out the hypocrisy of some black elites is not meant to deny the fact that some black youth engage in behaviors that are troubling.[3] In this chapter, once again, I am not concerned with naming those self-destructive behaviors. Others have taken on that project and have been quite successful.[4] Instead, I want to explore the contradictory space we all inhabit between the values we profess and the actual behaviors in which we engage.

This chapter will focus on how young black people think and talk about value-laden subjects such as sex, abortion, and rap music and how these professed beliefs seem to collide with reported behaviors among many in this group. Using data from the Black Youth Project and focus groups, I outline the complicated, and at times contradictory, thinking of black youth on two issues closely associated with their public image: sex and rap music. I will explore the attitudes and critical judgment of black youth about these two subjects. While sex and rap music may seem to stand outside the explicit forms of politics that undergird this book, they are illustrative of the moral and political judgment and behavior that is expected of participants in national and global political communities. Daily, individuals are asked to assess any number of sensitive moral issues, including those that require judgments about which individuals or citizens should receive support from the government, what subjects should be taught in public schools, and for what reasons persons should lose their freedom through incarceration. All of these issues involve not only attention to specific information but also the capacity to abstractly assess what is fair, reasonable, just, and equal. Without understanding the ways young black Americans define what is right and wrong, how they apply those assessments to their own lives, and how they engage in moral evaluation when assessing public policy, we will never comprehend the moral politics of young black people.

Another critical reason for exploring the attitudes and actions of black youth in the morally loaded domain of sex is that we know that the groups who are believed to be lacking moral judgment, as measured by adherence to dominant norms and values, are often construed as deficient citizens whose deviant behaviors threaten not only their own progress but that of the nation. These "deviant" subjects are marginalized socially, economically, culturally, and politically, inhibiting their ability to secure the resources and respect needed to achieve a basic standard of living, as well as the equality and opportunity promised in the Constitution. Thus, comprehending the moral and critical judgment of black youth will help us to understand their place as members of the political community. An exploration of how black youth think about, engage in, and explain their sexual choices also allows us to contrast their sense of sexual moral behavior with that of young people from other racial and ethnic groups, and assess whether their behaviors and attitudes correspond to the picture of black youth disseminated by those who are fomenting moral panics in black communities.

Far from endorsing the behaviors of black youth that underscore the black moral panics discussed in chapter 2, black youth seem equally, if not more, disgusted with the choices and behaviors of their peers. As noted at the end of chapter 2, when we asked respondents to the Black Youth Project if they agreed with the statement "too many young black people have the wrong morals about important things like sex and work," 80 percent of black youth agreed, compared to 32 percent of whites and 34 percent of Latinos. Ironically, many of the young black people who denounce the norms and values of other black youth are the same individuals who are more likely than white youth to engage in sexual intercourse and to have sex at an earlier age. This disjunction between what black youth do and what they think and say requires careful examination.

While from the outside it may seem that black youth have walked away from traditional norms and values thought to be critical to success and progress, it may be, instead, that black youth are struggling to reconcile their embrace of idealized dominant norms and values around sex and family with the visible limitations in their lives that prevent implementation of these dominant constructs. Philosopher Tommie Shelby, in his work on the black poor, argues that "when people criticize the ghetto poor for failing to play by the rules that others honor, they are assuming, if only implicitly, that these rules are fair to all who play. As we have seen, however, the fairness of the scheme is open to doubt."[5]

Much of the data from the Black Youth Project indicate that our black respondents hold quite conservative opinions about social issues when compared to other racial and ethnic groups. Similarly, in many of our focus group discussions we found black youth highly critical of the decisions their peers were making. At the same time, they also expressed a concern that the rules for advancement were not fair and the resources needed for progress were not equal. They described the often limited choices confronting young black Americans in their educational and economic pursuits and contrasted this condition with the desire among all young people, including blacks, to have success or expertise in some realm of their lives. They suggested, therefore, that we should not be surprised that when the opportunity to succeed in the economic or political realm is unavailable to them, they focus their attention and energy on "success" in other available domains, including sex, intimacy, and nontraditional forms of work.

Making the distinction between what black youth think and what they do even more problematic is the constraint on the discursive space available to this group in which to discuss their opportunities, challenges, and choices, especially in the realm of sex. In the United States there are very few spaces in which to talk openly and honestly about controversial issues such as sex and sexuality—a dialogue that could help to inform the decision-making of young people. In black communities, institutions such as the church have not promoted a full-ranging discussion of the truth of black people's sexual lives. Even in dominant institutions such as public schools, black youth have their discussions of sexuality channeled through legislated frameworks of abstinence or comprehensive sex education. Not surprisingly, proscribed ideas of what is appropriate rarely resemble what black youth are actually doing. They are taught a certain set of norms and values, which they internalize and reiterate when asked to judge behavior. They are rarely forced to push, however, beyond that prearranged normative script to think about and make sense of the sexual patterns, the culture, and the family structures that they are producing—arrangements often cast as deviant and at odds with normative and protected sexual citizenship.

With the election of President Obama and the growing acceptance of the marriage equality movement, which promotes marriage for gay and lesbian couples, we are witnessing a change in the discourse around family, sex, and intimacy, especially in black communities. This discourse is in some ways more limiting than what we experienced in the not-so-distant past. This statement may seem bizarre, given that we have a president who supports comprehensive sex education and thinks that family planning organizations should be able to discuss abortion. In fact, many would argue that in the age of Obama we are finally reclaiming and expanding the discursive space available to talk more honestly and openly about sex. And while indeed President Obama has supported more open discussions of sex education and family planning, there is a metanarrative taking hold throughout the country that puts forth a clear image of productive and valued families as those that not only are headed by two married parents—if need be of the same sex—but also, most important, are financially independent from the state.

The truth, of course, is that fewer white families than ten years ago and fewer than a majority of black families operate within such a structure.[6] However, in the absence of honest discussion about the truly representative forms of sexuality, intimacy, and family structure in black communities, the very public moral entrepreneurs, championing the black heteronormative family model, are allowed to mute important discussions about the multiple forms of family that structure black communities and the sexual decision-making of black youth. If we do not address the growing discrepancy between sexual storytelling and true sexual life, we will only exacerbate the negative consequences that result from such silences, including ineffective policies to support the families who actually populate black communities and inappropriate messaging in the fight against HIV/AIDS, all of which threaten the very survival of young black people.

SEX AND BLACK YOUTH

What They Do

Numerous studies and reports have cited the distressing statistics that detail the peril faced by black youth in the sexual realm.[7] In general, many of these studies find that African-American youth tend to initiate sex earlier, have more partners, and have higher rates of teenage pregnancy and sexually transmitted infections than youth in other racial and ethnic groups. A 2008 study released by the Centers for Disease Control and Prevention found much higher rates of sexually transmitted infections among black teenage girls. A press release from the Black AIDS Institute explained the findings and its implications:

> 838 14- to 19-year-old girls were tested for a handful of common sexually transmitted infections—chlamydia, herpes, trichomoniasis and human papilloma virus, or HPV. More than a quarter of the girls had at least one of the infections, as did 48 percent of Black girls. Twenty percent of both white and Mexican American girls (the only Latino group CDC broke down the numbers on) had one of the infections.... The study is the latest to show higher prevalence of STDs and STIs among Black youth. Syphilis rates, for instance, are holding steady or declining among other youth groups, but are increasing

among African American teens—and skyrocketing among Black males. Already, we know that Blacks account for 69 percent of new HIV/ AIDS cases among American teens every year. And this week's study suggests that number will get worse before it gets better.[8]

The data in table 3.1 from the Black Youth Project corresponds with those found by the CDC. For example, while black youth were almost 10 percentage points less likely to report engaging in oral sex than white youth—66 to 57 percent—and were only slightly more likely to indicate they had sexual intercourse overall, greater disparities exist between our younger respondents. Black adolescents and young adults aged 15–17 and 18–21 report higher rates of sexual intercourse than their white and Latino counterparts. One of the more troubling statistics to emerge from our data on the sexual lives of black youth was the age of sexual initiation. While 21 percent of black youth who engaged in sexual intercourse indicated that they had their first such sexual encounter by the time they were 13 years old, only 9 percent of white youth and 12 percent of Latino youth engaged in intercourse by that time.

There are other trends in the Black Youth Project data that are also of concern. In table 3.2, the data indicates that black youth have higher rates of having been or having gotten someone pregnant. They also report higher rates of having had an abortion or their sexual part-

TABLE 3.1   Sexual Experience among Respondents of the Black Youth Project

Respondent's answer to "Ever had…" by race/ethnic group and age	Oral sex (%)	Sexual intercourse (%)
Black youth	56.9	70.2
White youth	66.3	65.3
Latino youth	57.5	64.1
Black youth 15–17	29.6	42.0
White youth 15–17	35.3	32.3
Latino youth 15–17	25.2	26.6
Black youth 18–21	66.9	82.2
White youth 18–21	74.6	68.9
Latino youth 18–21	62.3	72.1
Black youth 22–25	74.7	88.7
White youth 22–25	85.2	91.6
Latino youth 22–25	78.9	84.5

Source: The Black Youth Project

TABLE 3.2 Reported Pregnancies and Abortions from the Black
Youth Project

Respondents by race/ ethnic group and gender	Ever been or gotten someone pregnant (%)	Ever had an abortion or someone you've gotten pregnant has had an abortion—percentage having an abortion of those who have been pregnant (%)
Black youth	43.1	37.3
White youth	34.4	18.3
Latino youth	36.4	16.2
Black females	53.0	37.8
White females	39.1	13.5
Latinas	48.7	15.5
Black males	32.1	36.4
White males	28.9	25.9
Latino males	25.2	17.5

Note: In the right-hand column, the percentage of respondents refers to the percentage of pregnant participants who had an abortion, not the percentage of all participants.
Source: The Black Youth Project

ners having had an abortion. The gap between blacks and whites in reported pregnancies is most stark among females and among those in the 22–25 age range, where 64.9 percent of blacks compared to 44.4 percent of whites report they have been or have gotten someone pregnant. The data on abortions suggest that significant gaps between blacks and whites are found consistently across age groups and sex.

The trends outlined in the tables 3.1 and 3.2, while disturbing, are not new. There are countless stories and reports that document the seemingly risky and self-destructive sexual behavior of this cohort.[9] And while national studies like the Black Youth Project and Youth Risk Behavior Surveillance Study provide important empirical information about the general patterns of sexual engagement and exploration among black youth, far fewer studies have closely examined the attitudes, norms, and decision-making of this population.[10] Indeed, many of the decisions about sex and intimacy made by black youth are troubling, and increase the probability of negative consequences for themselves and their families. However, it is often the contradictory nature of sexual decision-making that goes unexamined or is masked by extreme interpretations of their behavior. Absent from many of the

TABLE 3.3 Testing for Sexually Transmitted Infections (STIs) and HIV/
AIDS among Respondents of the Black Youth Project

Respondents, by race/ethnic group	Respondents who were willingly tested for ... (%)	
	STIs	HIV/AIDS
Black	64.6	57.4
White	49.1	39.8
Latino	51.0	47.7

Source: The Black Youth Project

discussions about the sexuality of black youth is any recognition of their attempts at sexual responsibility. For example, while black youth report higher rates of sexual activity, they also report higher rates of using protection to prevent pregnancies and sexually transmitted diseases. In all, 53.6 percent of black youth report using protection every time they have sex, compared to 39.8 percent of white youth and 41.7 percent of Latino youth. Similarly, table 3.3 shows that more black youth have willingly been tested for sexually transmitted infections and HIV/AIDS.

Thus, it is the question of representation that begins to emerge when trying to detail the complexity of the sexual lives of black youth. We might ask if black youth who make impulsive sexual decisions and experience the sometimes-unexpected consequences of their actions are given the same care and forgiveness often afforded white youth. Many in black communities would say no. As an example of this perceived double standard some might point to the June 1, 2009, cover of *People* magazine. Gracing the cover of this issue is Bristol Palin, daughter of 2008 Republican vice-presidential nominee Sarah Palin and a new, unwed, teenage mom. In a story that was supposedly part of Bristol Palin's campaign against teen pregnancy, Bristol is applauded for her focus, determination, and tenacity. Readers are given an insider's look at Bristol's life—a life we are told is full of sacrifice, hard work, and commitment to doing right by her child:

> Her mom may be governor, but there is no nanny in the Palin house. Bristol gets up—usually twice during the night—to feed Tripp, who sleeps in a hand-me-down crib in her bedroom, and she says she has tapped out at least one school paper with her son crying in the background. She pays for diapers and formula by working part-time. And while her parents help a lot, she shops for the whole family's

groceries and does the laundry. (Babies, she has discovered, make for a lot of laundry. She was the only senior with spit-up on her graduation dress.)[11]

Amazingly, later in the article Bristol Palin declares that she is glad she did not marry the father of her baby, Levi Johnston: "I'm thankful we didn't get married because if it wasn't going to work now, it wasn't going to work in five years." While for some, particularly those on the Left, Palin's statement makes perfect sense; it would seem antithetical to the beliefs about family espoused by many conservatives who supported her mother and John McCain in their bid for the White House. Yet there was little vitriolic reaction to her pregnancy by those on the right or left of the political spectrum.

Many in the black community were not surprised yet did notice the public's general acceptance of Palin's teen pregnancy and out-of-wedlock birth. The response to Bristol Palin's pregnancy and life as an unwed teen mom stands in direct contrast to the condemnation and disrespect that Fantasia Barrino, winner of *American Idol*, received when she released her single "Baby Mama" in 2005.[12] Upon release, critics took aim at Fantasia for what they called the shameless promotion of single parenthood. As one editorial noted, "from bloggers to columnists to NPR guests, critics have blasted the singer for one particular line: 'Nowadays it's like a badge of honor / to be a baby mama.'" Read in context, the lyrics, like Bristol Palin's story, are meant to highlight the sacrifice and hard work that single mothers endure in an effort to care for their children:

B-A-B-Y M-A-M-A
This goes out to all my baby mamas
I got love for all my baby mamas
It's about time we had our own song
Don't know what took so long
Cause nowadays it's like a badge of honor
To be a baby mama
I see ya payin' ya bills
I see ya workin' ya job
I see ya goin' to school
And girl I know it's hard
And even though ya fed up
With makin' beds up
Girl, keep ya head up

In an NPR interview, Fantasia clarified her intentions. "I wanted to shout them out and say, 'Look, I salute you for going to school, getting off at work, going home, taking care of those kids, cooking and cleaning.' You know, it gets heavy, it gets crazy, especially when a man walks off and say, 'Look, I can't do it. You do it. I've got to go.'...It looks cute, but it messes up a lot of lives. Only a fateful few come out. Some of them never make it."[13]

While readers of dominant media are regularly treated to stories of a faulty culture and rampant sex among black youth, the image of the exceptional teen mother, exemplified by Bristol Palin, is much harder to find when discussing sex and teenage pregnancy in black communities. Not surprisingly, considering the country's racial history, it is Fantasia's experience with the topic of teen pregnancy that best depicts how black teen moms and the sexual lives of black youth are generally represented in the public discourse. In light of the framing of black youth sexuality as deviant and out of control, it is not surprising that black youth articulate a very strict moral code when it comes to questions of premarital sex and abortion.

What They Believe

Beyond the data on what young black people do sexually, I wanted to understand what sex does for them or, to put it another way, why they have sex. A series of focus groups with black youth provided answers to this question, as did data collected from the Black Youth Project. Before discussing some of the detailed answers provided through our focus groups, I will quickly review the general trends found in the Black Youth Project data. We asked respondents to the survey how they feel about themselves when they have sex, and table 3.4 details their responses. Earlier, I argued that one of the reasons black youth engage in behaviors that from a distance appear to many to be immoral and reckless is the limited control or agency they have in other areas of their lives. Without real opportunities for a good education, fulfilling careers, and social and economic mobility, black youth may look for power and success in the few domains they believe to be available to them, including sex and rap music. The data from the Black Youth Project suggest that black youth, and especially young black men, are more likely to feel in control and good about themselves when having sex than their white counterparts. Thus, they might be seeking agency, control, and success through their sexual relationships.

TABLE 3.4   Sexual Control among Respondents of the Black Youth Project

Respondents who answered strongly agree or agree to "When I have sex..." by race, ethnic group and gender	I feel in control (%)	I feel good about myself (%)
Black youth	82.2	82.4
White youth	68.0	76.0
Latino youth	73.0	81.7
Black males	86.2	88.4
White males	65.5	75.8
Latino males	83.1	90.1
Black females	78.4	76.6
White females	70.2	76.2
Latinas	60.5	71.1

Source: The Black Youth Project

STATISTICAL ANALYSIS

Throughout the rest of the book, in particular in this chapter and chapters 4 and 5, there will be sections that are heavily data focused. I want to reassure the reader that most of this statistical analysis will be presented in a form that is accessible. Specifically, I will on occasion attempt to go beyond the presentation of percentages and explore whether some of the characteristics and attitudes of respondents in my datasets are related to or influence particular variables of interest such as respondents' reported feelings of sexual control—these variables of interest I will call dependent variables. To investigate such relationships we use a statistical analysis called ordered probit.[14] In the current example, an ordered probit analysis allows one to see (statistically) whether variables such as a respondent's age or sex or education—the variables I will call independent variables—are related to a respondent's feelings of control when having sex.[15] Generally, I will choose independent variables to explore (in my model) that in the past have been shown to be related to the dependent variable or that I believe, given all that we currently know, might be related to the dependent variable.

In the model exploring what factors are related to feelings of sexual control, I included demographic characteristics of the respondents such as their sex, their age, the socioeconomic status (SES) of their family, and their education level.[16] For example, one might imagine that young men are more likely than young women to feel more in control when having sex. It is also likely that older respondents feel more in control when engaging in sex. In addition to demographic variables, I also included in the model other factors such as the SES of the respondent's neighborhood, how religious the respondent is, how often they listen to rap music and watch rap music videos (rap exposure),[17] their level of self-esteem, their feelings of social support, their exposure to sex education in school, their level of political efficacy,[18] and their sense of political alienation.[19]

Many of these variables are examined because I believe they are related to and possibly shape how a young person thinks and their feelings of control when having sex. For example, it might be that young people from neighborhoods with lower SES have fewer opportunities to succeed in more traditional areas such as at work and therefore are more likely to feel good about themselves when they are having sex, since this is one of the only domains in which they can experience success. Similarly, individuals who have higher levels of social support may not need to depend on sex to provide them with a feeling of success and power and therefore they may be less likely to report feeling in control when having sex. Finally, being exposed to sex education may lead persons to make informed decisions about when to have sex, leading them to feel good about having sex.

Because we are primarily interested in understanding how all these characteristics impact feelings among black youth, but also want to be able to compare our findings among black youth to white and Latino youth, I divided the sample into three groups—blacks, whites, and Latinos—and ran the same model for each group. Finally, since the results from an ordered probit analysis are not easy to interpret, we have taken one additional step. To make the findings more accessible to the reader we have used the statistical program Clarify, developed by political scientist and methodologist Gary King.[20] Clarify allows us to present the findings in "a reader-friendly manner." I will use Clarify throughout the book when reporting the findings of ordered probit analysis for black youth. For example, findings for black youth when exploring their feelings of sexual control suggest the following:[21]

- Young black women are 13 percent *less likely* to feel in control and good about themselves when having sex than young black men.
- A 25-year-old black adult is 26 percent *more likely* to feel good about him- or herself and in control when having sex than a 15-year-old black youth.
- Black youth with the greatest exposure to rap music and rap music videos are 15 percent *more likely* to feel good about

themselves and in control when having sex than those with the lowest exposure to rap music and videos.

- Black youth who report the highest levels of self-esteem are 16 percent *more likely* to feel in control and good about themselves when having sex than those with the lowest levels of self-esteem.
- Black youth who express the highest opinions of government officials are 14 percent *less likely* to feel in control and good about themselves when having sex, compared to those black youth with the lowest opinions of government officials.

While many of the relationships between the characteristics of our respondents and their feelings of sexual control are in the directions we might expect, the last finding is in need of some discussion. I suspect that young people who expressed high opinions of the government probably ascribed to a conservative ideology, since this data was collected in 2005 when George W. Bush, a conservative Republican, was president. It might also be the case that young people, independent of race or ethnicity, who subscribe to a more conservative political ideology are less likely to feel good about themselves when having sex.

Some of the same relationships found among black youth are evident among white and Latino youth when we look at how they feel about sex. Among whites, older respondents and those with higher levels of social support were more likely to feel in control and good about themselves when having sex. In addition, white youth who offered positive evaluations of public officials were less likely to feel empowered when having sex. Among Latinos, those who were older, those with higher levels of self-esteem, and those with greater levels of rap exposure were more likely to report feeling good about themselves and being in control when they have sex.

In addition to asking young people to indicate what they feel about their sexual empowerment, we also asked our respondents their thoughts about a range of moral judgments dealing with sex. For example, we asked a series of questions about whether it is okay for teenagers to have sex under certain conditions: (1) if they are in a serious relationship, (2) if they are emotionally ready for it, and (3) if they use protection. As shown in table 3.5, the answers of black youth did not differ substantially from those of white or Latino youth. Thus, far from being the deviant moral outliers they are often portrayed to be, when providing evaluations of appropriate sexual behavior, black youth express values similar to those of other young people.

TABLE 3.5   Teenagers' Beliefs about When Sex Is Okay for Teens

Respondents, by race/ethnic group	Answered affirmatively to the question: "Is it okay for teenagers to have sex if they…" (%)		
	"Are in a serious relationship"	"Are emotionally ready for it"	"Use protection"
Black	43.1	47.7	55.0
White	43.0	47.5	48.4
Latino	42.1	51.7	58.4

Source: The Black Youth Project

To assess what factors are associated with young people's ideas about when it is all right for teens to have sex, we combined the three questions in table 3.5 to make up a "teen sex scale." We used ordered probit and Clarify to explore what variables significantly (statistically) relate to our respondents' views on teen sexuality. We found that three variables—sex, religiosity, and rap exposure—either increased or decreased a person's probability of agreeing with the idea that it was appropriate for teens to have sex under the conditions outlined above:[22]

- Black girls and young women are 4 percent *less likely* than black boys and young men to agree that it is appropriate for teens to have sex.
- Black youth who are the most religious are 13 percent *less likely* to agree that it is okay for teenagers to have sex, compared to those who are the least religious.
- Black youth with the highest rates of exposure to rap music and videos is 8 percent *more likely* than those young blacks with the lowest exposure to rap to agree that it is okay for teens to have sex.

Among our white respondents, being a young woman, being more religious, having higher levels of social support, and having more positive feelings about the government were all associated with being less supportive of teen sex. Higher rates of rap exposure made it more likely that a white respondent would support the idea that it was all right for teens to have sex under certain conditions. Many of the same variables were significant among Latino youth. Again, being a young woman and being more religious corresponded with less approval for teen sex. Similarly, more rap exposure corresponded with higher rates of support for teen sex under certain conditions. Interestingly, only among

TABLE 3.6   Responses to "Moral Absolute" Questions by Respondents of
the Black Youth Project

Respondents, by race/ethnic group	Responding affirmatively to "moral absolute" questions (%)		
	"It is always wrong to have sex before you are married"	"Homosexuality is always wrong"	"Abortion is always wrong"
Black	42.3	54.8	47.1
White	28.0	34.7	33.6
Latino	31.5	36.4	45.7

Source: The Black Youth Project

Latino youth did we find that higher neighborhood SES corresponded with the opinion that under certain conditions teen sex is acceptable.

When we take our questioning further and ask what we label "moral absolute" questions, we find an even more interesting pattern, namely, that black youth take a more conservative stand than white or Latino youth on whether premarital sex, homosexuality, and having an abortion are always wrong. As is detailed in table 3.6, black youth consistently hold the most conservative views on these three issues. On the question of homosexuality, black youth are the only racial or ethnic group in which a majority believes that it is always wrong. In fact, it is the only question among the three in which a majority of any group registered the belief that it is always wrong.

Our ordered probit analysis of a scale combining all three moral absolute questions finds that both religiosity and rap exposure are significantly related to young black people's views on moral issues.[23]

- Black youth who are more religious are 13 percent *more likely* than the least religious black youth to agree that all of the behaviors listed are always wrong.
- Black youth with greater exposure to rap music and videos are 6 percent *less likely* than black youth with the least exposure to rap music and videos to agree that the behaviors listed are always morally wrong.

I should note that since we used a scale combining the three variables, we are not able to discern if, for example, those with the greatest exposure to rap disagreed with the same vigor that all three behaviors were not always wrong or if, for example, they were more likely to believe that homosexuality and not premarital sex was always wrong.

Among white youth, many more factors were associated with their perception that sex before marriage, homosexuality, and abortion are always wrong. Specifically, being more religious, having the belief that everyone in the United States has an equal chance to succeed, and having positive feelings about government officials were associated with greater agreement that these three "moral absolutes" are always wrong. Again, these last two variables—feelings about government officials and the belief that everyone has an equal chance to succeed in the United States—are measures used to assess the level of political alienation young people feel. In light of these responses, it seems that young whites who are not politically alienated (at least in 2005 under the Bush administration, when data were collected) were more likely to believe that premarital sex, homosexuality, and having an abortion are always wrong. In contrast, being a young woman, being older, higher family SES, greater exposure to rap, and higher levels of political efficacy all corresponded with less agreement that the three acts were always wrong.

Finally, among our Latino respondents, being a young woman, having a higher family SES, greater rap exposure, and higher levels of political efficacy were also shown to correlate to disagreement that premarital sex, homosexuality, and abortion are wrong. Among Latino youth only greater religiosity and the belief that everyone in the United States has an equal chance to succeed corresponded with more support for the idea that homosexuality, premarital sex, and abortion are always wrong.

Given the social conservatism many black youth evidenced in their responses to our questions about the immorality and timing of sex, it is hard to square their answers with the numbers presented earlier in the chapter that suggest black youth are having sexual intercourse earlier, more often, and with more partners. If so many black youth believe sex before marriage is wrong, why are they having sex before they are married and in some cases during their teenage years? Responses to a series of questions on the possible consequences of teenage pregnancy or out-of-wedlock birth provide some insight on this matter.

We asked our sample what the consequences would be if they had a baby or fathered one either before they were married and/or as a teenager. Would it embarrass your family? Would it embarrass you? Would you have to stay with the baby's father or mother? Would you find it difficult to fulfill your goals? The answers to these questions are listed in table 3.7. Consistently, black youth were less likely than white or Latino youth to suggest that the negative consequences presented would affect them if they either had or fathered a baby. Just

TABLE 3.7   Consequences of Teenage Pregnancies

Respondents, by race/ethnic group	Respondents who answered affirmatively to questions about the consequences of teenage pregnancy (%)			
	"If you had/ fathered a baby before you were married, would it be embarrassing to your family?"	"If you had/ fathered a baby before you were married, would it be embarrassing to you?"	"If you had/ fathered a baby before you were married, would you have to stay with the baby's father or mother?"	"If you had/ fathered a baby while a teenager and before you were married, would it be difficult to fulfill your goals?"
Black	25.9	27.9	26.7	69.2
White	42.1	39.0	40.8	88.1
Latino	35.1	28.0	36.3	78.0

Source: The Black Youth Project

over 25 percent agreed that the circumstances presented would impact them. The only exception to this pattern is the question whether having or fathering a baby while a teenager *and* before one was married would make it difficult to fulfill one's goals. Under such monumental conditions, a majority of black, white, and Latino respondents agreed that the negative consequences would impact them; however, black youth had the lowest levels of agreement among these three groups.

To see what characteristics of young people are related to their views about the consequences of pregnancy, we built a scale from two of our questions—"If you had or fathered a baby before you were married would it be embarrassing to you?" and "If you had or fathered a baby before you were married would it be embarrassing to your family?"[24] We found the following:

- Black youth who are older are 8 percent *less likely* than those who are younger to ascribe to the idea that having a baby before getting married would be embarrassing to them or their families.
- Black youth from neighborhoods with the highest SES are 6 percent *less likely* than those from the poorest neighborhoods to believe that embarrassment results from having a baby before getting married.
- Black youth with the highest levels of religiosity are 4 percent *more likely* to agree that having a baby before getting married would be embarrassing to themselves and/or their families.

Among our white respondents, those who were older, had greater rap exposure, and had higher self-esteem were less likely to agree that having a baby before marriage would embarrass them or their families. Greater religiosity, higher family SES, and a feeling that one is a full and equal citizen were associated with white respondents' belief that having a baby before marriage could lead to embarrassment for them. Latino respondents who were older and had higher levels of rap exposure were more likely to downplay the negative consequences of having a baby before marriage. Latino youth, like white youth who were more religious or from families with higher SES, were more likely to agree with the assertion that negative consequences would result from having a baby before marrying.

Some readers will undoubtedly be appalled at the numbers in table 3.7. How, they might ask, can young people in general, and black youth in particular, demonstrate such reckless disregard for the impact of having a child during their teenage years or before they are married? This disregard may be bred by the circumstances in which these young people find themselves or at least perceive themselves to be. In the next chapter, I will review data that suggest that the majority of black youth believe that it is hard for black youth to get ahead because of the discrimination they face, that black youth receive a poorer education than white youth, and that the police discriminate against black youth much more than white youth. When we pair these perceptions with some of the gruesome facts of life for black youth, such as low graduation and high incarceration rates, disproportionately high rates of HIV and AIDS, double and triple unemployment rates compared to whites, and the 34 percent poverty rate, it is not hard to understand why a narrative of disregard resonates with this group of young people.

Such disregard may lead black youth to believe that given the circumstances they already confront, having a baby would not change their lives drastically. Many of the young blacks at the center of this book look around and see that having a baby doesn't hurt a friend's chances of fulfilling his or her goals, because the opportunity to fulfill those goals was eclipsed when they entered a subpar school in kindergarten. Finding themselves educationally behind middle-class white and black children at an early age, the decision to have sex, even though at some abstract level they believe it is wrong, seems not that far-fetched, in terms of the "rational" decision-making and limited agency of a 15-year-old.

Before turning to rap music, I want to take one more look at the political attitudes of black youth on government policies dealing with sex, abortion, and same-sex marriage. As was discussed earlier in this chapter, every member of the political community—young and old—is expected to exercise moral judgment. Through public opinion polls, contacts with public officials, and discussions with family, friends, and coworkers, everyone expresses his or her perspective or judgment on moral issues. Moreover, on occasion one is also asked to abstract from one's personal moral codes to form a position on value-laden policy in the public arena. It is therefore important to understand not only how young black Americans make moral judgments on a personal level but also how they transfer their moral analysis to public issues and policies, judgments that will define the inclusiveness of the American state in the future.

In the first set of such questions, we focus on the topic of marriage. We asked respondents about whether the government should be involved in (1) promoting heterosexual marriage, and (2) making it legal for same-sex couples to get married. Consistent with our earlier findings, most black respondents support the promotion of heterosexual marriage by the government and oppose the idea of making same-sex marriage legal (table 3.8).

When questioned about the government's role in setting abortion policy, young blacks provided nuanced responses. They overwhelmingly opposed allowing a teenager to get an abortion without the permission of her parents but disagreed with the proposition that the government should make abortion illegal under any circumstance (table 3.9). Thus, while almost half of black youth believed that abortion is always wrong and more than half rejected the idea that a teenager should be able to get an abortion without her parents' permission, a majority of black

TABLE 3.8   Views of Black Youth Project Respondents on the Government Agenda Concerning Marriage

Respondents, by race/ ethnic group	Believed that "the government should…" (%)	
	"Promote marriage by offering special benefits to married couples"	"Make it legal for same-sex couples to get married"
Black	65.8	33.9
White	56.1	47.1
Latino	56.8	46.8

Source: The Black Youth Project

respondents were not prepared to allow the government to outlaw abortion under any circumstances.

In our final set of policy questions about social issues, we asked our respondents about sex education programs and the distribution of condoms in high school, as well as what types of sex education programs the government should be funding. Overwhelmingly, as can be seen in table 3.10, respondents rejected the government funding of abstinence-only sex education programs and supported mandatory sex education and condom availability in high schools.

Numerous commentators have written with glee about the generational shift in attitudes around social issues occurring in the United

TABLE 3.9   Views of Black Youth Project Respondents on Government Policy toward Abortion

Respondents, by race/ ethnic group	Respondents who agree with the following statements (%)	
	"Abortion should be available to teenagers *without* the permission of their parents"	"The government should make it *illegal* to get an abortion under any circumstances"
Black	26.7	36.4
White	27.6	25.1
Latino	30.4	36.8

Source: The Black Youth Project

TABLE 3.10   Views of Black Youth Project Respondents on Sex Education and Condom Availability

Respondents, by race/ethnic group	Respondents who agree with the following statements (%)		
	"Sex education should be mandatory in high schools"	"Condoms should be available in high schools"	"The only sex-education programs the government should fund are abstinence-only programs"
Black	93.0	75.7	20.1
White	90.2	68.4	14.3
Latino	92.2	73.5	15.5

Source: The Black Youth Project

States. For example, a recent CNN story announced that there was a generational divide on the topic of same-sex marriage. The author writes: "Fifty-four percent of people questioned in a CNN/Opinion Research Corporation Poll released Monday said marriages between gay or lesbian couples should not be recognized as valid with 44 percent suggesting they should be considered legal. But among those 18 to 34 years old, 58 percent said same-sex marriages should be considered legal." The article closes with a quote from CNN commentator Bill Schneider, who said, "young voters strongly favor marriage equality. They're the future of American politics."[25] A *USA Today* story made a similar argument, stating, "younger Americans, more eclectic in their views on social issues and more likely to have friends or family members who are openly gay, are more tolerant of same-sex couples than their parents or grandparents and appear to be more interested in compromise."[26]

In the many articles that exist about the generational shift in attitudes on social issues, such as gay marriage, few, if any, take the time to disaggregate the data by race and ethnicity to see if there might be divergent trends among the many groups comprising "youth." There are significant differences in how young black adults think about same-sex marriage and abortion and how white youth think about these issues (see tables 3.6 and 3.8). If opinion leaders assume that white youth are the future of American politics, they are in for a rude awakening. As the demographics of the country continue to move from one dominated, in population and power, by whites to one increasingly populated by individuals of color, our analyses must start paying attention to the ideas, attitudes, and actions of young people of color. In the case of sensitive social issues such as abortion, sex, and homosexuality, black youth are signaling at best a position of limited tolerance. For those who support same-sex marriage or a woman's right to unconditional reproductive freedom, there is still more work to be done. Waiting for the generational shift will not be enough.

Those who are trying to intervene in policy debates about issues such as same-sex marriage and abortion should want to know what factors appear to be significantly related to young people's attitudes in this charged political domain. Instead of using a scale that includes all the variables in tables 3.8, 3.9, and 3.10, we focused on two issues independently: same-sex marriage and abortion.[27] Examining responses to the statement "The government should make it legal for same-sex couples to get married," we found the following:

- Young black women are 15 percent *more likely* to agree that the government should make it legal for same-sex couples to marry than young black men.
- Black youth with the highest exposure to rap music and rap music videos are 14 percent *more likely* to agree with making same-sex marriage legal, compared to those with the lowest exposure to rap music.
- Black youth who are the most religious are 43 percent *less likely* to agree with the legalization of same-sex marriages, compared to those black youth who are the least religious.

The findings for white and Latino youth were somewhat different. Among white respondents, young women and those with higher levels of political efficacy—those who believe they have the skills and knowledge to make a difference politically—are more likely to support the legalization of same-sex marriage. Those white youth who are religious, who believe that in the United States everyone has an equal chance to succeed, and who have positive feelings toward government officials are the least likely to support the legalization of same-sex marriage. Latino youth with higher levels of political efficacy are also more likely to support making same-sex marriage legal. Latino youth who are older and who have positive feelings toward the government are less likely to support the government making same-sex marriage legal.

When we examined which factors were associated with the statement "The government should make it illegal to get an abortion under any circumstances," we found a similar set of characteristics.

- A young black adult who was 25 is 15 percent *less likely* than a 15-year-old black person to agree that abortion should be illegal under any circumstance.
- Black youth with the highest exposure to rap music and rap music videos are 15 percent *less likely* than those with the lowest rap exposure to believe that the government should forbid access to abortions under any circumstance.
- Black youth who are the most religious are 16 percent *more likely* to agree that the government should make abortion illegal under any circumstance, compared to those black youth who are the least religious.

White respondents who are older and from families with higher SES are less likely to support such stringent restrictions on abortions. Those white youth who are more religious and believe that everyone in the United States has an equal chance to get ahead are more likely to support making abortion illegal under any circumstance. Latino youth, like those who are older and from families with higher SES opposed making abortions illegal under any circumstances. Predictably, those Latino youth who were more religious are more likely to support legally restricting access to abortions irrespective of circumstance.

As we have seen so far and as we might expect, youth in general— and black youth in particular—who are more religious express more conservative views on a range of issues, including teen sex, premarital sex, and same-sex marriage. This consistent finding is not surprising, especially given the role of religious institutions and clergy in black communities in promoting a strict moral code regarding sex. There is a long-standing tradition of articulated social conservatism in black communities. What may be a bit more surprising is the strength of such convictions on the part of young black people. Again, the influence of these factors on the actual behavior of black youth seems weak, but nonetheless, young black people, when asked, regularly respond with a conservative script about sexuality that seems to be a key component of their thinking, if not their behavior.

In contrast to the influence of religion is the consistent significance of exposure to rap music and rap music videos to the moral attitudes of black youth. Repeatedly, we have found that the young black people who have the highest rates of rap exposure are more likely to agree that under certain circumstances it is all right for teenagers to have sex and that abortion, homosexuality, and premarital sex are not always wrong. This group is also more apt to feel good about themselves and in control when having sex. To some, these findings suggest that rap exposure is related to more liberal and liberated ideas about sex and morality. Others will see rap exposure as corresponding with promiscuity and an anything-goes mentality regarding sex. Whatever your position, the findings suggest that a narrow understanding of the impact of rap music on the lives of black youth is misguided. While many of the videos and songs are undoubtedly drenched in misogyny and violence, they also push back at the constricting nature of public discourse on the topic of sex and morality. Given this important function of rap music and rap music videos, let's take a closer look at what young people do and think about them.

RAP MUSIC AND BLACK YOUTH

What They Do

As noted, black adults over 30 believe that rap music is at least partially responsible for many of the ills that threaten black youth. According to our data, a majority of black adults 30 and older believe rap music causes black youth to have sex too early, have multiple sex partners, take drugs, sell drugs, disrespect their elders, and have babies before they are married, to name just a few of the perceived negative effects. A *New York Times* article exploring the relationship between sex and hip-hop confirms the findings from our data, noting that "hip-hop, with its suggestive lyrics, videos and dance moves, has long been criticized by public health experts and parents, who fear that it leads to risky sexual behavior among teens."[28] Given such pervasive concern about hip-hop, and rap music in particular, one might suspect that black youth are uncritical consumers of rap music and videos, especially gangsta rap.

There is no doubt that black youth are avid listeners of this musical art form. When asked how often on average they listened to rap music, 58 percent of black youth said they listened every day. More than twice the percentage of black youth reported listening to rap music every day, compared to the percentage of white youth (see fig. 3.1).

A similar pattern emerged when we asked, "On average, how often do you watch rap music programming on television?" Far fewer young

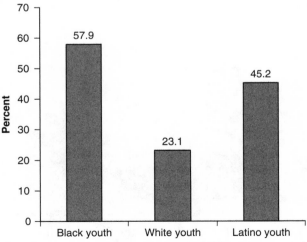

FIGURE 3.1 Number of respondents of the Black Youth Project who listen to rap music every day, by race. *The Black Youth Project.*

people in general said they watched rap music on television every day. For example, only 25 percent of black youth watched rap music on television daily, compared to the 58 percent who said they listen to rap music every day. However, the percentage of black youth who watched rap music on television several days a week was more than triple that of white youth, with 12 percent of white youth reporting they watched rap music several days a week and 48 percent of black youth and 35 percent of Latino youth so reporting (fig. 3.2).

What They Believe

While black youth are watching rap music videos and listening to their favorite rap artists, they are not doing these activities uncritically. When asked whether they agreed with a range of criticisms leveled against rap music videos, significant numbers of black youth and young people generally agreed that there were components of rap music videos that desperately needed improvement. Table 3.11 shows the percentage of young people registering concerns about the state of rap music videos. Interestingly, a majority of black, white, and Latino youth agreed that rap music videos contained too many references to sex and violence and portrayed black women and black men in offensive ways.

Among all three groups, more people agreed with the statement that rap music videos contained too many references to sex than with any other question we asked about rap music videos. At the other end

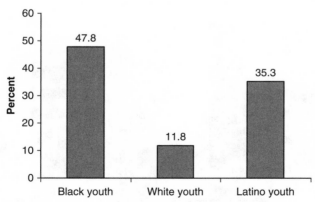

FIGURE 3.2 Percentage of respondents to the Black Youth Project who report watching rap music programming on television at least several days a week, by race. *The Black Youth Project.*

TABLE 3.11 Negative Views on Rap Music Videos among Respondents of
the Black Youth Project

Respondents, by race/ethnic group	Respondents who believe the following statements about rap music videos (%)			
	That they contain too many references to sex	That there are too many references to violence	That they portray black women in bad and offensive ways	That they portray black men in bad and offensive ways
Black	72.2	68.3	61.8	54.0
White	68.0	63.7	60.5	51.7
Latino	69.2	64.2	54.3	53.5

Source: The Black Youth Project

of the spectrum, the assertion that rap music videos put forth a negative and offensive portrayal of black men garnered the least amount of support among the four questions we asked. Examining the responses by race and sex, we have found that young black men were the group least likely to agree that black men are portrayed in bad and offensive ways in rap music videos, with only 48 percent agreeing. In contrast, young black women were more likely than any other group to agree that rap music videos portray black women in bad and offensive ways, with 66.3 percent agreeing.

Left unexplored through survey data is exactly what types of images black women find demeaning. As I have been reminded by a number of young black women, representations of sex in and of itself are not the problem in rap music and videos. It is instead the male-driven sexual imagery that represents black women as at best eye candy or the loyal girlfriend and at worst the powerless, undemanding "ho." Women and gender studies professor, Gwendolyn D. Pough, in her book *Check It While I Wreck It: Black Womanhood, Hip-Hop Culture, and the Public Square*, discusses the lack of honest discourse about black women's sexuality and the role hip-hop is playing in filling that void with problematic and stereotypical images:

What the conflicting images of Lil' Kim and Foxy Brown [two female rappers] represent is clear if we choose to see it. They have based their womanhood and sexuality on the images that men rappers rapped about.... With no real constructive conversations going on about sex, Black female identity, and the shaping of public gendered subjects outside of the academy, their lyrics and images are inevitable.... The images young Black women get from contemporary Hip-Hop culture and rap music tell them that they should be willing to do anything for their men. The "ride or die" chick who will do anything and everything for her man is placed on a Hip-Hop pedestal as the ideal woman.[29]

Not surprisingly, at least some young black men seem to embrace the hard, gun-shooting, money-having, women-grabbing representations of black men seen in too many videos. As others have noted, the detrimental images of masculinity found in many rap videos are common themes of American masculinity found throughout popular culture. Thus, we should not be surprised that such sexist and even violent portrayals of black masculinity are not only familiar but are embraced by substantial numbers of young men who listen to rap music. Tricia Rose, a leading scholar of hip-hop and popular culture, explains how some of the themes that are demonized when associated with hip-hop actually extend across American society:

> Although conservative values proponents sometimes talk about violence as if it is some kind of external threat to American society, violent behavior is, in fact, at the heart of the American values system and has been for some time. Throughout the twentieth century especially, violence was wedded to mainstream visions of manhood.…
>
> The symbolic resonance of Hollywood-action-hero-turned-Republican-governor-of-California Arnold Schwarzenegger's repeated use of the term "girlie men" to deride opponents—nearly making it a Republican battle cry—epitomizes the links between manhood, sexism, homophobia, and machismo.… What is the substantive difference between rappers' use of rhymes about men who are called "bitches" to signal male opponents' inferior masculinity and their own superior masculinity, on the one hand, and conservatives' embrace of Governor Schwarzenegger's use of "girlie men," on the other? Rappers' aggressive, sexist, and confrontational style of masculinity reflects a core American value, not an aberration of one.[30]

STATISTICAL ANALYSIS

Again, it is important to try and get a sense of what characteristics and attitudes of young people might be significantly associated with our respondents' ideas about rap. Toward this end, we used an ordered probit analysis to explore whether any of the variables included in our models of sex and morality were also associated with how black youth felt about rap music videos. We combined the four questions asking whether rap music videos had too many references to sex or violence or portray black women or black men in bad and offensive ways into one scale and used that as our dependent variable.[31] What we found was consistent with our analyses of sex and morality earlier:

- Black girls and young women are 10 percent *more likely* to agree with the negative assessments of the content of rap music videos.
- Black youth who are the most religious are 5 percent *more likely* to agree that rap music has too many references to sex and violence and portrays black men and women in bad and offensive ways.
- Black youth who have the highest levels of rap exposure are 25 percent *less likely* to agree that the content of rap music videos is problematic, compared to black youth with the lowest exposure to rap.
- Black youth with the highest evaluations of government officials are 6 percent *less likely* to believe that rap music videos contain disturbing content.

White girls and young women and those white youth who are most religious, like their black counterparts, are more likely to agree that rap music videos have too many references to sex and violence and portray black men and women in offensive ways. In addition, white youth with higher levels of social support are also more likely to find some of the content in rap music videos problematic. White youth who have higher levels of rap exposure are less likely to agree with the negative assessments of rap music videos. Latino youth with higher levels of political efficacy are less likely to agree that rap music videos were in need of attention and repair.

Interestingly, the one statement about rap music videos that generated only mild agreement and stood out statistically from our other questions about these videos was the idea that "rap music videos should be more political."[32] Black youth are significantly more likely than white and Latino youth to want rap music videos to be more political, even though less than half of black youth support this idea (fig. 3.3). It seemed that white and Latino youth are uninterested in having rap music videos motivate them or take a stand or comment on the power distribution in society any more than they already do. Instead, these young people are satisfied with the apolitical, entertaining, and often stereotypical images and messages found in commercial rap music videos today.

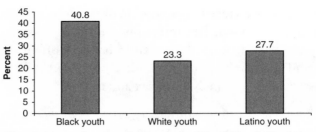

FIGURE 3.3 Percentage of respondents to the Black Youth Project who believe that rap music videos should be more political. *The Black Youth Project.*

As has been suggested by others, white youth in particular may enjoy a voyeuristic engagement with "black" life in the hood through rap music and videos; however, the same young men and women are not interested in having the videos become more political—commenting on the power distribution in American society from which many of these young whites will benefit. As Bakari Kitwana, author of numerous books on hip-hop, explains, "yes, a white kid engaging in the predominately Black medium of hip-hop is going to be deemed cool by his peers if he can pull it off, especially in a climate where hip-hop is mainstream youth culture. By doing so, however, that kid is not choosing race suicide. Eminem is not seeking to become Black and abandon whiteness. Instead, his being white is what makes him so attractive to the marketplace."[33]

As we found when comparing what young people did versus what they believed about sexuality, there was a big difference between listening to rap music every day and uncritically accepting the images, messages, and stereotypes associated with this medium. Black youth are critical listeners of rap music, if not critical consumers; they seem to have clear ideas about the failures of rap music, yet they continue to consume this musical form. The necessity of black youth being conversant in the culture of hip-hop should not be underestimated; the idea that black youth, because of their critiques of rap, and in particular gangsta rap, should walk away from the art form seems unrealistic. It would be like a stock trader refusing to read the *Wall Street Journal* because he or she disagreed with the political ideology of the paper. Hip-hop is the culture in which young black people have grown up and over which they have limited control. Hip-hop is like family: it is part of them and they are part of it; and in the end, you cannot make either family or hip-hop act right. There is no controlling the outside influences that lead your family astray, and in the case of hip-hop, these influences overwhelmingly include record companies in search of a profit. Miguel A. Munoz-Laboy, an assistant professor at Columbia University who studies hip-hop, explains that "hip-hop is not just music but a support system and social structure that dominates youth culture."[34]

Again, the point is not to diminish the agency of black youth, especially those who are more marginalized, but instead to be realistic about how much agency these young people actually have. Of course, there are black youth who make traditionally rational and seemingly appropriate decisions about sex, culture, and even listening to rap music. Often, however, those young people are able to get ahead not only because they have made good decisions but also because they have had additional resources that help along the way—a teacher who takes extra time, a friend or family member who has access to financial resources, networks and information that facilitate the navigation of foreign and sometimes hostile institutions, or peers who are similarly focused on getting ahead. What I have found through talking to, working with, and researching black youth throughout my life, but more intensely for the last five years, is that young black people—like other young people—make good decisions and bad decisions, but too often do not have the resources, buffers, and opportunities to recover from them. It is, in the end, their limited resources and constrained agency that make righting a ship going in the wrong direction that much more difficult.

LET'S TALK ABOUT SEX

Focus Group Data

While the data from the Black Youth Project are helpful in peeling back some of the layers of how young blacks think about sex and rap music, responses to survey questions can only tell us so much. In an attempt to explore in greater detail the attitudes and norms of black youth about the multiple dimensions of their decision-making, I conducted three focus groups with young black people aged 18–21, living in Chicago, in early 2004. One group consisted of eight black males who identified as heterosexual. Another group consisted of seven black women who also identified as heterosexual. Another group included nine black youth who identified as gay, lesbian, or bisexual. This final group included four females, two of whom identified as lesbian and two whom identified as bisexual. The five males in the group also varied in their sexual identity; three identified as gay and two as bisexual.[35]

In each group, the participants represented diverse demographics. Some were employed, some were currently unemployed, and some were attending colleges, universities, and vocational schools. Participants generally lived with either their mother or father, with most living with their mother. Only a few lived with both parents, on their own, or with a partner. None of the participants were married, and just over 33 percent had children. While the findings from the focus groups provide a glimpse into the norms, attitudes, and decision-making of participants, they are in no way representative of black youth aged 18–21. Our discussion focused on their sexual lives, and rap music was only mentioned in reference to the topic of sex. We explored a number of issues that corresponded with some of the Black Youth Project data I reviewed earlier in this chapter, including influences on their sexual decision-making, when and under what conditions they have unprotected sex, and when and why they get tested for sexually transmitted infections. Some of the general points made by participants are detailed below.

The facilitator began each session by asking participants what they thought was the most pressing issue facing young African Americans like themselves. Overwhelmingly, participants in all three groups began answering by naming structural issues such as drugs in their neighborhoods, police brutality, poverty, and the subpar quality of education. Repeatedly, respondents evoked a broader analysis or approach, describing what it meant to grow up in a failing educational system or to be routinely stopped by the police because of how they looked. One heterosexual male discussed his concern with police brutality. "They are hard on a young black brother. For one they stereotype us. They think we do not know anything because of the way we look." A heterosexual female explained the impact of growing up in "a real urban neighborhood" on the decisions people make, for example, about work:

> I feel like my peers are faced with drugs, violence, sex, teenage pregnancy, STDs, and things of that nature. And I feel that nowadays people become a product of their environment. People my age maybe can't find a job. So they think they can make a couple of bucks selling crack or whatever. That's why I think they become a product of their environment.

A heterosexual black male focused his concern on the poor education children living in urban areas receive:

> The average urban child, especially in the Chicago area, does not have a good education. The schools do not get the funding. The teacher has so many students that she cannot concentrate on one if he or she has a particular problem so he or she gets passed over. Either that or they get tested, they fail, and they are stuck there again. They are just going to fail again because they are not getting the personal credit they need. Either that or they get transferred to LD [learning disabled classes], but they are not getting taught anything in there. It is basically just a holding room for attendance.

A heterosexual female also discussed education. She, however, highlighted the differences in resources between schools on the city's predominately white North Side and those on the South Side, which serve primarily black students:

> A lot of the schools that African Americans go to don't have what other students have, the other white kids. I've been to some different high schools. Those places [that white students attend] look like one of the buildings that belong to a college campus. That's a shame. If you go far north, it's so much better than the schools I've seen. It's all the same district and we're not getting the same money.

Interestingly, while respondents were initially quick to offer structural responses, very soon in every group the discussion turned to and was dominated by the topic of personal responsibility and the failings of individual black people. For example, one heterosexual female, in response to the articulated concern with differential educational spending, offered this rebuttal:

> That's true, but I think the nice stuff we [African Americans] actually get, they end up messing up; even the little minor things. They're putting the new bus stops up and everything further south, trying to make our neighborhood look more like up north. Within a week's time they've put the graffiti up there, wrote this or done that, and the city is like why keep throwing money to this part of the city when they are just going to destroy it anyway. I think it has a lot to do with how a person raises their kids and who their friends are. Those little things really count.

According to a significant number of participants in all three groups, many of the problems faced by young blacks could be addressed by better parenting, more respect for each other, and a general desire to do right. A heterosexual male put it this way:

> I mean, some of these parents just keep their children alive. That is not enough. You have to teach them. They think that as long as they feed them that is enough. You have to teach these kids or else they know no better. Or else someone else is going to teach them. Or they will learn from television. For a lot of people, the television teaches their kids. If the television says Master P is this... a lot of blacks have the perception that if you look a certain way you are successful... That is why a lot of people are going into debt buying Escalades just to look cool. Why not be rich inside a Grand Prix instead of halfway making it inside an Escalade? I really think it starts at home.

A focus on personal responsibility did not prevent respondents from also commenting on structural constraints evident in black communities, but most seemed to feel more comfortable stating the oft-heard themes and partial truths of bad personal behavior and nontraditional norms. Thus, even in the early part of the focus group conversation, before we turned our attention to direct questions about sex, participants in all three groups modeled how most of their answers would be organized, namely, with both a structural and personal failing component, but heavy on the personal failing element.

Sex

When participants were asked direct questions about sex, their concentration on personal decision-making was even more evident. For example, nearly every participant believed that black youth are having sex too early. Interestingly, their concern was not with having sex in and of itself, or how young or old someone was. Instead, they focused on the belief that most black children having sex are not prepared for the consequences—in particular, the prospect of having and taking care of a baby. The reality of this concern is evident in table 3.7, showing that black youth registered the lowest levels of worry about the negative consequences of a teenage or premarital pregnancy. One gay male participant explained that one should start having sex when "you're able to be mature enough to handle it and put on your condom or your birth control or whatever you got to do, then you're okay." A heterosexual female respondent only half jokingly suggested that boys and young men, in particular, do not think about the consequences of sex and should be made to take a test:

I think they should have a paper they gotta sign after they take a test that will tell you they're ready. A little bit of everything [would be on the test]. If the female becomes pregnant, are you willing to take responsibility for your child? Are you financially ready? Are you ready and prepared to have [an] STD? I ain't going to say STD, I'm going to tell you all the STDs, the herpes, the warts, we're going to have it all written down so he'll know this is what you can get and this is what you can give me.

When asked why they thought young black people were having sex before they were ready, many participants suggested there was pressure, especially on girls. A number of respondents first listed structural or commercial pressures such as the messages found in movies and videos. Quickly, however, the respondents once again turned their attention to the personal decision-making of young people, especially young women. For example, it was generally agreed that although black girls were more mature than black boys with regard to sex, they were being pressured to have sex for fear of losing their boyfriends or partners. As one heterosexual female explained, young women have sex before they want to "because they don't want to make this man mad. Some of them are scared that he will hit them in the eye. Some of them are scared that he won't want to be with them no more or they aren't going to get the so-called dough he was giving them." In this answer, we find the reality of limited agency in the sexual lives of young blacks. Of course, a young person can decide to not have sex, but it may be difficult to implement such a decision if you are also concerned with being accepted and having access to resources and your personal and intimate relationships are a primary means for securing the status and resources that all young people seek.

When one consults the numerous articles and studies documenting the shrinking number of black men who are not incarcerated, have continuous employment, or are what William Julius Wilson deems marriage-eligible, one finds structural forces, like the labor market and the criminal justice system, working to limit the power and sexual decision-making of young black women.[36] These systems of regulation and control, by limiting the number of black men available for partnership, put pressure on young women to do whatever is necessary to find and keep a partner. This is especially true if they believe that having a partner is important to their lives and will affect what others think of them. Participants in all three groups, but especially the female respondents, believed that young black heterosexual women, faced with the prospect of being alone and without the additional resources and status of a male partner, were willing to engage in sexual practices that they might not desire.

A number of respondents across the three groups also commented on how public representations affect decisions about sex. One heterosexual male explained that young black men have sex because they believe that is what they are supposed to do. The images on television and their social networks promote the idea that guys are supposed to be players, and young men care what other people think about them. "A lot of people go out and have sex just because they want people to think he is the party guy or he is the player. It is all in the songs and it is all that you see." In contrast to the pressures put on young men to have sex, respondents suggested that the public imagery surrounding black women had a different effect. They believed that because the sexuality of black women has repeatedly been demonized and used to justify their secondary status and treatment, young black women are rightly concerned with their reputations and with the negative consequences, in particular, to women when they have multiple sex partners. In this case, both societal and community norms about what is proper sexual activity for young people, especially young women, was thought to limit their sexual self-presentation, if not their sexual decision-making. One heterosexual male respondent put it this way: "They [society] have a double standard. If a guy does it, he is a player and if a girl does it, she is a ho." Similarly, a gay male respondent stated, "I think it is more acceptable for a man to have multiple partners, but if a woman has multiple sex partners, she is labeled a ho." One consequence of this double standard, as will be discussed later, is that it shuts down much-needed open dialogue about the sexual decision-making of young black people, especially young black women, as they attempt to perform an idealized chastity that is not true, or necessarily healthy.

In addition to the differential pressure felt by men and women to engage in sex, most respondents believed that other factors such as parental relationships, peer group pressure, and religiosity also played a significant role in the sexual decision-making of young black Americans. One heterosexual female commented, "Friends give you a lot of pressure. They're like, 'Girl, come on.'" Participants confirmed what researchers have long argued: that peer groups, family, neighborhood, and networks shape expectations, desires, and sexual choices. Interestingly, one factor that was repeatedly offered by the participants as a major influence on the sexual and intimate lives of black youth—one that has yet to withstand consistent and rigorous examination—was rap music. Respondents expressed concern about the messages imparted by rap music and suggested that for young adolescents, rap music was a major source of information on topics ranging from sexual expectations to HIV and AIDS. One young lesbian respondent said, "I think as far as rap music having something to do with it [having sex]; I think if you are over 17 or 18, it doesn't affect you. It affects those under us because they probably haven't experienced it [sex] yet and they are hearing all this [and they think] 'I wonder what it's going to be like if I did have that done to me.' But as far as someone older, it is just talk." A heterosexual male respondent said explicitly, "These videos have a real big influence on kids now." Another heterosexual male agreed and offered his own analysis. "That is how you get your little 'in' and 'out' groups. The guy like the one from the video is a cool guy and the other guy that has penny loafers and corduroys is not and no one wants to hang with him."

As mentioned earlier, one criticism that has been aimed at black youth by both their peers and older adults is that they do not think about the consequences of their sexual encounters and guard against pregnancy or sexually transmitted infections, representing yet another example of their disregard for dominant norms concerning family and sex. The criticism is most often posed in the form of the question: Why don't young people who are sexually active use protection to avoid unplanned pregnancies? As I discussed previously, black youth report using protection more often than white or Latino youth. Moreover, when respondents in all three groups were asked under what conditions they would have unprotected sex, an overwhelming number of respondents, especially heterosexual male respondents, indicated that they would engage in such behavior only when in a relationship. Specifically, most of the participants in the heterosexual male group suggested that a relationship of anywhere from six months to two to three years was necessary to "know" someone and know that one's female partner "doesn't have anything." One heterosexual male explained: "I would say six months. It doesn't have to be an exact year or something like that, but you have to fully know a person to where you could say if I get her pregnant, she is not going to bring a disease or if we do have a kid, I have to deal with her being the child's mother."

Most participants in the heterosexual female group agreed that it was generally when they were in a relationship that they engaged in more unprotected sex. One explained, "Like my boyfriend, we've been together for four years. I feel I should protect myself more with him but I trust him.... Yeah, we go to the same doctor, whatever. So I be feeling comfortable having sex without a condom." Another heterosexual female responded, "I've only had one partner and we've been together four and a half years. Me and him, we go and get tested every three months. I trust him, but he's a man." All the members of the heterosexual female group had been tested, and even those in relationships said they continued to be tested for HIV and STDs. These respondents noted that while they trusted their partners, they realized that it was possible they could be cheating on them. It was a risk they were willing to take to communicate their own sense of trust in the relationship.

Members of the gay, lesbian, and bisexual focus group also made a distinction between sex with those with whom they are or have been in a long-term relationship and those with whom they are not. One gay male participant stated:

> The guy I am with, I have been with since I was 13 and we were together until I was 19. We were together for some years and now he is gone away to school. When he comes home, I might have sex with him without a condom, but we keep up with each other so it is like "show me." With him, it is like I can trust him. But if I was to sleep around with someone else, I would use it [a condom].

While some members of the gay, lesbian, and bisexual group agreed that long-term relationships built on trust might merit unprotected sex, others thought it was never all right to have sex without protection. As one bisexual male respondent said, "I don't think there is anyone that I would have unprotected sex with. I am not ready for nothing. I don't like dirty [people]." Given the devastating impact of AIDS on black gay, lesbian, bisexual, and transgender communities, it is not surprising that more participants in this group asserted that it is never a good idea to have unprotected sex. Overall, respondents in all three groups were not recklessly engaging in unprotected sex. They all were able to articulate the issues they considered when deciding whether to have unprotected sex and the conditions under which they would do so. And while these young people's definitions of trust and long-term relationships might differ from those of people in their forties, they did have an evaluation process that came into play when they considered engaging in unprotected sex.

Focus group participants were also asked if they believed there was a lot of pressure to have unprotected sex. Most heterosexual male participants indicated that there was no pressure to have unprotected sex. As one young heterosexual man quipped, "Who is going to tell you not to put a condom on?" Another stated, "I think people would think differently [of me] if I didn't use a condom." In contrast, over half of those in the heterosexual female group indicated that they believed there was a great deal of pressure to have unprotected sex. And while many of the respondents in the heterosexual female group believed that most of the impetus in heterosexual relationships for unprotected sex came from men, a few also suggested that increasingly more women desired unprotected sex. One participant stated:

> The first thing that comes out of their [men's] mouth is that "it feels better without the condom. You don't feel nothing." Now to be honest, now that we have these female condoms, I'm not going to just put it on the men anymore. The females say exactly the same thing. "You don't get the feeling, you feel better without it." Actually, when I think about it, it's mostly the females that don't want the condom.... I would be like, do you use condoms? "Girl, hell no, I ain't using no condom. I can't feel that."

Another heterosexual female explained that it is more difficult for girls to ask for safe sex because "the guy looks at it and says, 'you don't trust me. You think I'm going to give you something?' That's the first thing that comes out of his mouth. She don't want to tell him her true feelings because she don't want him to leave her. Lot of your girls have self-esteem [issues]." Finally, a female heterosexual participant noted, "Most women use the excuse that the condoms [have] given them a yeast infection and I'm allergic to latex.... It's always an excuse or the guy says he ain't got no condom or we just going to have to do without. I'm going to pull out."

Members of the gay, lesbian, and bisexual focus group mirrored the division of the heterosexual groups. Some in the group believed there was pressure to have unprotected sex because it feels better. One gay male respondent explained, "Most people feel with a condom there is no feeling. A lot of people say it feels better. It is the sensation of it. Even though it is safe and protected, it is the feeling of it." One bisexual female member of the group repeated the difficulties experienced by women when asking men to wear a condom. "I know with me it is difficult because I am thinking, 'Man, I want to be with this person. If I ask them to put on a condom, he is going to be thinking I don't trust him. I don't know if I am going to ask.'" Others, however, believed there was little pressure to have unprotected sex, especially with the availability of condoms.

Respondents from all three groups were then asked whether they believed that most of their friends were practicing safe sex. While many confessed to not knowing, most of the participants in the heterosexual male group and those in the gay, lesbian, and bisexual group believed that their friends were practicing safe sex. One heterosexual male respondent explained that in these times people have to protect themselves. "Back in the times when disco was going, they were just having sex all the time. After AIDS and STDs started up then it's like, okay we have to protect ourselves. We don't want to die early." In contrast, most of the heterosexual female respondents thought their friends probably were not practicing safe sex regularly.

Generally, most studies, including the Black Youth Project, find that black youth are more likely to report having been tested for HIV/AIDS. Most respondents across our focus groups indicated that they had been tested and suggested that testing is increasingly part of the process of starting new relationships. One heterosexual male respondent offered, "If I start a relationship with somebody and we get real serious I would say let's both go get checked out so were both sure." It was generally agreed that today you do not know who is "clean," even though participants offered up indicators such as whether someone keeps themselves up or has a clean house or has a nice appearance. But in the absence of clear indicators that someone is disease free, young blacks pursue different strategies, including, as one heterosexual male respondent suggested, "get tested or you wrap yourself up."

Interestingly, while respondents in all three groups generally viewed testing as a necessary part of taking care of themselves, there was a much more mixed response to the idea of one's partner asking that one get tested. One heterosexual male respondent proclaimed in a dismissive and angry tone, "I wish some girl would come over and ask me to [be tested]." Another heterosexual male responded to his indignation, stating, "There is nothing wrong with asking." Participants in the gay, lesbian, and bisexual focus group seemed to express the most accepting views about being asked to get tested for HIV. One gay male respondent indicated that if someone he was dating asked him to be tested for HIV, he would interpret it to mean "they are serious [about me]." One of the lesbian respondents said, "I don't mind being tested for HIV, [however], I also want them to do it." Everyone in the gay, lesbian, and bisexual group agreed that if someone is given the opportunity to be tested, they should take that opportunity.

I have concentrated my examination of the attitudes of black youth about sex in areas where their personal decisions are often represented as lacking and leading to dire individual and community consequences. While the data presented are not conclusive or generalizable, they do provide a glimpse into the complicated and at times contradictory thinking of young blacks. The young people we talked to are clearly aware of the larger political, social, and economic realities they and their peers face. They are able to point to discrepancies between the opportunities available to white youth and the economic, social, and political challenges they, as young black people, face. These young people experience life at the intersection of multiple regulating systems and, when asked, are able to articulate an intersectional analysis that details their complicated lives.[37] At the same time that the young people in this study have a sense of the larger context in which sexual decision-making happens, they seem most comfortable or capable of focusing on the individual behavior of others. Thus, while they recognize, for example, the lack of choices many black youth face in terms of opportunities for progress and mobility, they are quick to blame individuals and their parents for their poor choices and seemingly deviant behavior.

There are a number of interesting points to take away from the discussion among our focus group participants. First, these young people remind us of the varied perspectives of black youth on issues such as sex and intimacy, even among youth from one region of the country—the Midwest. For example, some participants believe that black youth, and in particular young black women, experience high levels of pressure to have sex from boyfriends, peers, and rap videos. Other black youth acknowledge the existence of some pressure but do not believe that it is excessive or pervasive. Second, black youth find fault with the individual decision-making of other black youth. In contrast to the argument that black youth embrace the position of the victim, these young people express very traditional liberal notions of the personal agency and responsibility of their peers. While acknowledging the structural difficulty many black youth experience, there is still the expectation that individuals should make the "right" decision. Third, however, there is also real nuance in what these young people consider to be the right decision. In the realm of sex, the idea that black youth should not have sex just on principle was not embraced as a sensible position. Instead, our participants suggested that young black people—and all people—should only have sex when they were ready and prepared for the consequences. In general, through our focus groups we are able to see how young black people are abstractly aligned with dominant norms about when one should have sex and under what conditions, but we also are allowed to witness how those norms are contextualized. Just as we discovered through our analysis of the Black Youth Project data, the attitudes of black youth about sex and other moral issues are contradictory and nuanced, but not pathological. Given the limited options available to many black youth, we see how abstract thinking about dominant norms evolves into pragmatic and inconsistent judgments and decision-making about their sexual lives. Ironically, such inconsistency exists in all our lives, but usually the faulty decision-making of groups with more resources is less visible, and when it is examined less scrutiny and fewer generalizations result.

DEVIANCE AS RESISTANCE REMIXED

In previous work on the decision-making of black youth, I argued that what many view as deviance in the behavior of significant numbers of young blacks might actually be resistance.[38] I wondered if it might be possible to understand the decisions, family structures, and norms surrounding intimacy, sex, and culture as somehow forming an act of resistance against the normative or societal expectations that are largely unavailable to these young black people. Central to my argument—or actually, the component that limited the veracity of the argument—was the idea that for young black people to be engaging in acts of resistance through *their* restructuring of normative understandings of family and sex, they had to do so willingly and with conscious intent. As is evident in both the Black Youth Project and focus group data, far from expressing intentional deviance, black youth are quite scripted in dominant norms and traditional moral judgments. They seem not to be engaged in intentional resistance to dominant norms, at least not rhetorically.

In that earlier work I introduced what might be considered a compromise position, namely, that short of resistance, what these young people were engaged in was defiance. For example, young black men and women who are faced with the reality of the end of low-skill, good-pay manufacturing jobs turn to alternative forms of income production so that they might be able to participate in our consumer culture. In an act of defiance, these young people create alternative spaces for income production—the "underground economy"—but they do so not with the intent of challenging or resisting dominant norms of work but for the normative goal of consumption. They want to participate in, not restructure, the consumer culture that in many ways defines their status and worth.

The fact that black youth are actively engaged in defying dominant norms is evident in much of the data on their sexual lives and alternative family structures, but the question of intent still seems to be unresolved. Interestingly, the words of the young black people featured in this chapter suggest that they do have a different understanding about what constitutes being ready for sex, how the consequences of an unplanned or teenage pregnancy will impact their lives, and what is involved in responsible sexual behavior. However, this new normative set of ideas about sex, which has evolved from dominant norms as a way for black youth to make sense of the social context in which they find themselves, is joined in their responses with familiar tropes of blame assigned to "failed" parenting and personal decision-making. It is the disjuncture between what young black people say and what they do that makes any easy labeling of their actions difficult—whether the label is deviance, resistance, or defiance. Similarly, the gap between their actions and attitudes makes many of the moral panics described in the last chapter seem reductive or simplistic, ignoring the moral and normative nuance of black youth.

Fundamentally, the data presented in this chapter suggest that black youth do, in fact, have an analysis and critique of the decisions they make and those made by their peers, contradicting those who represent them as not engaged in their own moral evaluations. Thus, one problem for the black crusaders intent on improving the ways of black youth is that they have misunderstood the problem. The issue is not that black youth do not share or at least articulate the same values, norms, and concerns of older generations of black Americans. The issue is that their articulated norms do not exist in a vacuum. They have to be implemented in a larger context that dictates that these norms become more relativistic and adaptable. Sadly, for many, there is no opportunity to discuss and debate the different moral frameworks and contextual environments they must navigate in their attempts to be moral people, engaging in moral politics. As Pough has argued, "with no real constructive conversations going on about sex," the simplistic and traditionally patriarchal representations of, for example, black women's sexuality found throughout the dominant society, including in rap music videos, are inevitable. My concern is that with the election of President Obama, the discursive space available for black youth to discuss alternative practices when it comes to sex, family, and intimacy may become limited, if not completely silenced, facilitating a greater disjunction between what black youth do, what they think, and what they say.

THE INCREDIBLE SHRINKING SPACE
FOR HONEST DISCOURSE

Sociologist David Snow argues that the meanings we learn or assign to events or people are not permanent but are able to change in response to the social context in which we find ourselves. "Shifting patterns of interaction, discourse, and identification are especially likely to alter the meanings one attaches to persons, groups, nations, events, experiences, material objects, and even to one's biography and self."[39] Discourse is not static but contested, shaped in part by the politics and political institutions, as well as by the personal interactions, in which priorities are set and attitudes and biases are supported or challenged. It is the space in black communities for conversation and debate about such important topics as sex, intimacy, and family that I worry is being constrained by elite and commercial speech seeking to crowd out any utterance thought to promote or engage activities and ideas that do not conform to dominant frameworks and norms. By now, most are familiar with the continuous attacks on the supposed nonnormative family structure and patterns of sexuality found in black communities. From the narrative of hypersexuality rooted in justifications for slavery to the attacks of the Moynihan Report to the literature of the underclass, there has been a constant barrage of condemnation of single mothers, absent fathers, and deviant and sexualized children. The most recent examples of such attacks have been initiated by black elites like Bill Cosby.[40]

As noted, Bill Cosby's seemingly annual rant about the failings of the black poor may be the most familiar of such diatribes, but he is not the only person with access to the airwaves who proselytizes about the importance of two-parent families and the failure of parenting and culture among those commonly known as the "underclass." I could recite any number of vitriolic public attacks against unmarried black mothers and fathers, but I am interested instead in the move toward a kinder, gentler, more rational promotion of the heteronuclear family in black communities by prominent individuals, including President Obama and director and producer Tyler Perry, who have the attention of black people, including black youth. Again, my concern is that both the imagery and the narratives being promoted by and through these individuals do not correspond to but actually contradict the true normative reality of family and sex in black communities. Moreover, when elites such as Obama and Perry promote traditional or dominant norms of what is appropriate family structure to the exclusion of alternative forms of intimacy, their speech crowds out honest and reflective discussions about sex, family, and parenting among black Americans.

Indigenous sources of information such as black radio, magazines, and even politicians are often seen as more valid and authentic by black audiences. This is where black people turn when they do not trust the mainstream or white press. Black leaders are also positioned as being able to speak the truth about and to black people, with the intent of bettering "our" position. So when Obama gave his "Father's Day Speech" to the black congregation at Apostolic Church of God in Chicago during his candidacy, he was interpreted by many in black communities as not simply attempting to solidify his credentials with white voters but also as speaking a truth that needed to be spoken to black people. Many inside and outside black communities hoped his speech might help end what are perceived as the destructive patterns of having children out of wedlock and men failing in their role as fathers that many believe bring down the black community, especially the black poor. In his talk that day, candidate Obama stated:

> Of all the rocks upon which we build our lives, we are reminded today that family is the most important. And we are called to recognize and honor how critical every father is to that foundation. They are teachers and coaches. They are mentors and role models. They are examples of success and the men who constantly push us toward it. But if we are honest with ourselves, we'll admit that what too many fathers also are is missing—missing from too many lives and too many homes. They have abandoned their responsibilities, acting like boys instead of men. And the foundations of our families are weaker because of it. You and I know how true this is in the African American community. We know that more than half of all black children live in single-parent households, a number that has doubled—doubled—since we were children.[41]

President Obama's proselytizing about the ideal heteronormative family is not limited to a Father's Day speech. His Christian faith in the heteronormative nuclear family is also visible both in his support of civil unions for gay couples and his opposition to same-sex marriage—because according to his Bible, marriage is only between a man and woman. President Obama has stated repeatedly that as a public official he feels it is his duty to ensure that gay and lesbian couples have equal access to the same rights and benefits that married heterosexual couples have—that is, short of the right to marry. However, it is in this seemingly small objection to same-sex marriage that we see his commitment to the heteronormative ideal overriding his expansive commitment to a boundless equality that includes lesbian and gay couples. Specifically, he stated on the floor of the Senate in 2006: "personally, I do believe that marriage is between a man and woman." He also stated on *Larry King Live* in 2006: "I am somebody who has not embraced gay marriage. I've said that it's not something that I think society is necessarily ready for. And it strikes me that in a lot of ways for a lot of people; it may intrude in how they understand marriage."

However, beyond his position on same-sex marriage, President Obama's most powerful support of the heteronormative nuclear family may be in a realm he does not totally control, namely, the media coverage of his family. One does not have to search hard to find a magazine cover featuring President Obama, Michelle Obama, and often their two girls (see fig. 3.4). In a recent *Chicago Tribune* article entitled "Reality, Carefully Scripted: First Family Imagery Part of Strategic Plan," Peter Wallsten and Faye Fiore write: "like a reality show set on the glorified soundstage at 1600 Pennsylvania Ave., the details of one family's life have captivated the country—if not the world—making the Obamas seem within reach, an ordinary family that just happens to be living an extraordinary existence." They go on to argue that

> these glimpses into President Barack Obama's household are far from spontaneous. Instead, they are part of a careful strategy that has helped bolster the new president's popularity and political clout.…Since November, American magazine readers have seen a steady stream of coverage lionizing the Obamas and their marriage—with access parceled out to *Vogue, People, Essence* and *O*, Oprah Winfrey's magazine.…[E]mbracing celebrity news outlets is nothing new for presidents or political figures, eager to relate to average Americans.…But White House aides and celebrity-news executives say the Obamas are taking this engagement to a new level.

It is his reasonable tone, his beautiful family, and his quiet, dignified, and accessible presentation of the heteronormative ideal that marks the effectiveness of President Obama's proselytizing. He has shifted the tone but not the message of the primacy of a normative nuclear family structure, monopolizing the discursive space in black communities. What is ironic—or possibly sad—is that President Obama, who was raised without really knowing his father, could tell a more nuanced story about the support children need from adults and family beyond the two-parent family. He could ask the nation to think about new forms of family and explore policies needed to support our evolving

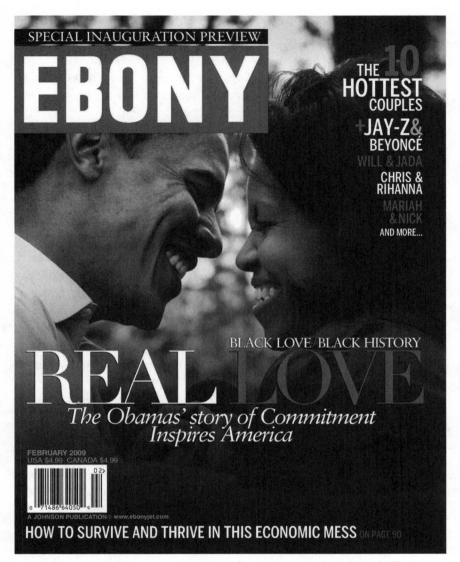

FIGURE 3.4 *Ebony* February 2009 cover featuring Barack and Michelle Obama. *Ebony* magazine. *Johnson Publishing Company, Inc. All rights reserved.*

reality around family, parenting, and even sex. Obama could engage the sexual decision-making and family organization of young black people, not with disdain, but with a sense of understanding for the complexities they face in their political, economic, social, and intimate lives. He could present himself as an example of the positive outcomes that are produced from alternative family structures that involve grandparents, aunts, uncles, and close family friends. Instead, it seems that President Obama has decided to fill the discursive space with rhetoric of longing for a return to a family form that he was denied and that, truthfully, has been obtained in only a minority of families in black communities for some time.

Of course, it is not just a nostalgic memory that drives such discourse about the importance of a two-parent family. It is also the political and economic reality in black communities that the idealized nuclear family receives the stamp of approval from both the dominant society and the state. Yet at the same time, the family is increasingly expected to take on the responsibility for providing basic services that were once the domain of government. When the nation can assume—or at least assert—that two-parent families have the resources necessary to pay for child care, health care, and other basic resources such as food, shelter, and safe physical space, then the role of the state or the government can be lessened in these matters. Thus, it is in the interest of the state and those concerned with its breadth, power, and cost to promote the idea that families, in particular familiar two-parent nuclear families, are able to provide for the needs of family members. In contrast, those outside the nuclear family are constructed as deviants. Their "choice" to not conform to the nuclear family ideal is communicated as generating negative consequences, including the need for financial assistance and moral guidance from the state.

Bill Cosby and President Obama are not the only forces promoting a return to the two-parent, Christian family in black communities. Major institutions such as black religious organizations, civil rights groups, and popular culture deliver a similar message. For example, Tyler Perry's proselytizing for the heteronormative Christian family in black communities is probably just as forceful as the president's words in constraining the discursive space in black communities that could allow for open and broad discussions of sex and family. The success of Tyler Perry is now mythic. He has turned the production of what some would call, at best, corny gospel stage shows into a multimillion-dollar pop culture institution. A recent *New York Times* article counts Perry one of two black directors who can get their films made and distributed. The other is Spike Lee.[42] Andre Willis writes: "ten years after his start doing gospel plays in black theaters, Mr. Perry has made $500 million and is the most prominent Black conservative evangelical on earth."[43]

Almost every Perry film tells the story of a troubled black woman who must turn back to or restore her faith in the Lord in order to be rescued by a good black man. Clearly, for Perry, religion and honorable black working-class men are what is needed to mend all that is ailing black communities. My intent is not to minimize the impact of his work, but his reach and the size of his audience in black communities concerns me. In the scripts Perry produces, it is difficult to find the reality of black family structure, sex, and intimacy reflected on the screen. Instead, we find the idealized heterosexual family in black church face. *New York Times* film critic A. O. Scott writes: "His films are hardly realistic, but they aren't exercises in pure escapism either. They offer comic relief and moral correction."[44]

Of course, it isn't just the public viewing of the Obamas or of Tyler Perry's films that sends limiting and conflicting messages about sex and family to young black people. Reality television programs these days function as a sort of heterosexual boot camp where young men are made into "gents" worthy of marriage and young women are instructed in how to be ladies so that they might attract a husband. And if all else fails, young women are offered up in groups out of which one lucky guy—Ray Jay, Flava Flav, or some eligible bachelor—is encouraged to pick and choose one who just may be wife material. But along the way to finding his "ride or die chick," not only is he allowed to rename the women on the show, stripping them of any identity and existence independent of him, but he is also encouraged to engage in forms of intimacy and sex that will both satisfy him and the viewing public. In such a strange, distorted, and demeaning popular culture, how can we expect any young person to have consistent, informed, and functioning moral judgment and behavior?

What seems to be left out of the new discourse on "black love," as scripted by Perry and performed by the Obamas, is the reality of "the declining significance of the two-parent family in most black communities," as well as other complicated truths about sex, love, and intimacy in black communities in America in the twenty-first century. The popular narrative about black love is idealized and selective and ignores many urgent concerns, including violence in our intimate partner relationships—until it erupts in the lives of young celebrities such as Chris Brown and Rhianna. Largely missing from these scripts is any mention of the devastating effect of compulsory gender conformity and bullying in black communities that can result in death, as we witnessed when Carl Joseph Walker-Hoover, an 11-year-old African-American boy, hung himself because of the bullying and homophobia he endured at school. Ignored in our discussions about the new black love in D.C., namely, Michelle and Barack Obama's relationship, are the devastating rates of HIV/AIDS in black D.C. communities, estimated to be as high as 5 percent.[45]

My intent in this chapter has been to explore the question of sex as a way to understand moral judgment among black youth, because

I believe that such a capacity is necessary to the public functioning of our democracy. I worry that we have abandoned the responsibility of providing spaces for honest discourse and deliberation, elements essential to the development of moral reasoning and informed decision-making among young people. I am not interested in the capability of reiterating moral "rules" that have been passed down from generation to generation. Instead, I am interested in the ability of young people to use the limited agency and constrained rationality available to them, to work their way through moral dilemmas, and to make decisions that contextually and politically make sense. If we do not create the opportunity or space to talk about, for example, single mothers raising our children, then we cannot develop effective policies that will empower those families. If we cannot talk about men who have sex with men in black communities, then we will never fully challenge the transmission of HIV/AIDS. If we are not able to provide black youth with the space to discuss their sexual lives and moral dilemmas, we will never adequately arrive at an understanding of family and intimacy that facilitates the empowerment of black communities.

Given this dangerous predicament, we must intervene in the discourse and change it from a rhetoric of striving—striving to be married, striving to have two-parent households, striving to be heterosexual—to a discourse that highlights the true norms of family life in black communities with a focus on acceptance and empowerment. Ironically, it is because of President Obama that this moment can be rescued and transformation in our thinking can occur. We sometimes have to be reminded that President Obama is an example of the true normative picture in black communities and, increasingly, the country: he is the child of a single-parent household. The images of that reality are much more difficult to find though no less important (see fig. 3.5). He was raised by his mother, and different men along the way, with the help of his grandparents. By all accounts, while he seemed to struggle with many of the issues children, adolescents, and young adults confront, all in all he turned out okay. It is that story that we need to highlight—not to glorify single-parent households but to present that life narrative as America's and especially black America's reality. We must remember that in 2006, for the first time in U.S. history, 50 percent of births to women under 30 were to women who were not married. Nearly 80 percent of births to black women under 30 are to women who are not married. Those trends are not going to turn around significantly in black communities any time soon, if ever. We can continue to spend time and energy preaching about

FIGURE 3.5 "Raising Obama" cover from *Time* magazine, 2008. *PARS International Corp.*

the rapidly disappearing two-parent household, or we can spend our energy, time, and resources developing policies that will support the reality of family life without trying to transform these families into the heterosexual model that ineffectively guides our current policy around family, sex, and intimacy.

In a recent speech to schoolchildren on what for many was their first day of the school year, President Obama talked of his experience as a child being raised by a single mother. Specifically, he focused on his childhood without a father:

> My father left my family when I was two years old, and I was raised by a single mother who struggled at times to pay the bills and wasn't always able to give us things the other kids had. There were times when I missed having a father in my life. There were times when I was lonely and felt like I didn't fit in. So I wasn't always as focused as I should have been. I did some things I'm not proud of, and got in more trouble than I should have. And my life could have easily taken a turn for the worse. But I was fortunate. I got a lot of second chances and had the opportunity to go to college, and law school, and follow my dreams.[46]

President Obama was quick to follow up his revelation of making mistakes and having second chances with the declaration that one's station in life is no excuse for not trying, since we make our own destiny in the United States:

> But at the end of the day, the circumstances of your life—what you look like, where you come from, how much money you have, what you've got going on at home—that's no excuse for neglecting your homework or having a bad attitude. That's no excuse for talking back to your teacher, or cutting class, or dropping out of school. That's no excuse for not trying. Where you are right now doesn't have to determine where you'll end up. No one's written your destiny for you. Here in America, you write your own destiny. You make your own future.

In this speech, President Obama demonstrated both the promise of talking openly about our varied structures of family and support and the instinct to pull back from honest discourse about the challenges to mobility in this country that are faced especially by children of color. It is safe and reassuring to engage in neoliberal discourse of endless possibility in a country where we all make our own destiny. I understand that as a politician and more specifically as a black man running for the presidency Obama was limited in his ability and willingness to stray too far from the dominant discourse about the superiority of the heterosexual two-parent family. Those of us less constrained by political ambition can, however, facilitate a more honest discussion of family structure, sex, and intimacy in the U.S. and specifically in black communities. We can engage in more truthful and transformative talk about the inequality that must be tackled if one's destiny is truly to be determined by what one does and not who one is.

Appendix

TABLE A3.1 Determinants of Sexual Control among Respondents

Sexual control	White (SE)	Black (SE)	Latino (SE)	First difference	Max difference
Gender	-.11	-.46***	-.61***	-.05	-.13
	(.11)	(.10)	(.16)		
Age	.04*	.09**	.06*	.16	.26
	(.02)	(.02)	(.03)		
Family SES	.01	-.01	-.01	-	-
	(.02)	(.01)	(.02)		
Education	-.02	.01	-.05	-	-
	(.03)	(.03)	(.04)		
Neighborhood SES	-.00	.00	-.00	-	-
	(.00)	(.00)	(.00)		
Religiosity	-.07	-.04	.00	-	-
	(.06)	(.06)	(.08)		
Rap exposure	-.03	.05**	.03	.05	.15
	(.02)	(.02)	(.02)		
Self-esteem	.07	.10*	.14*	.06	.16
	(.05)	(.05)	(.07)		
Social support	.15***	.04	.02	-	-
	(.04)	(.04)	(.06)		
Sex education	-.07	.03	-.02	-	-
	(.12)	(.11)	(.19)		
Political efficacy	-.03	-.02	.04	-	-
	(.09)	(.08)	(.11)		
Political community	-.01	-.01	.03	-	-
	(.06)	(.05)	(.07)		
Equal opportunity	-.01	.03	.02	-	-
	(.05)	(.05)	(.06)		
Government orientation	-.11*	-.08	-.06	-.07	-.14
	(.05)	(.04)	(.06)		
Sample size	376	456	204		

Note: Data is imputed.
* Denotes statistical significance at .05 level.
** Denotes statistical significance at .01 level.
*** Denotes statistical significance at .001 level.
Source: The Black Youth Project

Determinants of Respondents' Beliefs about Sex

Teens and Sex	White (SE)	Black (SE)	Latino (SE)	First difference	Max difference
Gender	-.32***	-.37***	-.40***	-.02	-.04
	(.09)	(.09)	(.12)		
Age	-.01	-.01	-.02	-	-
	(.01)	(.01)	(.02)		
Family SES	.01	-.00	.02	-	-
	(.01)	(.01)	(.02)		
Education	-.04	-.01	-.00	-	-
	(.03)	(.03)	(.03)		
Neighborhood SES	-.00	.00	.00**	-	-
	(.00)	(.00)	(.00)		
Religiosity	-.41***	-.28***	-.17**	-.01	-.13
	(.05)	(.05)	(.07)		
Rap exposure	.05***	.10***	.04*	.03	.08
	(.01)	(.02)	(.02)		
Self-esteem	.04	.05	-.02	-	-
	(.04)	(.04)	(.06)		
Social support	-.07*	-.02	.02	-	-
	(.04)	(.03)	(.05)		
Sex education	.06	.08	.25*	-	-
	(.10)	(.09)	(.14)		
Political efficacy	.12	-.05	.02	-	-
	(.07)	(.06)	(.09)		
Political community	.04	.05	.00	-	-
	(.05)	(.04)	(.06)		
Equal opportunity	-.07*	.04	.00	-	-
	(.04)	(.04)	(.05)		
Government orientation	-.12**	-.04	.01	-	-
	(.04)	(.03)	(.05)		
Sample size	548	619	302		

Note: Data is imputed.
* Denotes statistical significance at .05 level.
** Denotes statistical significance at .01 level.
*** Denotes statistical significance at .001 level.
Source: The Black Youth Project

Morality	White (SE)	Black (SE)	Latino (SE)	First difference	Max difference
Gender	−.28**	−.11	−.24*	-	-
	(.09)	(.08)	(.12)		
Age	−.04**	−.02	−.01	-	-
	(.01)	(.01)	(.02)		
Family SES	−.04***	−.01	−.05***	-	-
	(.01)	(.01)	(.02)		
Education	.03	.01	−.00	-	-
	(.03)	(.02)	(.04)		
Neighborhood SES	−.00	.00	−.00	-	-
	(.00)	(.00)	(.00)		
Religiosity	.57***	.52***	.43***	.05	.13
	(.05)	(.06)	(.08)		
Rap exposure	−.03*	−.04*	−.04*	−.01	−.06
	(.01)	(.02)	(.02)		
Self-esteem	−.06	−.05	−.08	-	-
	(.04)	(.04)	(.05)		
Social support	−.01	.04	−.03	-	-
	(.04)	(.03)	(.05)		
Sex education	−.11	−.08	−.06	-	-
	(.10)	(.09)	(.14)		
Political efficacy	−.15*	−.07	−.17*	-	-
	(.07)	(.06)	(.09)		
Political community	−.01	−.01	−.04	-	-
	(.05)	(.04)	(.06)		
Equal opportunity	.19	.07*	.12*	.02	.04
	(.04)	(.04)	(.05)		
Government orientation	.14	−.04	.07	-	-
	(.04)	(.03)	(.05)		
Sample size	550	619	302		

Note: Data is imputed.
* Denotes statistical significance at .05 level.
** Denotes statistical significance at .01 level.
*** Denotes statistical significance at .001 level.
Source: The Black Youth Project

TABLE A3.4   Determinants of Respondents' Understanding on Pregnancy Consequences

Pregnancy consequences	White (SE)	Black (SE)	Latino (SE)	First difference	Max difference
Gender	-.03	.06	.13	-	-
	(.09)	(.09)	(.12)		
Age	-.09**	-.10***	-.07***	-.04	-.08
	(.01)	(.01)	(.02)		
Family SES	.07***	.02	.03*	-	-
	(.01)	(.01)	(.02)		
Education	.02	.02	.02	-	-
	(.03)	(.02)	(.03)		
Neighborhood SES	.00	-.00**	-.00	-.02	-.06
	(.00)	(.00)	(.00)		
Religiosity	.21***	.24***	.19**	.01	.04
	(.05)	(.06)	(.07)		
Rap exposure	-.06***	-.02	-.06**	-	-
	(.01)	(.02)	(.02)		
Self-esteem	-.08*	-.06	.04	-	-
	(.04)	(.03)	(.06)		
Social support	-.00	-.06	-.01	-	-
	(.04)	(.03)	(.05)		
Sex education	.07	-.14	.05	-	-
	(.10)	(.09)	(.14)		
Political efficacy	.11	-.02	-.06	-	-
	(.07)	(.07)	(.09)		
Political community	.10*	.01	.07	-	-
	(.05)	(.04)	(.06)		
Equal opportunity	-.03	-.04	.01	-	-
	(.04)	(.04)	(.05)		
Government orientation	.03	-.00	-.04	-	-
	(.04)	(.04)	(.05)		
Sample size	549	619	301		

Note: Data is imputed.
* Denotes statistical significance at .05 level.
** Denotes statistical significance at .01 level.
*** Denotes statistical significance at .001 level.
Source: The Black Youth Project

TABLE A3.5 Determinants of Feelings toward Same-Sex Marriage

Legalizing same-sex marriage	White (SE)	Black (SE)	Latino (SE)	First difference	Max difference
Gender	.30*	.39**	.32**	.08	.15
	(.09)	(.09)	(.13)		
Age	.01	.00	−.05*	-	-
	(.02)	(.01)	(.02)		
Family SES	.01	.00	.03	-	-
	(.01)	(.01)	(.02)		
Education	−.01	.03	−.01	-	-
	(.03)	(.03)	(.03)		
Neighborhood SES	−.00	.00	.00	-	-
	(.00)	(.00)	(.00)		
Religiosity	−.38***	−.37***	−.11	−.06	−.43
	(.05)	(.02)	(.07)		
Rap exposure	.01	.04*	.02	.05	.14
	(.02)	(.02)	(.02)		
Self-esteem	−.07	−.01	.02	-	-
	(.04)	(.04)	(.06)		
Social support	.03	−.00	−.03	-	-
	(.04)	(.03)	(.05)		
Sex education	.13	−.03	.15	-	-
	(.11)	(.09)	(.14)		
Political efficacy	.30	.02	.23*	-	-
	(.08)	(.07)	(.10)		
Political community	.06	.01	.06	-	-
	(.05)	(.04)	(.06)		
Equal opportunity	−.11	−.06	−.04	-	-
	(.04)	(.04)	(.05)		
Government orientation	−.15	.02	−.11*	-	-
	(.04)	(.04)	(.05)		
Sample size	546	614	302		

Note: Data is imputed.
* Denotes statistical significance at .05 level.
** Denotes statistical significance at .01 level.
*** Denotes statistical significance at .001 level.
Source: The Black Youth Project

TABLE A3.6   Determinants of Feelings on Government Policy
              toward Abortion

Government should make abortions illegal	White (SE)	Black (SE)	Latino (SE)	First difference	Max difference
Gender	-.12	-.14	-.09	-	-
	(.09)	(.09)	(.13)		
Age	-.08***	-.04**	-.05**	-.08	-.15
	(.02)	(.01)	(.02)		
Family SES	-.05***	-.01	-.04*	-	-
	(.01)	(.01)	(.02)		
Education	-.01	.02	-.02	-	-
	(.03)	(.02)	(.03)		
Neighborhood SES	-.00	.00	-.00	-	-
	(.00)	(.00)	(.00)		
Religiosity	.37***	.17**	.27***	.03	.16
	(.05)	(.06)	(.07)		
Rap exposure	-.00	-.04**	-.01	-.04	-.15
	(.02)	(.02)	(.02)		
Self-esteem	.05	.04	-.01	-	-
	(.04)	(.04)	(.06)		
Social support	.02	-.01	-.03	-	-
	(.04)	(.03)	(.05)		
Sex education	-.05	.08	-.10	-	-
	(.11)	(.09)	(.15)		
Political efficacy	-.06	-.05	-.06	-	-
	(.08)	(.07)	(.10)		
Political community	.05	.04	.02	-	-
	(.05)	(.04)	(.06)		
Equal opportunity	.11**	.06	.09	-	-
	(.04)	(.04)	(.05)		
Government orientation	.07	-.04	.03	-	-
	(.04)	(.04)	(.05)		
Sample size	547	613	302		

Note: Data is imputed.
* Denotes statistical significance at .05 level.
** Denotes statistical significance at .01 level.
*** Denotes statistical significance at .001 level.
Source: The Black Youth Project

Rap attitudes	White (SE)	Black (SE)	Latino (SE)	First difference	Max difference
Gender	.23**	.33***	.13	.07	.10
	(.09)	(.08)	(.12)		
Age	.00	−.02	−.01	-	-
	(.01)	(.01)	(.02)		
Family SES	−.02	−.01	.00	-	-
	(.01)	(.01)	(.01)		
Education	.01	.00	.04	-	-
	(.02)	(.02)	(.04)		
Neighborhood SES	−.00	−.00	.00	-	-
	(.00)	(.00)	(.00)		
Religiosity	.15**	.13**	.11	.01	.05
	(.05)	(.06)	(.07)		
Rap exposure	−.10***	−.12***	−.07***	−.04	−.25
	(.02)	(.02)	(.02)		
Self-esteem	−.03	.02	−.01	-	-
	(.04)	(.04)	(.06)		
Social support	.09**	.04	.05	-	-
	(.04)	(.03)	(.05)		
Political efficacy	.13	.09	.32***	-	-
	(.07)	(.06)	(.09)		
Political community	.05	.06	.02	.01	.03
	(.05)	(.04)	(.06)		
Equal opportunity	−.07	.03	−.02	-	-
	(.04)	(.04)	(.05)		
Government orientation	−.02	−.07*	−.02	−.03	−.06
	(.04)	(.03)	(.05)		
Sample size	538	620	299		

Note: Data is imputed.
* Denotes statistical significance at .05 level.
** Denotes statistical significance at .01 level.
*** Denotes statistical significance at .001 level.
Source: The Black Youth Project

CHAPTER 4

"Minority Report"

Kanye West, Barack Obama, and Political Alienation

(with Jamila Celestine-Michener)

O NLY THREE DAYS after the tragedy that would become known simply as Katrina, NBC News secured some of the top performers in the entertainment industry to participate in a one-hour live special to raise money for the survivors of the catastrophe. All donations would be funneled to those in need through the auspices of the American Red Cross Disaster Relief Fund. The lineup on that particular Friday evening included stars of film and music from multiple genres, with the hope that such an eclectic show of celebrity power would not only attract fans from across the spectrum of pop culture but also stand in visible contrast to the disproportional devastation Katrina had wrought on the lives of poor black people who had lived only days before in the Lower Ninth Ward of New Orleans.

The show began with performances from two New Orleans natives, Harry Connick Jr. and Wynton Marsalis. Other performers who appeared that evening included Randy Newman, Aaron Neville, Chris Tucker, Lindsay Lohan, Glenn Close, Richard Gere, and Leonardo DiCaprio. Despite the presence of such sought-after celebrities, the most reported-on moments of the evening came about halfway through the hour, when

Kanye West, who was paired with Mike Myers, went off-script and began denouncing the portrayal of the black people devastated by the flood and the racism of the Bush administration. West said:

I hate the way they portray us in the media. You see a black family, it says, "They're looting." You see a white family, it says, "They're looking for food." And, you know, it's been five days [waiting for federal help] because most of the people are black. And even for me to complain about it, I would be a hypocrite because I've tried to turn away from the TV because it's too hard to watch. I've even been shopping before even giving a donation, so now I'm calling my business manager right now to see what is the biggest amount I can give, and just to imagine if I was down there, and those are my people down there. So anybody out there that wants to do anything that we can help—with the set-up the way America is set up to help the poor, the black people, the less well-off, as slow as possible. I mean, the Red Cross is doing everything they can. We already realize a lot of people that could help us are at war right now, fighting another way—and they've given them permission to go down and shoot us![1]

Following the stage directions, the cameras returned to Myers, who, although visibly stunned by West's deviation from the script, began to read his lines on the teleprompter about the possible destruction of the spirit of people devastated by the flood. He then stopped, naively expecting West to dutifully return to the script. Instead, Myers and all those watching were confronted with West's most succinct and controversial statement of the night: "George Bush doesn't care about black people." At this point it seemed no one knew what to do, so the cameras turned to a shocked Chris Tucker, the event's emcee, who made no reference to West or his comments and went back to NBC's planned script for the one-hour program.

The responses to West's comments came fast and furious. The NBC network issued a statement that evening distancing themselves from West's statements: "His opinions in no way represent the views of the networks." They went one step further, pitting West against the other artists on the program (those who had stayed on script) and those individuals who had called in to donate money, writing: "It would be unfortunate if the efforts of the artists who participated tonight and the generosity of millions of Americans who are helping those in need are overshadowed by one person's opinion." Commentary on West's remarks could be found just about everywhere: in the print media, on the evening news, in the blogosphere, and, of course, on YouTube. Some have noted that before he had said a word, West had been visibly nervous and that his demeanor should have been a tip-off that something was about to erupt. Others have downplayed the sincerity of his comments, highlighting the fact that he has a reputation for such off-the-cuff rants.[2] Not surprisingly, blacks and whites differed significantly in their evaluations of his comments. In a study on attitudes about Hurricane Katrina led by political science professor Michael Dawson at the University of Chicago, Dawson found that while 56 percent of white respondents believed that West's comments were unjustified, only 9 percent of blacks agreed with that position.[3]

In spite of his history of outbursts, Kanye West's comments about Katrina provide insight into the struggles, frustration, fear, and disillusionment of not only West but many other young black Americans today. When young black adults and adolescents are interviewed or asked about their lives and political views, Katrina is just one more example of what many believe to be their secondary position in the American political community. It is also a reminder of the existence of structural racism in the lives of black people in contrast to neoliberal and color-blind discourse that would have us focus almost exclusively on individual effort and decision-making. For many in this group, Katrina, the racial discrimination faced by six black high school students in Jena, Louisiana, who came to be known as the Jena Six, and the exponential rates of both HIV/AIDS and incarceration disproportionately affecting black youth all serve as reminders that they can never depend on the government to fully recognize their contributions or respond to their needs and concerns.[4] As one 19-year-old black woman from Chicago explained, Hurricane Katrina reminded her that she really can't count on anyone—the government or other people. "Just like with Hurricane Katrina, you know it took a disaster for people to open up, and 'Oh I'm going to help you' and this and that. And now you got people from Hurricane Katrina that's poor, that's still in Chicago, out in the street, you know, so it's like, I don't know. They just [out there] for themselves."[5] A 15-year-old black girl from Chicago explicitly mentioned the secondary position of black people: "We [black people] come second, and, like, the rich and stuff comes first before we do."

For this generation of young black people, Katrina is their "Rodney King moment," that visible rendering of black people and the black body as expendable, especially in the eyes and behavior of the state. In the case of Rodney King, it was not only the physical beating of yet another black man at the hands of the police witnessed around the world but also the vindication of those white police officers who took part in the attack (also witnessed around the world). Both components of this event served as a reminder to black Americans across the life course that although the formal laws of the United States may have changed, the ideologies and instruments of brutality used historically against black people were still employed and available to those in power.

Young black Americans today view Katrina as a reminder that although the rhetoric of a supposedly color-blind society has come to dominate ideological and political discussions of race, especially in light of Barack Obama's historic campaign for the presidency and victory and the expansion of the black middle class, in general, black people are still thought of and treated like second-class citizens on any given day. And so on August 29, 2005, this generation of young people turned on their televisions, radios, and computers and found a barrage of images and news stories that highlighted the disproportionate impact of Katrina on poor black people, the mistreatment of the same people in evacuation centers, and finally the vindication of those in charge, who had displayed great ineptitude and discrimination. One need only recount President Bush's proclamation that Michael Brown, then head of the Federal Emergency Management Agency, was dealing effectively with this calamity: "Brownie, you're doing a heck of a job."[6]

The importance of young people to our current political process was highlighted at every rally for Obama, where thousands of young people, especially those in college, showed up to visibly demonstrate their support for his candidacy and their eventual influence, with black youth voting in record numbers, almost exclusively for Obama. However, beyond the college-kids-for-Obama crowd, other segments of the youth population in this country, especially marginalized black youth, serve as an important indicator of the current strength and future functioning of our democracy. While this generation of young black Americans did not live under Jim Crow or experience the harshest realities of systematic economic, political, and social exclusion, they represent the generation of black Americans that has been expected to benefit the most from the country's attempts at societal transformation. Without the participation of young black Americans and other marginalized populations, our democracy is left vulnerable to the continued and increasing control of those with more power, more access, and more status, reinforcing and exacerbating divisions that will only lead to greater disparities and violent recourse. Moreover, our democracy is left vulnerable to decreasing support not only for politicians and policies but for the fundamental political order meant to ensure equality, justice, and opportunity.

Barack Obama and Kanye West both call Chicago home, and both are favored sons. President Obama delivers a message of hope, inspiration, and tough love to "urban youth," suggesting that if he can make it, so can they. The trade-off, of course, is that to succeed these young people (and their parents) have to do some soul-searching and decide to embrace traditional priorities, such as getting an education and performing at their highest ability. But to truly pursue these higher goals, Obama and others repeatedly emphasize the role of personal responsibility and the need to ascribe to dominant cultural norms. Their message is centered on the belief that young black people, with their parents' help, have to channel their agency, turn off the television and video games, pull up their pants or pull down their skirts, and stop buying and listening to most rap music.

Kanye West's message is less about hope and more about learned skepticism and cynicism. His directive to young people and their parents is not about pulling up their pants but instead about lowering their expectations of what the government will do for black Americans. West also believes that young black people must harness their agency, for the simple reason that the U.S. government has no desire to protect the basic rights and survival of black people. Interestingly, while clearly not a "hope monger," West does believe in hope and fortitude. As he recounts in one of his hit songs: "That don't kill me / Can only make me stronger."

As we continue to examine the lives of young black people in the United States, it is important to know which messages and—informally—which messengers resonate with this group. Will these young people who never experienced the harshest realities of Jim Crow express the hope in government, country, and citizenry made popular by Barack Obama? Or will these young people who daily confront the "new Jim Crow" replicate the political cynicism, alienation, and measured "hope" of Kanye West? Given the popularity of rap music and rap music videos among this group, one might suspect that we are more likely to find attitudes similar to those of West. However, given the historic election of 2008 resulting in the nation's first African-American president, the tide of cynicism toward the government may be changing. In this chapter we will focus on the attitudes of young black Americans prior to the election of Obama with some brief exploration of how those attitudes might be shifting in the "age of Obama."

Interestingly, when black youth talk about their political status today, their concerns do not start or end with Katrina, Kanye West, or Barack Obama. One is as likely to hear mention of the suppression of black votes during the 2000 and 2004 presidential elections, the constant and increasing attacks on rap music and hip-hop culture, the mass incarceration—or what I have deemed the "domestic deportation"—of black men and women, as well as the treatment of blacks in the aftermath of Hurricane Katrina as reasons that many young black people feel like secondary citizens in this country, fifty years after the civil rights movement and the passage of the Voting Rights Act.

Far from feeling that Kanye West's moment of "speaking truth to power" was unjustified, these young people welcomed and largely agreed with his comments. West said what millions of young black people believed—namely, that the government does not care about people like them, that black people in general and young black people in particular are not treated as full citizens in the political community of this country, and that young black people face so much discrimination that it is hard for them to get ahead. As one 21-year-old black woman explained, "To me, I really don't think that they [the government] care about black people. They put us up there up front and say, 'Oh, we got a lot of black people in high places.' But things would be different if they were actually, if they had any power. You know, or if the power they had, they used it." A 21-year-old black male from Chicago succinctly stated that when he hears the word "politics," he thinks of "a bunch of white people just trying to get together and just trying to get Blacks back into slavery."[7]

Even when respondents to the Black Youth Project in-depth interviews were asked, years before the election of Barack Obama, about the importance of having a black president to the lives and condition of black communities and black youth, most respondents were clear to point out that just having a black person in the presidency does not guarantee substantial change. Most of the young black people who were interviewed focused not on the race of the president but on his or her policies, intellect, and ability to govern. One 24-year-old black woman from Chicago explained: "I don't think that it can't just be a black president. Just like, that's going to solve the problems. Just him being black...being black is one thing, but what's up here, what's, what's your thought process and your ethics and your morality and all that stuff ties into it...George Bush could have a black counterpart, we never know." Another young black man from Chicago provided a qualified yes to the question, stating: "Yes, I do [believe a black president could make life better for black people] to a certain extent, but he can't change too much of nothing because he still has to go through the House of Representatives." It was an understanding of the process of governing, in which the president can help to set the agenda and push legislation but must secure the cooperation of the entire governing apparatus, that gave young people pause in terms of the potential impact of a black president and made them skeptical about the possibility of significant changes occurring in the way the government approaches young black people.

It is important to highlight that although the comments from black youth interviewed through the Black Youth Project may seem extreme, especially in their sense that black people have been neglected, marginalized, and made into secondary citizens by the government, the same young people, like Kanye West, are quick to point out their own personal faults and responsibilities. In conjunction with attacking the government for its inaction, West also acknowledged that he was a hypocrite, because "I've been shopping before even giving a donation."[8] Although the balanced nature of his attack was lost on the media, West's willingness to publicly berate himself for his own shortcomings is a trait witnessed over and over again in my discussions with young black people. Specifically, when asked what has led to the often dangerous and devastating condition that many black youth face, the young people in our study first articulated the personal failings of black youth and then proceeded, sometimes after prompting, to outline the structural circumstances that make it hard for young black people to get ahead. Unlike their critics, who seem focused only on the personal shortcomings of black youth, this group seems to have a more comprehensive and nuanced understanding of themselves, their communities, and politics in this country.

Given the insight of young black people, their centrality to some of the most important issues facing the country, and their often early and consistent engagement with the state, it is ironic that they should feel so tangential to the operation of American democracy. Increased access to information through the Internet, television, and popular culture, as well as the constant presence of the state in the lives of vulnerable populations, means that the age of significant political engagement with the state and other political entities, if not formal political citizenship, comes early in the lives of young people from marginal communities, especially black youth. Young black Americans interact daily with the state and its representatives, and these interactions inform their opinions about themselves, their communities, and their government. For example, young black people engage with the state on a regular basis through state-run health-care policies such as Medicaid; through their own experiences or their children's experiences in the public schools;

through the payment of taxes; and through all-too-familiar encounters, personal and observed, with the police. Thus, politicians, policy-makers, and even researchers are sorely misguided if we proceed as if young people, who are often the targets of institutional and state campaigns, programs, and policies, do not have strong opinions about their position in society, their life chances, and the distribution of power in their communities and the country.

Generally, data gathered over the years suggest that on most traditional markers of affect toward the government, young black Americans, like the public in general, are cynical, distrust politicians, and feel alienated from the government.[9] However, little recent scholarship has attempted to understand the nature of that discontent. Specifically, is there something different about the political alienation registered by black youth compared to other young people? Are black youth upset with government policies or do their negative feelings extend deeper to question the fundamental fairness of opportunity and inclusion in the political community or citizenry? And finally, if severe and differently structured political despair is evident among black youth, what are the consequences of such a condition for them and the country at large? It is time to once again focus on the politics of young people, not with an eye toward how such attitudes will influence their behavior when they are older adults, but with a determination to understand their sense and practice of politics today, given that they are critical members in our democratic experiment. To explore these questions, we will once again examine data from the Black Youth Project collected from July to November 2005.

THE POLITICAL LIFE OF YOUNG BLACK AMERICANS—IDEAS MATTER

Since the late 1970s and until very recently, there has been a dearth of rigorous research and careful reporting on the political attitudes and actions of black youth.[10] Instead, much of the writing, whether by academics or journalists, has sought to describe the lives, challenges, and choices of young black people, often exploring the impact of a marginal existence on the norms, sexual choices, and cultural vehicles of this group.[11] Most of the scholarly and journalistic studies of black youth published during this era pay no attention to their politics and political agency. In recent years, however, led primarily by the Center for Information and Research on Civic Learning and Engagement

(CIRCLE), some researchers are once again turning their attention to the political and civic engagement of young people. Even with this jolt to the academic research agenda, though, problems still remain. For example, most of the research focuses on civic engagement or voting, and the presumed normative population of study is still white youth.

In spite of such limitations, one important question has reemerged and is being explored: To what degree do we find racial and ethnic differences in the political behaviors and attitudes of young adults and adolescents? Ironically, as in studies of black political participation in the past, current researchers argue that black youth "out-participate" other young people, at least in the civic arena. Peter Levine, in *The Future of Democracy*, writes, "[While] education and income generally promote participation, and African American youth continue to have lower average levels of education and income than whites...[n]evertheless, African American youth are well ahead of whites on several measures of civic engagement."[12]

Levine's bottom line when discussing the civic engagement of blacks is that being young and black is currently a positive predictor of civic engagement. Furthermore, he attributes their larger rates of engagement as possibly being tied to political organizing and mobilization learned in the African-American church.[13] It is important to note that while Levine is correct that on many measures, black youth are more *civically* engaged than other young people, we should remember that in general, the majority of all youth are disengaged, both civically and politically, so the advantage that black youth hold is a slight one. Furthermore, while black youth might report slightly higher levels of civic engagement, such as volunteering regularly for a nonpolitical group or raising money for a charity, data from the Black Youth Project indicate that very few young people reported engaging in politics and, in general, black youth, prior to the election of Barack Obama, tended to trail their white counterparts in reported political activity.

FEELINGS ABOUT THE GOVERNMENT

Differences in rates of civic and political participation tell us something about the political life of young black Americans and how their patterns of political activity differ from those of other groups of young people. However, this only reveals part of the story. We still have no sense of how young blacks think and feel about the political system. When we posed such questions to adolescents and young adults participating in

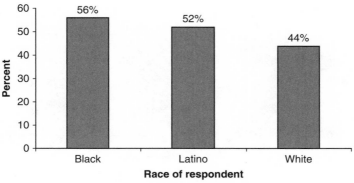

FIGURE 4.1 Percentage of respondents who agree that "the leaders in government care very little about people like me." *The Black Youth Project.*

the Black Youth Project, striking differences emerged among different racial groups. On most measures, black youth, more than any other group of young people, hold negative views of the government. For example, the majority of black youth—56 percent—believe that "the leaders in government care very little about people like me." This is compared to 52 percent of Latino youth and 44 percent of white youth (fig. 4.1).

Interestingly, in additional analysis when we disaggregated the data on the basis of race and gender, the largest gap emerged between black women and white women, with 58 percent of black females and only 41 percent of white females believing that the government cares little about people like them.[14]

Similarly, we can see in figure 4.2 that black and Latino young people are more likely than white young people to agree that "the government is run by a few big interests looking out for themselves and their friends." Sixty-six percent of black youth, 62 percent of Latinos, and 50 percent of whites agree with this assessment.[15]

Again, when the data are disaggregated by sex, the greatest disparity is found between young black women and young white women, with 66 percent of black women and 49 percent of white women believing that the government is run by a few big interests. These negative orientations toward the government were clearly on display in our in-depth interviews with black youth. When we asked a 22-year-old black woman from Chicago what came to mind when thinking about the government, she responded that the government was "a whole bunch of guys in suits that represent people that they don't necessarily help. And, I think about a small population of so-called, maybe rich or wealthy people,

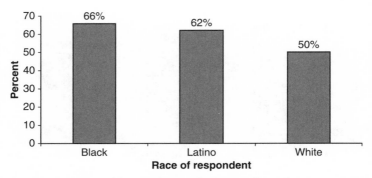

FIGURE 4.2 Percentage of respondents who agree that "the government is run by a few big interests looking out for themselves and their friends." *The Black Youth Project.*

men predominantly, controlling or making decisions about millions of people, and they have no idea what those people want or need."[16] One 19-year-old black woman from Chicago explained that politicians and politics are "scams...just scams. A bunch of scams, con artists."[17]

Interestingly, not only was such contempt expressed about wealthy, white, male politicians but similar feelings of disappointment and cynicism were also expressed about black politicians. A 24-year-old black woman from Chicago reluctantly said, "I hate to say a lot of, but a lot of black politicians are normally in it for them...or themselves. You know, not necessarily for what they can do and change about their race and how their race [is] perceived or how things are being dealt with in relation to their race. But I think they're more into it for themselves. And that...that sucks. It's like, why are you even bothering to run?"[18]

New information suggests that the political cynicism toward the government evident in the previous quotes and findings from the Black Youth Project actually might be on the rise among black youth. For instance, data from CIRCLE's Civic and Political Health of the Nation Survey (fig. 4.3) indicate that between 2002 and 2006, African-American youth registered the greatest increase among those groups agreeing that the government is not responsive to the genuine needs of the public. Thirty-five percent of African-American respondents believed the government to be unresponsive in 2002, while 52 percent called it unresponsive in 2006. African-American youth were also the only group of young people in which a majority indicated that they believed the government to be unresponsive. More recent data on this issue will be discussed later in this chapter.

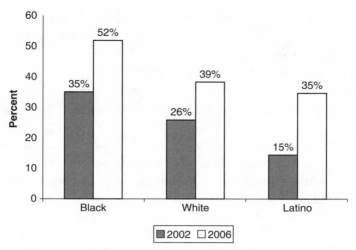

FIGURE 4.3 Percentage of respondents to a CIRCLE survey who believed the government to be unresponsive. *Data from CIRCLE Civic and Political Health of the Nation Survey, respondents ages 15–25.*

There are, of course, many examples of the government failing to act that would explain the declining faith of black youth in the government. These young people, however, are not suggesting that the failing of the government in their lives is only a story of race and racism. Instead, as was evidenced most clearly in the in-depth interviews, this is a familiar tale for these young people, who see those with power, whether white, black, male, or female, ignoring the most vulnerable people, who are thought to hold little political power and even less political worth.

RACE AND THE GOVERNMENT

During his speech at the Democratic National Convention in 2004, Barack Obama made the statement, "There's not a black America and white America and Latino America and Asian America; there's the United States of America." Again, after his victory in the South Carolina primary race, he underscored his color-blind approach to viewing the United States: "I did not travel around this state over the last year and see a white South Carolina or a black South Carolina. I saw South Carolina." While the social positioning and political ambitions of Obama that helped generate his color-blind politics surely will be debated for years to come, I call attention to his comments to draw out the contrast in how then senator and candidate Obama saw the United States and how many of the young black people we surveyed understand the United States. Most of these young people not only see a black and white America; they would contend that they live and negotiate the consequences of such a racial ordering every day.

When respondents to the Black Youth Project were asked more racially explicit questions about the government's treatment of blacks and black youth, we found even greater disparity between the attitudes of black youth and, in particular, white youth. For example, nearly half of young black people—48 percent—agreed with the statement "The government treats most immigrants better than it treats most black people born in this country." As we would expect, much smaller proportions of young Latinos (18 percent) and whites (29 percent) agreed (fig. 4.4).[19]

In addition, like Kanye West, it seems that the majority of young black people believe that in times of crisis, the government is prone to do more when the victims are white. Figure 4.5 shows that the overwhelming majority of black youth (68 percent) agreed with the statement "If more white people had AIDS, the government would do more to find a cure." Again, smaller proportions of Latinos (but still substantial at 50 percent) and whites (34 percent) agreed.[20] Much of this perspective is probably fueled by the lived reality of these young people—a reality in which African Americans aged 13–19 comprise only 16 percent of all people aged 13–19 in the United States but made up 69 percent of reported AIDS cases among that age group in 2006. Unfortunately, the infection rate for black youth aged 20–24 reflects

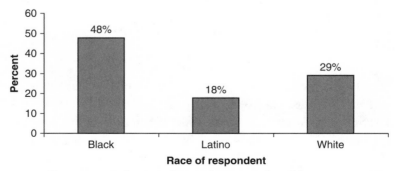

FIGURE 4.4 Percentage of respondents who agree that "the government treats most immigrants better than it treats most black people in this country." *The Black Youth Project.*

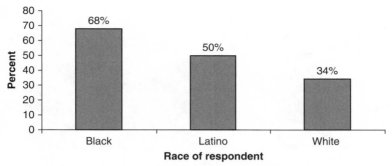

FIGURE 4.5 Percentage of respondents who agree that "if more white people had AIDS, the government would do more to find a cure." *The Black Youth Project.*

a similar disparity. African Americans represented 14 percent of all those 20–24 years of age in the United States in 2006 and 57 percent of reported AIDS cases among the same age group. In comparison, whites made up 62 percent of those aged 20–24 and only 17 percent of reported AIDS cases in this age group in 2006.[21]

When we probed the perceived discrimination that black youth experience in other aspects of their lives, we found a similar pattern of large gaps in attitudes between white and black youth, reflecting what might be called the viewpoint of young white America versus that of young black America. For example, 61 percent of black respondents agreed with the statement "It is hard for young black people to get ahead because they face so much discrimination," 45 percent of Latino respondents agreed, and 43 percent of white respondents agreed (fig. 4.6).[22] The largest intrasex gap was found between young black men and young white men, with 65 percent of black males agreeing with the statement while only 45 percent of while males agreed.

Again, this is not just a difference in perspective but, more accurately, a difference in experience. Recent research has shown that black job applicants can expect to face greater scrutiny and often less employment success than whites with prison records when applying for the same job. A recent study by sociologists Devah Pager, Bruce Western, and Bart Bonikowski demonstrated "that whites and Latinos are systematically favored over black job seekers. Indeed, the effect of discrimination is so large that white job seekers just released from prison do no worse than Blacks without criminal records."[23]

When we asked respondents if they agreed with the statement "On average, black youth receive a poorer education than white youth," 54 percent of young black people concurred, compared with

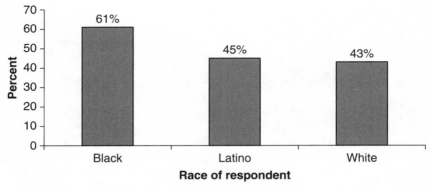

FIGURE 4.6 Percentage of respondents who agree that "it is hard for young black people to get ahead because they face so much discrimination." *The Black Youth Project.*

31 percent of white youth and 40 percent of Latino youth (fig. 4.7).[24] Worthy of note is the fact that the gap in support between black males (56 percent) and white males (33 percent) was 23 percentage points. This substantial gap was less than the 25 percentage-point difference between black females (53 percent) and white females (28 percent). One need look no further than the Chicago public school system to understand the racial gaps in youths' opinions about the type of education many black youth receive. For example, in 2007 it was reported that 54 percent of black students in the Chicago public school system met or exceeded state educational standards. That figure was up from 30 percent in 2001. And while the progress made is to be commended, black parents and students wonder why, in the same school system, 85 percent of white students in 2007 met or exceeded state standards, up from 66 percent in 2001.[25]

The persistent belief articulated among young black people is that they are receiving a substandard education. As one young male from Chicago explained, "White people have laptops and we have a pen that don't work with paper." Another young man from Chicago argued that part of the reason for the poorer education of blacks had to do with teachers' expectations. "These white kids can get the extra help or whatever. Black people can, too, but it's like white people [teachers] already expect black people to only do a certain amount. You know, just do enough. So they don't ever push them to, you know, go above that limit."

Perceptions of the treatment of blacks in the health-care system also registered interesting racial and ethnic differences among respondents. When asked if they agreed with the statement "In the health-care system, blacks are treated less fairly than whites," the majority of black

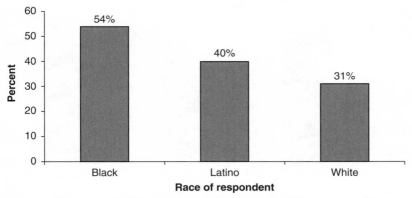

FIGURE 4.7 Percentage of respondents who agree that "on average, black youths receive a poorer education than white youths." *The Black Youth Project.*

(59 percent) and Latino (52 percent) youth indicated their agreement, while only 32 percent of whites agreed (fig. 4.8).[26]

Among racialized questions concerning the treatment of black youth at the hands of state entities, the one area where there is overwhelming agreement among all young people surveyed is in their assessment of how the police treat black youth. As figure 4.9 shows, the majority of all young people across racial groups agreed with the statement "On average, the police discriminate much more against black youth than they do against white youth." Seventy-nine percent of young black people, 73 percent of Latinos, and 63 percent of whites agreed.[27]

It is a sad fact, but there are a plethora of examples of black youth being harassed, beaten, and killed by the police. Of course, there are the extreme stories that receive national attention, like the killing of

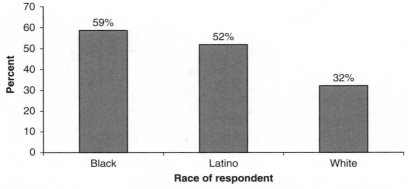

FIGURE 4.8 Percentage of respondents who agree that "in the health care system, blacks are treated less fairly than whites." *The Black Youth Project.*

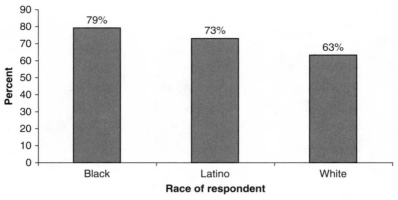

FIGURE 4.9 Percentage of respondents who agree that "on average, the police discriminate much more against black youths than they do against white youths." *The Black Youth Project.*

Sean Bell on November 26, 2006, by three New York City police officers the evening before he was to marry. Bell, aged 23, and two friends were fired at fifty times by plainclothes New York City police detectives who suspected a member of Bell's entourage of reaching for a gun. Again, while many know the story of Sean Bell's sad and unconscionable death, young black people experience daily what they perceive to be harassment by the police. In their responses to questions on the Black Youth Project survey, over half of black males (54 percent) reported being treated unfairly by the police, compared to 42 percent of Latino males and 38 percent of white males.[28]

During the in-depth interviews, nearly all the young people discussed how the police stereotypically defined the motives and behavior of black youth. As one 17-year-old black male from Milwaukee explained, "If they see four or five black young dudes standing on the corner, we gotta be selling dope and stuff like that. So, they just already got us labeled." When asked if he had ever seen the police physically harass anyone, he responded, "I seen them harassin' people every now and then....Like if you run and they catch you, they beat you up. Rough you up a little bit. Stuff like that."[29]

POLITICAL ALIENATION

There are myriad factors in the daily life experiences of black youth that might prompt them to disengage from political and civil society. But in this chapter, I want to focus on the role of political alienation—

not just the feelings of black youth toward the government, but their assessment of the entire political landscape—as one reason many of them have been largely disengaged, actively and emotionally, from the political process.

I am interested in the role of political alienation because it is so prevalent in our data and because the topic has been shown to be relevant for so long. One need only read the sociological classics of Durkheim and Marx to underscore the significance of the concept of alienation for our understanding of how individuals exist and interact in the world.[30] In political science, much of the work on alienation emerged in the 1960s, in part because of the availability of survey data through the Survey Research Center at the University of Michigan. Over the years, alienation has been conceptualized and measured in various ways. Most political science scholars take political alienation to be a subjective condition in which feelings of inefficacy or the belief that formal political decision-making is impenetrable to the average citizen conjoin with feelings of cynicism and distrust toward the government. The combination of low efficacy and high cynicism has often been viewed in political science studies as the signal of political alienation.[31]

Early data gathered through the Michigan Survey Research Center Presidential Election Studies showed increasing levels of political alienation among the populace in the 1960s and 1970s.[32] Although the Michigan data were central to the expansion of alienation studies, concern over the social and political uprisings of the 1960s and 1970s, encompassing the civil rights movement, the Black Power and Brown Power movements, opposition to the Vietnam War, and the women's movement, also fueled work in this area. Alarm was voiced over what impact growing levels of political alienation would have on the political system and, more specifically, the political behavior of the masses.

Some argued that rising alienation, especially among the young and the disadvantaged, would lead to political uprisings, riots, and greater political activism.[33] Others suggested that amplified alienation would lead to broad disengagement from the political system, possibly most evident among the middle class, since their absence would be noticed.[34] Still others suggested that mounting alienation would have little or no effect.[35] Basically, those who had participated in the past would once again find their way to the polls or the office of a public official to voice their concerns. In the end, researchers generally concluded that while certain demographic groups, such as blacks and college-educated youth, seemed to be more willing to engage in extrasystemic political behavior, such as protesting, across the public there was a rise in political alienation, but without a significant withdrawal from politics or support of the underlying political structure.[36]

The majority of people were fed up with political officials they viewed as corrupt and unresponsive; however, they continued participating at about the same rates. Feelings individuals held toward political authorities and specific policies would come to be labeled *specific support* by social scientists such as David Easton. Ironically, the same individuals who held limited specific support for the political authorities and their policies still harbored what Easton called *diffuse support* for the larger political order. Easton explains the difference between specific and diffuse support:

> Some types of evaluations are closely related to what the political authorities do and how they do it. Others are more fundamental in character because they are directed to basic aspects of the system. They represent more enduring bonds and thereby make it possible for members to oppose the incumbents of offices and yet retain respect for the offices themselves, for the way in which they are ordered, and for the community of which they are a part. The distinction of roughly this sort I have called "specific" against "diffuse" support.[37]

For Easton and other scholars, diffuse support may be the most important form of support a political system both generates and depends on. Diffuse support exists independently, to some degree, of the specific policies of any one administration. It is instead an attachment or bond that members of the political community develop to or with the broader or underlying political order. Diffuse support is an attachment to what has been called the political regime—constitutional order or political structures that design how authorities are elected, how policies emerge and are validated, and how participants contribute to the work of the government. Diffuse support, which develops during childhood, is durable and acts as a buffer when the authorities do not meet the demands of the political community, generating system stress.

Diffuse support is the component that can curb violent outbursts and sustained collective action among the masses, because it calls on a reservoir of goodwill and faith in the government and the political order during times of specific discontent. Fundamentally, diffuse support is an underlying belief that the political system is fair and that one's concerns will, on balance and over time, be recognized and addressed by those in power. Easton's insights about the difference between specific and diffuse support necessitate that scholars today, when thinking about and attempting to measure political alienation, be cognizant of what I believe to be the multiple dimensions of political alienation.

Building on the work of Easton, I conceptualize political alienation as having three dimensions. One dimension is what I call *government orientation*, or the feelings individuals hold toward government officials. This dimension in many ways maps onto a number of studies that measure political alienation by asking respondents questions about their feelings toward political officials and their sense of efficacy. The second dimension is what I label *political community*. This measure is more closely aligned with the idea of diffuse support. Through this dimension, I explore respondents' feelings of connectedness to and membership in the larger political community. The third dimension is that of *equal opportunity*. This dimension seeks to interrogate one's feelings of fairness and opportunity in the country. Again, this last measure is thought to be a marker for diffuse support, the idea that citizens may not agree with every decision or policy of political officials but overall believe the "system" to be fair, providing everyone with an equal chance to succeed. When we include in our analysis of political alienation all three of these dimensions, we engage in a much more comprehensive interrogation of the feelings black youth hold toward the political system and the overall political landscape. Furthermore, while the first of the three dimensions centers on traditional conceptualizations of political alienation, we are especially interested in also exploring the more stable notion of diffuse support among black youth and young adults.

In his own work, Easton concedes that largely stable diffuse support can be altered. He provides two scenarios in which diffuse support may erode either over time or quickly. In one case, if people's dissatisfaction with the decisions and actions of the government extends over time, it may slowly and gradually chip away at the diffuse and fundamental attachment people have to the political system. In another scenario, a very quick and intense rise in unhappiness with the government can severely wound people's belief in the system and send their diffuse support "into a precipitous decline."[38] Easton warns that these scenarios are not as rare as people may believe.

Researchers in the 1960s and 1970s worried that events such as the civil rights and Black Power movements, the Vietnam War, the 1968 Democratic Convention, and Watergate would not only diminish specific support among most Americans but might also provide a significant and defining shock to diffuse support, putting political stability and persistence into question. Eventually, however, most scholars breathed a sigh of relief when they concluded that while the white populace was registering increasing alienation toward elected officials (declining specific support), they still strongly supported what they believed to be the fundamental structure and fairness of the political system (diffuse support).

The same was not true of black Americans, who repeatedly pointed to deep-seated flaws in the political process, questioned the legitimacy of foundational political documents such as the Constitution, and believed it their right, if not their patriotic duty, to take to the streets to demonstrate their lack of diffuse support for the political system. Many black Americans had been socialized politically since childhood to hold greater distrust of public officials and the political system. Early researchers in the field of political socialization repeatedly found that black schoolchildren registered lower levels of trust in the government and political efficacy and higher levels of cynicism than white schoolchildren.[39] Some researchers and politicians worried that black Americans could work to destabilize the political system if their specific and diffuse support became too weak. The feared revolution of black Americans never occurred, in part because of the social mobility experienced by some in the group. As educational, employment, political, and residential opportunities expanded for some black people, diffuse support for the promise of equality and opportunity through our current political structure stabilized among black Americans.[40]

Ironically, nearly forty years after the heyday of political alienation studies, the political attitudes of black youth raise some of the same questions asked by a previous generation of scholars concerning both specific and diffuse support for our political system. Specifically, why is it that over forty years after the Civil Rights Act and the Voting Rights Act were passed, black youth continue to feel alienated from the government? Do their rates of discontent continue to exceed those of their counterparts in other racial and ethnic groups? Moreover, does their alienation toward government officials, or what I will label *government-oriented alienation*, mirror their feelings in other dimensions of political alienation, such as their feelings of full inclusion in the larger political community of presumed equals and their sense that all are given an equal chance to succeed?[41] Finally, what factors are related to these dynamics, and are they the same across racial and ethnic groups?

It has long been noted by scholars that black Americans exhibit more distrust and skepticism of the government than do other groups.[42] However, many believed that the current generation of young black people would no longer hold the levels of government alienation witnessed among previous generations of blacks who withstood pervasive marginalization by systems such as Jim Crow. As discussed earlier, prominent commentators and figures in black communities, including Bill Cosby, Stanley Crouch, Oprah Winfrey, Juan Williams, and John McWhorter, have all complained that the current generation of black youth, including those who are middle and upper class, have a tight grasp on the victim mentality, leading them to be alienated from, and unproductive in, a society in which opportunity is greater than it ever has been for black people. For example, black elites ask why young black adults at some of the nation's most prestigious colleges and universities with nothing but earning power in their futures would be alienated from politics and the state? This question will undoubtedly be amplified now that the state is headed by a black president. Yet while those of an older generation might be frustrated with the attitudes and behaviors of young black people, the data from the Black Youth Project suggest that black youth are not the only ones exhibiting feelings of alienation. If we refer to two questions discussed previously, we can explore and compare the levels of alienation held among white, black, and Latino youth.

ALIENATION AND THE NUMBERS

We used two questions to measure attitudes concerning government officials, comprising the government-oriented dimension of political alienation. One question asked if respondents agreed with the statement that leaders in government care very little about people like them—a traditional efficacy/trust question. As noted, we found that 56 percent of black youth, 52 percent of Latino youth and 44 percent of white youth agreed with the statement.[43] The second question was whether respondents agreed with the statement that the government is run by a few big interests looking out for themselves. Sixty-six percent of blacks, 62 percent of Latinos, and 50 percent of whites agreed with the statement, suggesting that all young people, and especially black youth, harbor feelings of inefficacy and cynicism directed, in particular, at political officials.[44] These questions are similar to questions used to assess alienation in previous studies that have focused on feelings of efficacy and trust. Thus, if one does not trust government officials and feels that they have little ability or power to influence government decisions, they tend to be alienated.

Again, traditional studies of political alienation have often limited their target of inquiry to public officials, serving as a referendum on the government—"Do you trust them and are you able to impact their decisions?" Such questions are thought to tap into respondents' feelings about political authorities, which are often represented as their specific support for the outputs generated through the political system. I believe that the political alienation that black youth feel extends beyond their thoughts about government officials. So while most young people (and adults) agree that political officials are not to be trusted and just want to "throw the bums out of office," black youth are also questioning the fundamental fairness of the political order and their standing in the larger political community. Thus, borrowing from Easton's delineation of the political system, which includes political authorities, the political community, and the regime, I investigate whether there are significant differences in the feelings that young people from different racial and ethnic groups have not only toward politicians but also in the two additional dimensions of alienation I outlined earlier: political community and their sense that everyone has an equal chance for success under the current political order. It is only when we explore black youths' attitudes toward political officials, their feelings of inclusion in the political community, and their sense of equal opportunity under the current state order that we are truly able to assess their feelings of *political* alienation, not just *government-oriented* alienation.

To more fully interrogate how young people think about their place in the political community and the structure of opportunity, I turn to two questions in the Black Youth Project data set. The first question we asked respondents was to what extent they agreed with the statement "Generally, I feel like a full and equal citizen in this country with all the rights and protections that other people have." This measure I label the *political community* dimension of political alienation. This question is an indicator of how fully integrated and respected black youth feel as members of the political community. While there might be shared skepticism toward elected officials among young people, their experiences with the government and their general life experiences may differentiate their feelings of political status and equality. Findings from our national survey suggest that a significant number of black respondents—60 percent—feel like full and equal citizens; however, this was 23 percentage points less than the 83 percent of white respondents who stated they felt like full and equal citizens and the 70 percent of Latino respondents who did (fig. 4.10).[45]

A similar important distinction in the attitudes of young black people toward the political system is also found in their sense of the provision of equal opportunity to all citizens. Do they believe that generally

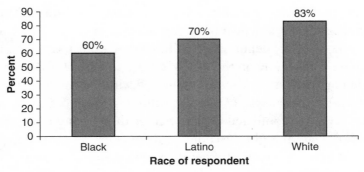

FIGURE 4.10 Percentage of respondents who agree that "generally, I feel like a full and equal citizen in this country with all the rights and protections that other people have." *The Black Youth Project.*

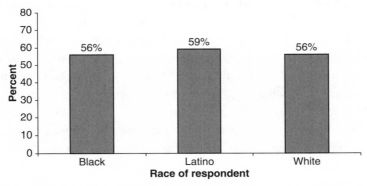

FIGURE 4.11 Percentage of respondents who agree that "in the United States, everyone has an equal chance to succeed." *The Black Youth Project.*

the system provides means so that everyone has an equal chance to get ahead? To explore these feelings, we used another question: "Do you agree with the statement that in the United States, everyone has an equal chance to succeed?" (fig. 4.11). This question is an indicator of what we call the *equal opportunity* dimension of political alienation. Interestingly, for this question there was less marked disparity among racial and ethnic groups. We found that 56 percent of whites, 56 percent of Blacks, and 59 percent of Latinos all agreed that in the United States, everyone has an equal chance to succeed.[46]

For many, it is this last question and the general consensus evidenced among young people that causes the greatest pause. How is it that young blacks, who are more alienated from government officials and who are less likely to believe that they are fully included as equal citizens in the democracy, similarly feel that everyone has an equal chance to succeed—however they define success? To provide even a partial answer to this puzzle, I again rely on the idea of diffuse support. It is possible that while young black Americans are disgusted with the current running of the nation's political system and are willing to withhold their specific support, they are conflicted about whether there is any hope, short of revolution, that can right the country's democracy. These young people seem torn between a feeling of being secondary in the political community, as expressed by Kanye West, and the promise of opportunity and mobility they hear from politicians like Barack Obama.

I daresay that while one component of political alienation—namely, disgust with political authorities—seems to be standard fare, the feelings of black youth about being full members of the political community and about fundamental equality of opportunity are still up in the air. These young people are at a crossroads, and possible changes in attitudes around race and class may determine whether young black Americans are to be decidedly alienated from the entire political process or are to revive their faith in the country and the possibility of a fully functioning democracy. If we are to intervene and gently push black youth in one direction or another, we will need to answer at least one substantial question: What characteristics and experiences are most closely correlated with the *political* alienation expressed by black youth?

TRYING TO UNDERSTAND POLITICAL ALIENATION

The data available through the Black Youth Project can help us to statistically examine what variables are closely related to and possibly influence how black youth feel about the three dimensions of political alienation detailed previously—government, political community, and equal opportunity.[47] Because we are primarily interested in the structure of political alienation and diffuse support among black youth, but also want to understand how their feelings of political alienation might differ from those of white and Latino youth, we again divided our sample into three groups—blacks, whites, and Latinos—and ran the same model of the three dimensions of political alienation for each group. The first dimension of political alienation explored focused on one's trust and feelings of efficacy toward the government. For this analysis, we created a measure of government-oriented alienation. The measure or variable is a scale that combines the responses from the two questions highlighted earlier in this chapter: "The leaders in government care little about people like me" and "The government is pretty much run by a few big interests looking out for themselves and their friends."[48] As noted, the second dimension of political alienation, as we conceptualize it—political community—is measured by the statement "I feel like a full and equal citizen." Likewise, for the third dimension of political alienation—equal opportunity—we use the statement "Everyone has an equal chance to succeed in the United States as an indicator of this dimension of alienation."

As in the analysis discussed in the previous chapter, we included in our models of political alienation essential control variables that, in this case, constituted four overlapping groups. In *Voice and Equality*, political scientists Sidney Verba, Kay Schlozman, and Henry Brady use a four-step process to explore the complex factors that result in political and civic activity.[49] While we will not replicate the same statistical model, we believe these authors' grouping of their control variables into categories makes them more instinctively comprehensible to the reader. We will, therefore, borrow this approach.

We call the first group of variables—as do Verba, Schlozman, and Brady—initial characteristics. These are largely demographic variables representing characteristics of our respondents over which they have little to no control. Variables in this group are age, sex, family SES,[50] and immigrant status.[51] A second group of variables included in our model are those we label political socialization variables. These are experiences thought to shape the political socialization a young person receives. Variables in this group include the respondent's education level, parental interest in politics, levels of exposure to rap music and videos,[52] personal experience with discrimination,[53] neighborhood SES, and neighborhood racial diversity. A third set of variables included in our model are those measuring institutional involvement. Numerous studies have found that individuals who are enmeshed in organizations and structured environments are provided with not only greater political information, often in the form of political discussion, but also the opportunity for political mobilization, positively impacting the probability of their engaging in politics.[54] In this model, we include variables that measure whether the person is in school or working, belongs to an organization or group, and is active at his or her place of worship.[55] The final group of variables included in the model is largely attitudinal, measuring respondents' perceptions, not experiences. In this category of variables are one's perceived political efficacy,[56] one's sense of linked fate,[57] and how one believes others outside of his or her racial group view their racial group.

THE FINDINGS

When exploring the factors thought to be related to negative orientations toward the government among black youth, it is the absence of family SES that jumps out initially (see appendix A). Amazingly, there is no direct relationship between the education and income of one's parent(s) and the degree to which one is distrustful and cynical toward government officials. This is not to say that young black Americans do not hold negative views toward the government, as discussed earlier. Instead, it seems that family SES is not closely related to which black youth will be alienated and which ones will not. Across the class divide in black communities, one can find young black people fed up with government officials. Consistently, across racial and ethnic groups we find that family SES is not related to the attitudes youth hold about government officials. In some ways this is not that surprising, since it seems that nearly all Americans today, regardless of race, ethnicity, sex, or class, seem to be frustrated and unhappy with elected officials.

Black youth, however, who are older seem to have more negative attitudes toward government officials. The impact of age is relatively significant:

- Young black adults who are 25 years old are 8 percent less likely to hold positive attitudes toward the government than those who are 15.[58]

The difference between being 15 and 25 is only 10 years, but during that time period, some young people start families; some graduate from college and start their first full-time jobs; others leave home and establish their residences—while others come to know the daily frustration of not being able to find or keep a job, being hassled by the police, or worse yet, spending time incarcerated. Given the range of experiences that occur during this period, it is not surprising that age is related to feelings toward the government among black youth. It might also be that as they grow older and have more interactions and experiences with the government through entities such as the police or the court system and possibly service agencies (many of which could be negative), they develop negative assessments of government officials.

A bit more surprising is the relationship between exposure to rap music and feelings toward government officials. As young black Americans experience greater rap exposure, we find a corresponding increase in levels of alienation toward the government.

- Black youth who listen to more rap music and watch more rap music videos are 4 percent less likely to register positive feelings toward the government than those black youth who have little to no exposure to rap music and rap music videos, if everything else remains stable.

Although this is a relatively mild effect, it is still an especially interesting finding, because numerous articles have crowned hip-hop as the defining cultural form in the lives of young people, not only in the United States but in many other parts of the world. By all reports, hip-hop culture—rap music, graffiti, break dancing, and deejaying—comprises much of what young African Americans listen to, watch, talk about, and possibly emulate. As noted, our data confirm that a majority of black youth (58 percent) indicate that they listen to rap music every day. And while a substantial literature has emerged detailing the history and current manifestations of hip-hop culture, there has also been a surge in substantial writing and some research warning of the possible negative impact of hip-hop culture on young African Americans, stemming from its perceived focus on and promotion of sex, drugs, crime, misogyny, consumerism, and nihilism. There is, however, very little systematic work that has empirically tested such propositions. Our data suggest that there is an impact on political attitudes but that the force of rap exposure is constrained when it comes to attitudes about the government.

In addition to rap music and videos being related to greater alienation, so are experiences with personal discrimination and feelings of linked fate among black youth. Again, we find relatively mild effects for both influences.

- Black youth who report the highest levels of experiences with personal discrimination are 5 percent less likely to hold positive feelings toward government officials than black youth with no experience with personal discrimination.
- Similarly, a young black person who feels that what happens to other black people will affect him or her is 3 percent less likely to hold positive feelings about government officials than a young black person who does not feel this sense of linked fate.

It is only a feeling of political efficacy that can bolster the positive feelings black youth have about government officials. The belief that one is politically efficacious diminishes negative feelings toward the government.

- A young black person with the highest level of political efficacy is 5 percent more likely to hold positive feelings toward government officials than a young black person with little to no political efficacy.

The model for white and Latino youth found similar and different patterns for variables related to attitudes toward the government. Among whites, experience with personal discrimination was related to negative feelings toward the government. There were, however, a number of other factors that corresponded with positive feelings toward the government for white youth. Those whose parents were interested in politics, those who were engaged in activities at their place of worship, and those who had a sense of political efficacy were likely to have more positive attitudes toward government officials. Latino youth were similarly positively impacted by feelings of political efficacy. In addition, among Latino youth, experiences with personal discrimination and being older corresponded to less positive evaluations of government officials similar to those of black youth. Interestingly, Latinos were the only group where sex was statistically significant in our models, with Latina or Hispanic young women and girls demonstrating less alienation from government officials than young Latino men and boys.

When we perform a similar analysis to understand what factors are related to the political alienation dimension of feeling fully included in the political community, far fewer clues materialize (see appendix A). Interestingly, while the number of variables in our model that demonstrated statistical significance is much smaller, the magnitude of the effects is much larger. For example, personal experience with discrimination once again emerges as a significant component related to feelings of full inclusion in the political community. Specifically, one's daily experiences with discrimination based on factors such as race, gender, age, or class seems to have a negative impact on one's feelings of inclusion.

- Black youth who score the highest in terms of experiences with personal discrimination are 34 percent less likely to feel like full and equal citizens, compared to black youth who score the lowest on the personal discrimination scale.

The only good news in this finding is that by far, the majority of black youth do not score at the highest level in terms of experiences with personal discrimination. In fact, only 9 percent of black youth indicate they have experienced personal discrimination often or very often. The bad news is that even when we look at the differences between the black youth who are average or at the mean in terms of their experiences with personal discrimination and those who indicate that they have never experienced discrimination, there is a substantial difference in the probability of them feeling like full and equal citizens.

- Black youth who register an "average" number of experiences with personal discrimination are 10 percent less likely to feel like full and equal citizens, compared to those black youth who report having experienced no discrimination.

In contrast to declining feelings of inclusion, our data suggest, black youth who feel politically efficacious are also more likely to report feeling a part of the political community. Of course, it is difficult to decipher whether political efficacy leads to greater feelings of inclusion or if feeling included leads to greater efficacy. And while some statistical tests allow us to try and disentangle the question of causality, for this analysis we will be content to highlight the relationship without making claims about what is causing what.

- Young black Americans who register the highest levels of political efficacy are 29 percent more likely to feel like full and equal citizens, compared to those black youth at the lowest levels of our political efficacy scale.

Luckily, most black youth (79 percent), like most white youth (79 percent) and Latino youth (77 percent), believe themselves to be politically efficacious.

Among white and Latino respondents, a number of interesting variables seem to be related to feelings of inclusion. White youth who have higher levels of family SES and who are more politically efficacious are more likely to feel like full and equal citizens. In contrast, white youth who have more experiences with personal discrimination or who themselves or whose parents are immigrants are less likely to feel included in the political community. Latino respondents who are immigrants or whose parents are immigrants feel less included in the political community. So, too, do those Latino youth who have experienced personal discrimination. However, Latino youth who are in school or are older exhibit higher feelings of inclusion in the political community.

The third dimension of political alienation as conceptualized here is that of equal opportunity (see appendix A). As in previous models, black youths' personal experiences with discrimination correspond with more negative perceptions of the opportunity available to all in the United States. Moreover, experiences with personal discrimination are related to a substantial decline in the belief that there is an equal chance to succeed.

- Black youth who register the highest rates of personal discrimination are 46 percent less likely than those black youth who report no experiences with personal discrimination to believe there is equal opportunity for success in the United States.
- Black youth who report an "average" number of experiences with personal discrimination are 14 percent less likely to believe there exists equal opportunity to succeed in the United States than black youth who have had no experiences with personal discrimination that they can identify.

And while the general impact of personal discrimination is not surprising, our knowledge of the reverberations of such experiences, which cause black youth to be less likely to feel part of the political community and believe in the equal opportunity to succeed, should reinforce our commitment to ending personal discrimination—not only because of the destructive nature of such experiences to an individual's self-esteem and pride but also because discrimination undermines the functioning of our democracy, increasing alienation among a new generation of political participants.

Also shown to be related to young black people's lower likelihood in believing that everyone has an equal chance to succeed in the United States are age, a sense of linked fate, and exposure to rap. Specifically, black youth who are older indicate less agreement with the idea that everyone has an equal chance to succeed. In fact, age in this case has one of the strongest effects on the beliefs of black youth.

- Black youth who are 25 years old are 54 percent less likely to believe that everyone has an equal chance to succeed than those who are 15.

Similarly, the more black youth see their life as tied to what happens to other black people (linked fate) the less likely they are to accept the idea that there is an equal chance for success among all Americans.

- Black youth who register are the highest levels of linked fate are 18 percent less likely to believe in equal opportunity than those black youth who do not believe that what happens to most black people in the country will affect them.

Young black Americans who listen to more rap music and watch more rap music videos are also less likely to agree that there is an equal chance for success in the country.

- Black youth who record the highest levels of rap exposure are 17 percent less likely than black youth who do not listen to rap music or watch rap music videos to believe that in the United States everyone has an equal chance to succeed.

Undoubtedly, many of the messages found in rap music underscore the inequality found in American society, directing listeners to try and get theirs because nothing is promised or guaranteed.

- Black youth who are members of organized groups also are 8 percent less likely to agree with the premise of equal opportunity than young blacks who are not in a group.

While there is no obvious explanation for this finding, we might imagine that in many organized groups young people are told that one has to work hard to succeed and that they have been encouraged to join a group by an adult or mentor because there is the understanding that one needs an advantage to get ahead in society in which significant inequality exists. Similarly, black youth might get involved in a group or organization to rectify the inequality they believe exists, thus underscoring their belief that everyone does not have an equal chance to succeed in the United States.

There were two variables that corresponded positively with the idea that in the United States everyone has an equal chance to succeed: political efficacy and religious activity.

- Black youth who are the most politically efficacious are also 23 percent more likely to agree that everyone has an equal opportunity to succeed in the United States than those with the lowest levels of political efficacy.
- Young blacks who are the most active religiously are 13 percent more likely to believe in equal opportunity in the United States, compared to those who are the least religiously active.

Again, we cannot make claims about which factors might be driving the relationship. In the case of religiosity, we might expect that those individuals who are participating in the activities of their religious institution come to this work with a fundamental belief in the equality of all human beings and the ability of such individuals to succeed in the country.

White youth exhibit interesting relationships in terms of their belief in the equal opportunity to succeed in the United States. Among young white people, those with higher levels of family SES are less likely to agree that in the United States everyone has an equal opportunity to succeed. Possibly seeing up close what it takes to get ahead, these young people are more skeptical of any claims about equal opportunity. In addition, those white youth who have experienced some form of personal discrimination are less likely to believe that equal opportunity is available in the United States. Finally, as we found with our black respondents, religious activity and political efficacy were related to a higher probability of agreeing with the idea that everyone has an equal chance to succeed in the United States. Latino respondents provide a scaled-down version of what we found among both black and white youth. Specifically, experiences with personal discrimination decreased the probability that Latino respondents would agree that there is equal opportunity to succeed, while higher political efficacy bolstered the belief that there is equal opportunity among them.

WHY ARE BLACK YOUTH SO ALIENATED?

Even given the findings we just discussed, it may seem puzzling—if not disturbing—to most people that in a historical period when black youth have more opportunities than ever before, as some would argue was evident in the election of Barack Obama, they are still alienated, at least politically. Why should a population of young people who benefit from policies such as affirmative action (or at least its remnants) feel that on average, black children receive a poorer education than white youth? Why should young black Americans who never formally experienced the poll tax or other legal mechanisms that denied black people the right to vote feel that the government will work to deny them the right to vote and that even though they are given the chance to cast a ballot, their votes (literally) won't be counted?

Part of the answer to these questions is undoubtedly rooted in the daily lived reality of far too many young black Americans. As discussed in

chapter 1, by now most people know that black youth suffer disproportionately in economic, political, and social realms, compared to young
people from other racial and ethnic groups. But how can we explain the
alienation of young black people across class categories? It might make
sense that someone who lives in poverty and attends a school with few
of the necessary resources would feel alienated from the government
and maybe the political process in general, but why should middle-class
black youth hold similar feelings of distance and disgust?

Here I believe the answer lies in the systemic pathologizing of all
black youth. It is the rare young black person who has not experienced
being pulled over by the police because he or she looks suspicious,
being followed through a store under the assumption that he or she is
there to steal something, or being chastised by the media for listening
to what is presented as a denigrating, misogynistic, and commercial art
form—rap music. Surveillance and demonization of black youth are
pervasive in this country and extend across class lines and across racial
and ethnic communities, although clearly concentrated in poor communities. Even young black people with privilege and access talk about
how they believe race and racism structure and limit their experiences
in the classroom and boardroom alike. One recent example might better illustrate our current willingness to criminalize black youth culture,
often independent of class.

In 2007, the *New York Times* and the *Miami Herald* published articles on the emergence of sagging-pants laws across the country.[59] It
seems that city councils and state legislatures are debating, and in some
instances passing, laws that criminalize wearing one's pants too low
below the waist. As Robert Samuels of the *Miami Herald* wrote in his
article, there is a "nationwide movement to curb youth from being too
small for their britches." The penalties for such an offense range from
a mere admonishment to community service to a fine of $500 and up to
six months in prison. It seems the supporters of such laws believe that
it is part of the tough love that black youth need to get them on the
straight and narrow. As one state representative from Louisiana said,
"Hopefully, if we pull up their pants we can lift their minds while we're
at it."[60] Interestingly, many of these laws originated in black communities with the backing of the local black leadership

We should note that not just cities are seeking to ban sagging
pants; at least one institution of higher education and a night club in
Chicago have also gotten into the act. In 2009, historically black and
all-male Morehouse College adopted a new dress code for its students.
Among the eleven outlawed forms of dress, including caps, do-rags,

hoods while indoors and women's clothing, also on the list were sagging pants. On October 29, 2009, Chicago Public Radio reported that a local Chicago night club—The Original Mother's—had agreed to apologize to six black college students from St. Louis who were denied entry into the club because their pants were deemed "too baggy."[61] The students were not allowed to enter the establishment even though some of their white classmates with baggier jeans were allowed entrance to the club.

So, in a time of war, when the housing market is in a free fall, black youth face depression-like unemployment, and many cities face economic shortages, some city, business, and a few college officials have decided that the issue that needs addressing is how low many youth, in particular black males, wear their pants. The concern over the sagging pants worn by many young black people, especially young men, has become so central that it entered into the 2008 presidential campaign. While being interviewed by MTV, Obama was asked his views on laws criminalizing sagging pants. Obama responded saying:

> Here's my attitude: I think passing a law about people wearing sagging pants is a waste of time. We should be focused on creating jobs, improving our schools, getting health care, dealing with the war in Iraq. Any public official who is worrying about sagging pants probably needs to spend some time focusing on real problems out there.... Having said that, brothers should pull up their pants. You're walking by your mother, your grandmother, and your underwear is showing.... What's wrong with that? Come on. There are some issues that we face that you don't have to pass a law [against], but that doesn't mean folks can't have some sense and some respect for other people. And, you know, some people might not want to see your underwear—I'm one of them.[62]

While Obama's laughing response underscores the belief of many that public officials who are focused on sagging pants should redirect attention to matters that really are important to the future of the country and the future prospects of young people, it is the level of concern surrounding this aesthetic as it is directly associated with black youth that gives us a glimpse into the fragile positioning of black youth as citizens. First, remember that of all the questions that could be asked of the likely winner of the upcoming presidential election, one of them was about sagging-pants ordinances. Second, only ten days after Obama was elected president, the *New York Times* thought the question of sagging pants and the "Obama effect" was important and funny enough to warrant publication of an article. Under the title "Can Obama Help Kill Baggy Pants Look?" Clyde Haberman begins what is meant to be a tongue-in-cheek article by linking sagging pants to criminal behavior and the economy—two critical and serious areas of concern for the populace. He writes:

> Two robbery suspects, hands cuffed behind them, were taken from a police station house in the Bronx a few days ago. Like many young men, they wore baggy trousers. They wore them low, very low, so low that the beltless jeans of one suspect slid down almost to his knees. Guilty or innocent, he looked ridiculous. President-elect Barack Obama, we're willing to bet, would have agreed.... The first order of business for the new president will no doubt be to get America to hitch up its pants and give the economy a kick-start. It will be interesting to see if he can also get America to hitch up its pants, period. This is a matter of no small concern to New York, where changes in fashion mean jobs, reputations and—count on it—money.[63]

At the heart of this move to criminalize sagging pants is the belief that this style of dress is the marker of truly dangerous and deviant individuals. As Niko Koppel has written in the *New York Times*, "behind the indecency laws may be the real issue—the hip-hop style itself, which critics say is worn as a badge of delinquency, with its distinctive walk conveying thuggish swagger and a disrespect for authority."[64] Of course, criminalization of what is perceived as an oppositional, deviant, often racialized male style is part of our history. Thus, sagging-pants laws should be understood in the context of moral panics that surrounded zoot suits and the black leather jackets and berets worn by the Black Panthers and their followers. The example of sagging-pants laws helps to illustrate both how quickly both those with dominant power and those with indigenous, or community-based, power can unite to criminalize young blacks and black youth culture, as well as use that power to generate feelings of alienation among black youth across any class divide. Such targeting of black youth contributes to their feeling of cynicism and alienation and to the lessening of their diffuse support for the legitimacy of our democracy.

We must remember that the criminalization of black youth is just one component of the systematic pathologizing of them. Even among those who we might argue have a commitment to bettering the condition of young black people, one hears an almost instinctive return to stereotypes and partial truths when they describe this group of adolescents and young adults. We might take Barack Obama as an example. *Before* running for president, Obama worked as an organizer working among the poor and young people. It was in part his experience in

Chicago as a community organizer that provided many of the reasons he turned to politics—to improve the condition of those most marginalized, including and especially black youth. And while candidate Obama dismissed legal ordinances criminalizing the wearing of saggy pants while in front of an MTV audience, the following exchange between Obama and a voter in Iowa is illustrative of the possibly unintended but still detrimental pathologizing of black youth that happens daily both inside and outside of black communities, even by those who are concerned and want to improve the condition of young black people. A woman complained to Obama about how "inner-city" kids don't know how to dress for a job. Below is Obama's response, as reported in the *Washington Post*:

> "Pull up your pants!" Obama interjected, as the crowd laughed. "Pull up your pants!" Appearance is key to urban youth succeeding, he stressed. You've got people coming in, heads hanging down, hat cocked. They're mumbling. [Obama mutters a few nonsensical words.] You can't understand what they're saying. The employer asks them to do something and they've got an attitude. "Why do I got to do it? Why didn't you ask Pookie to do it?" They come in late. The employer says, "why are you late?" "I don't know." The crowd laughed and cheered as Obama spoke.[65]

THE OBAMA EFFECT

Our discussion of political alienation among black youth has largely been based on data that were gathered prior to the arrival of Obama in the White House. Barack Obama is now the country's forty-fourth president and the nation's first African-American president. And as we might expect, such a first has brought with it an infinite number of expectations, not only for the country but also for how the Obama presidency might impact young black Americans, those at the heart of this book. As I will discuss in the chapters that follow, there is no denying the symbolic power of the election of Obama to affect the hopes and dreams of most black Americans. One need only refer to the stories and tears of older black Americans as they watched his inauguration, having believed that they would never in their lifetimes witness such an event in the United States of America. Such hope, optimism, and pride in Obama was also displayed among young black Americans as they wore "my president is black" T-shirts, wrote poems and performed spoken word pieces about Obama, and wrote and performed rap songs describing their pride in "Barry," their president.

The question we will briefly explore in this section is the degree to which Obama has altered, even temporarily, the political alienation many young blacks feel, as data from the Black Youth Project suggested. This analysis was undertaken early in the Obama presidency so this analysis can only tell us about the initial effect of Obama on the political psyche of young people and young black Americans specifically. The data we use in this section come from the MCPCE Study.[66] For this analysis, however, the data will be restricted to those respondents between the ages of 18 and 25 so as to most accurately approximate the respondents to the Black Youth Project.[67] Because of the limited number of respondents in this study's data set who are 18–25, our analysis can only hint at possible attitudes held among black youth more broadly. However, even a brief and temporary peak into how the election of Obama is playing among young black citizens might give us some indication of the potential impact of his presidency on their attitudes.

When we asked respondents if they agreed with the statement "The leaders in government care very little about people like me"—a question we also used in the Black Youth Project, among other questions, in measuring the dimension of *government-oriented alienation*—we found that as in the case of the Black Youth Project, black youth were more likely to agree with this statement than white, Latino, or Asian youth. There was, however, very little difference between black and white youth. Data in figure 4.12 indicate that 47 percent of black youth, 44 percent of white youth, 38 percent of Latino youth, and 32 percent of Asian youth agreed with the statement.[68]

For our Black Youth Project analysis, we used the question "Do you agree that the government is run by a few big interests looking out for themselves and their friends?" as the second indicator of the *government-oriented* dimension of alienation among young people. In the analysis of the Black Youth Project data, we found that again, black youth were more likely to agree with this statement; but here, the difference between blacks and Latinos was not statistically significant. In the MCPCE data collected just weeks before the 2008 presidential election, we find that white respondents were more likely to agree with this statement, but only by 4 percentage points more than blacks. Specifically, in figure 4.13, 56 percent of blacks, 60 percent of whites, 46 percent of Latinos, and 52 percent of Asians agreed with this statement.

Again, direct comparison with the Black Youth Project is difficult because of the different answer categories available to respondents

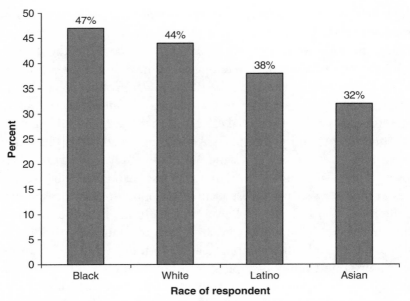

FIGURE 4.12 Percentage of respondents who agree that "leaders in government care very little about people like me." *2008 Mobilization, Change, and Political and Civic Engagement.*

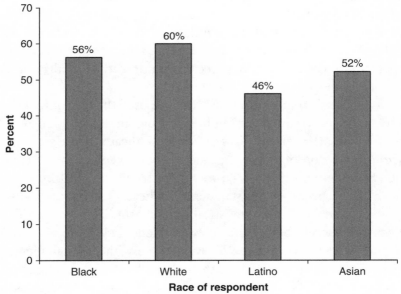

FIGURE 4.13 Percentage of respondents who agree that "the government is run by a few big interests looking out for themselves and their friends." *2008 Mobilization, Change, and Political and Civic Engagement.*

in each study. Moreover, in this analysis we are looking at respondents aged 18–25, while the Black Youth Project data included respondents who were 15–17. Given such differences, we would be reluctant to attribute the 10–percentage-point drop in the number of black youth agreeing with this statement to Obama or any other factor.

In an attempt to measure whether black youth felt equally included in the *political community*, we asked the question "Do you agree with the statement, generally I feel like a full and equal citizen in this country with all the rights and protections that other people have?" Unlike our previous comparisons with earlier Black Youth Project data, in this case and the next, the answer structures are the same for both data sources, with the answer set including the option of not responding. Again, earlier data reported from the Black Youth Project indicated that while a substantial number of black respondents—60 percent—felt like full and equal citizens, this percentage was 23 points lower than the 83 percent of white respondents who feel like full and equal citizens and 10 points lower than the 70 percent of Latino respondents who agree with the statement.

In the MCPCE Study, we find similar results, although the general number of those agreeing with the statement across racial and ethnic groups is down. This may be due to the ages of our MCPCE respondents (18–25). Specifically, we find that in 2008 there was a substantial split in the level of inclusion black and white youth felt, as detailed in figure 4.14, with 42 percent of black youth agreeing with the statement that they felt like full and equal citizens, compared to 66 percent of white youth, nearly the same 23–percentage-point difference registered with the Black Youth Project data. Also interesting is the split between Asian and Latino respondents, with 63 percent of Asian young adults agreeing with the statement, compared to only 43 percent of Latino young adults.[69]

Days before the country was poised to elect its first black president, there still was not only a sizeable gap in how fully included in the political community black and Latino youth felt compared to white and Asian young people, there was also a significant reduction in the number of youth more generally who felt included in the political community. This result may reflect the nature of the end of a political campaign, when nearly everyone is tired of the partisanship of the campaign and few feel unified in some larger political community. The results also suggest that President Obama and the rest of the country still have significant work to do to make all young people, but especially

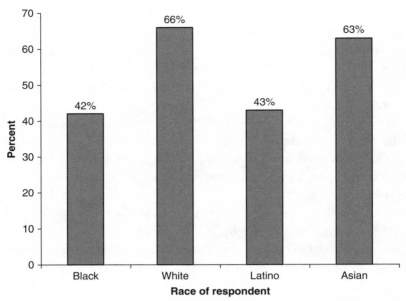

FIGURE 4.14 Percentage of respondents who agree that "generally I feel like a full and equal citizen in this country with all the rights and protections that other people have." *2008 Mobilization, Change, and Political and Civic Engagement.*

black and Latino youth, feel like full citizens with all the rights and protections that others have.

Finally, to assess what we have called the *opportunity dimension* of political alienation, we asked respondents of both studies if they agreed that in the United States everyone has an equal chance to succeed. As noted, the answer set in both studies is comparable, including the option of "neither agree nor disagree." In our earlier analysis of Black Youth Project data, we found very little difference among our black, Latino, and white respondents, with 56 percent of blacks and whites and 59 percent of Latinos agreeing that everyone has an equal chance to succeed in the United States. The results from the MCPCE Study stand in stark contrast to the findings from our Black Youth Project analysis. This time, just weeks and days before the election and the onset of the most devastating economic crisis in their lifetime, black youth registered significantly lower agreement with the idea that everyone has an equal chance to succeed in the United States. In fact, agreement with the statement was down among all young people, a phenomenon that could have been caused by the daily intensification of the economic recession. Of course, the downward push on the data could have been caused by any combination of things, including the different sample and survey technology of the MCPCE Study. The bottom line is that in our 2008 study, only 18 percent of black youth agreed with the statement that everyone has an equal chance to succeed, compared to 29 percent of whites, 34 percent of Asians, and 43 percent of Latinos (fig. 4.15). One of the more interesting findings here is not only the low numbers of black respondents who agreed with the statement but the comparatively higher rates of agreement among Latinos and Asians, two groups whose communities include substantial proportions of recent immigrants. It is possible that some members of these two ethnic groups still believe that their chances for success are better in the United States than in their home country.[70]

The data suggest that while young people have embraced Barack Obama and his promise of "Change You Can Believe In," they also recognize the limited ability of any president to fundamentally change their perceived secondary relationship to the state. These are young people who may feel proud of Obama and the country's ability to elect the first black president but who also recognize that an evolving racial order continues to shape which and how many opportunities they will be able to access. Many of these young people stand at the crossroads

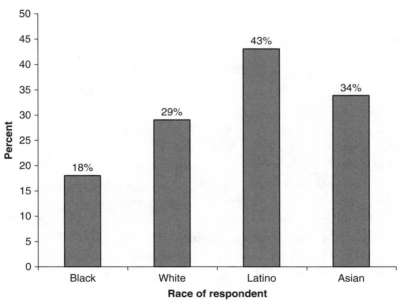

FIGURE 4.15 Percentage of respondents who agree that "everyone has an equal chance to succeed in the United States." *2008 Mobilization, Change, and Political and Civic Engagement.*

of a symbolic hope embodied in the election of President Obama and an often pained reality of failed or merely adequate schools; constant policing and incarceration; pervasive violence in their neighborhoods; shrinking economic opportunities; and demonization of their choices, cultures, and selves. They stand at this crossroads waiting to see which way the tide will turn. These young people have not given up on the promise of our democracy, but they are sorting out the conflicting messages this country is sending—on the one hand the uplifting promise of equality witnessed in the election of Obama and on the other hand the renewed second-class citizenship of black people, witnessed in the country's and specifically the government's unwillingness to devote the resources needed to save and support the survivors of Hurricane Katrina.

Of the scholars who have labeled black youth nihilistic, Cornel West has probably been the most evenhanded and genuinely concerned. In *Race Matters*, he suggests that nihilism needs to be a concept that researchers concerned with African-American youth make central to their analyses. He argues that we must tread "into the murky waters of despair and dread that now flood the streets of black America. To talk about the depressing statistics of unemployment, infant mortality, incarceration, teenage pregnancy, and violent crime is one thing. But to face up to the monumental eclipse of hope, the unprecedented collapse of meaning, the incredible disregard for human (especially black) life and property in much of black America is something else."[71]

While the prospect of nihilism among black youth is a plausible fear, especially given the daily circumstances in which they live, young black people seem to be resisting a descent into nihilism by holding onto the belief that opportunity and inclusion either are or may be available to them if they play by the rules. It is just this teetering on the brink of full-blown political alienation that I believe stands in contrast to the nihilism of black youth predicted by scholars such as West. For those young people who have seen a few, or maybe more than a few, family members benefit from the lessening of racial restrictions on jobs, housing, health care, and education, this optimism probably makes sense. Others who have not experienced such mobility directly may have come one step closer to accepting such hope and possibility as they watched Obama get elected president or witnessed economic transformation in the life of their favorite rap artist or sports hero. This is a generation that witnessed both the continuing marginalization of black people—in particular poor black Americans—while also witnessing the growing power and prosperity of some African Americans. This is a generation that continues to be confronted with the reality of police brutally killing young black people while also seeing the country for the first time headed by a black president. It is simultaneously the best of times and the worst of times for black people, and the political attitudes of this generation of young people reflect the confusion, unease, and disjuncture generated from such dueling narratives.

It is also important that we qualify our understanding of the willingness of black youth to embrace the idea of equal opportunity in the United States. During our in-depth interviews in the Black Youth Project, young black respondents explained their belief in the fairness of the United States as true relative to other countries. Many of the young black people we interviewed compared the United States to other countries that they believed were less well-off and afforded fewer rights to their citizens. In more than one interview, a respondent pointed out the discrimination black youth face in the United States but qualified that criticism by mentioning the greater sense of fairness they believed exists in America. One 24-year-old black woman from Chicago explained what she meant by the relative fairness of the United States: "I think it's a lot more fair than other countries. I don't think it's a lot, like, *so* great as they make it out to be. But if you compare it to other countries, I think it is *a lot* better than those other countries." A 17-year-old black female went further: "I see a lot of different countries that seem like they have more freedom than a lot of countries. And, like, they're more, hmm, like they more strict, but the United States, to me it seems like a 50/50. Like you free but then again you're not."[72]

Some might predict that the higher levels of political alienation that black youth hold will drive them away from any civic or political activity, believing that the system is not only closed to them but out to get them. While that might be true, another interpretation of this very basic data might be that such feelings of anger and frustration function as a motivator, leading young black people to act: we need only look at the mobilization surrounding the Jena Six as an example. So we are now left with the question of how political alienation impacts black youth. Does the political alienation evident among young black Americans hinder their political engagement? This is a question I pursue in the next chapter. But as we move forward in our investigations of black youth and their politics, let us not forget the continuing and disproportionate social, political, and economic marginalization of too many African-American youth. Without serious investigation and intervention regarding how living with constrained opportunities, fewer resources, and systematic racism impacts their feelings about this country and their resulting political engagement, we will never completely comprehend or address the political lives of African-American youth.

Appendix

TABLE A4.1   Determinants of Negative Orientation toward Government

Government orientation	White (SE)	Black (SE)	Latino (SE)	First difference	Max difference
INITIAL CHARACTERISTICS					
Family SES	.00	−.02	.02	-	-
	(.02)	(.01)	(.02)		
Gender	.09	.03	.27*	-	-
(0 = male)	(.10)	(.09)	(.14)		
Age	−.02	−.08***	−.08***	-	-
	(.02)	(.02)	(.03)		
Immigrant status	−.01	.03	−.02	-	-
	(.03)	(.03)	(.03)		
POLITICAL SOCIALIZATION					
Education	.00	−.0	.03	-	-
	(.03)	(.03)	(.04)		
Parent interest	.11*	−.03	.03	-	-
	(.06)	(.04)	(.06)		
Rap exposure	.00	−.05**	.00	−.01	−.04
	(.02)	(.02)	(.02)		
Personal	−.06***	−.06***	−.06***	−.02	−.05
discrimination	(.02)	(.01)	(.02)		
Neighborhood SES	−.00	−.00	−.00	-	-
	(.00)	(.00)	(.00)		
Racial diversity	.01	−.03	−.00	-	-
	(.06)	(.04)	(.06)		
INSTITUTIONAL INVOLVEMENT					
In school	.11	−.06	−.16	-	-
	(.14)	(.12)	(.20)		
Organization/group	.05	−.05	−.13	-	-
	(.11)	(.10)	(.16)		
Religious activity	.05*	.01	.08	-	-
	(.03)	(.02)	(.04)		

Government orientation	White (SE)	Black (SE)	Latino (SE)	First difference	Max difference
POLITICAL ATTITUDE					
Political efficacy	.47***	.29***	.27**	.03	.05
	(.09)	(.07)	(.11)		
Linked fate	.08	−.10*	−.09	−.01	−.03
	(.05)	(.05)	(.07)		
Positive view	.01	−.05	.01	-	-
	(.01)	(.04)	(.01)		
Sample size	458	548	258		

Note: Data is imputed.
* Denotes statistical significance at .05 level.
** Denotes statistical significance at .01 level.
*** Denotes statistical significance at .001 level.
Source: The Black Youth Project

TABLE A4.2　Determinants of Feeling a Part of the Political Community

Political community	White (SE)	Black (SE)	Latino (SE)	First difference	Max difference
INITIAL CHARACTERISTICS					
Family SES	.03*	.01	.01	-	-
	(.02)	(.01)	(.02)		
Gender	−.10	−.04	.05	-	-
(0 = male)	(.11)	(.10)	(.14)		
Age	.03	.00	−.07**	-	-
	(.02)	(.02)	(.03)		
Immigrant status	−.12***	−.02	−.10***	-	-
	(.04)	(.02)	(.03)		
POLITICAL SOCIALIZATION					
Education	−.01	−.02	−.00	-	-
	(.04)	(.04)	(.04)		
Parent interest	.02	−.01	−.06	-	-
	(.06)	(.05)	(.07)		
Rap exposure	.02	−.01	−.03	-	-
	(.02)	(.02)	(.02)		
Personal	−.04*	−.06***	−.07***	−.24	−.34
discrimination	(.02)	(.01)	(.02)		
Neighborhood SES	.00	−.00	−.00	-	-
	(.00)	(.00)	(.00)		
Racial diversity	.10	−.07	−.04	-	-
	(.07)	(.04)	(.07)		

(continued)

Political community	White (SE)	Black (SE)	Latino (SE)	First difference	Max difference
INSTITUTIONAL INVOLVEMENT					
In school	.18	.21	.65***	-	-
	(.15)	(.13)	(.21)		
Organization/group	.09	.04	–.26	-	-
	(.12)	(.11)	(.17)		
Religious activity	.02	.03	.06	-	-
	(.03)	(.02)	(.04)		
POLITICAL ATTITUDE					
Political efficacy	.46***	.25***	.16	.09	.29
	(.09)	(.07)	(.11)		
Linked fate	.00	–.08	–.08	-	-
	(.06)	(.05)	(.08)		
Positive view	.00	–.01	–.02*	-	-
	(.01)	(.00)	(.01)		
Sample size	458	555	259		

Note: Data is imputed.
* Denotes statistical significance at .05 level.
** Denotes statistical significance at .01 level.
*** Denotes statistical significance at .001 level.
Source: The Black Youth Project

TABLE A4.3   Determinants of Believing Everyone Has an Equal Chance to Succeed in the United States

Equal opportunity	White (SE)	Black (SE)	Latino (SE)	First difference	Max difference
INITIAL CHARACTERISTICS					
Family SES	–.03*	–.02	–.02	-	-
	(.02)	(.01)	(.02)		
Gender	–.06	–.08	–.18	-	-
	(.11)	(.10)	(.14)		
Age	–.03	–.06***	.02	-	-
	(.02)	(.02)	(.03)		
Immigrant status	.02	.00	–.02	-	-
	(.04)	(.03)	(.03)		
POLITICAL SOCIALIZATION					
Education	–.01	.01	–.02	-	-
	(.03)	(.03)	(.04)		
Parent interest	.02	–.00	.08	-	-
	(.06)	(.05)	(.07)		

Equal opportunity	White (SE)	Black (SE)	Latino (SE)	First difference	Max difference
Rap exposure	-.01	-.04*	-.03	-.05	-.17
	(.02)	(.02)	(.02)		
Personal discrimination	-.07***	-.08***	-.09***	-.32	-.46
	(.02)	(.01)	(.02)		
Neighborhood SES	-.00	.00	-.00	-	-
	(.00)	(.00)	(.00)		
Racial diversity	.03	.05	-.05	-	-
	(.06)	(.04)	(.06)		
INSTITUTIONAL INVOLVEMENT					
In school	-.06	.08	.25	-	-
	(.15)	(.13)	(.21)		
Organization/group	-.19	-.21*	-.13	-.05	-.08
	(.11)	(.11)	(.17)		
Religious activity	.09***	.05*	.05	-.06	-.13
	(.03)	(.02)	(.04)		
POLITICAL ATTITUDE					
Political efficacy	.33***	.19***	.35**	.08	.23
	(.09)	(.07)	(.11)		
Linked fate	.08	-.11*	.08	-.07	-.18
	(.06)	(.05)	(.08)		
Positive view	.00	-.01	.00	-	-
	(.01)	(.04)	(.01)		
Sample size	459	557	261		

Note: Data is imputed.
* Denotes statistical significance at .05 level.
** Denotes statistical significance at .01 level.
*** Denotes statistical significance at .001 level.
Source: The Black Youth Project

CHAPTER 5

"Fight the Power"

From Jena to the White House

O N SEPTEMBER 20, 2007, an estimated 15,000 to 50,000 largely black protestors descended on the town of Jena, Louisiana. Individuals, groups, and organizations from across the country, primarily black, made the trek to Louisiana to protest the racist distribution of justice handed down to a group known as the Jena Six: six male African-American high-school students who were charged with attempted second-degree murder after a fight with a white student, Justin Barker. While the larger context for this encounter stems from centuries of racial discrimination, this particular instance was thought to have begun when a small group of black students at the high school sat under the "white tree," located on the side of campus "claimed" by white students, who dominated the 460-person student body.[1] Unhappy with the distribution of power and in this case the distribution of land rights, a black freshman asked the principal for permission to sit under the "white tree" during a rally. School officials told the student to sit wherever he wanted, so a group of black students did just that. The next day, three nooses were found hanging from the tree.

Later, it was determined that three white students had placed the nooses on the tree. The white students said that the nooses were not directed at the black students who sat under the tree but instead were a prank directed at the school's rodeo team. The internal school investigation seemed to suggest that the three white students were unaware of the symbolic legacy of nooses and the lynching of thousands of black men and women as an indelible part of their country's history. The superintendent's disciplinary recommendation for the three white students involved in the incident was three days of in-school suspension. Many black residents in Jena saw this relatively mild punishment as another example of the consistent and visible double standard at the high school, such that black students received severe punishments for the same offenses for which white students barely received reprimands.[2]

Tensions between black and white people in the small town continued to escalate after the two incidents—the black students' sitting under the tree and the white students' display of the nooses—with physical violence resulting. For example, it was reported that a black student, Robert Bailey Jr., was trying to enter a party of primarily white students when he was beaten by whites at the party. The white youths accused of beating Bailey were charged with simple battery. Days later, when Bailey, accompanied by friends, confronted one of these white students, Bailey alleges that the white student pulled a gun on them and that he and his friends chased the white student and took the gun. Bailey was later charged with theft of a firearm, second-degree robbery, and disturbing the peace.[3] No charges were made against the white student who it was alleged originally pulled the gun.

On December 4, 2006, Justin Barker, age 17, a white student, was at school and was said to be boasting about the beating of Bailey at the party. A group of six black students overheard Barker's declarations and attacked him when he ventured into the school courtyard. Barker was knocked unconscious and fell to the ground. The black students then kicked him a number of times in the head. His injuries were minor, and he spent only a few hours in the emergency room. Later that evening, he attended the school's annual ring ceremony. Barker testified in court that he left the event early after receiving his ring because of pain from his injuries. In response to the fight, six black students were arrested, who later came to be known as the Jena Six. Five of them were initially charged with aggravated assault, but district attorney Reed Walters increased the charges to attempted second-degree murder, an offense that carries a maximum punishment of one hundred years in prison.[4] All six were also expelled from school.[5] Again, the black community was outraged. They and many others saw the charges as extreme and the dispersal of justice as unfair, biased, and blatantly racist.

Mychal Bell, age 17, was the first student charged to go on trial, on June 26, 2007, in front of an all-white jury. The day before the trial, the charges against him were lowered from attempted second-degree murder to aggravated second-degree battery and conspiracy to commit attempted second-degree battery. The prosecution called seventeen witnesses; Bell's public defender rested his case without calling a single one.[6] The all-white jury found Bell guilty, and the judge scheduled his sentencing for September 20, 2007. It was in many ways Bell's trial that drew national attention to this case.

News of the Jena Six and calls for mobilization in support of these young black men were spread initially and largely through black media venues—black radio stations, Internet sites, YouTube videos, MySpace pages—as well as via campus student groups and the everyday talk of black people.[7] It was the indigenous resources, media outlets, and discourse vehicles controlled and used by black people that moved this story, from one originally located in Jena, to the larger black community and then to the mainstream, demanding attention from the dominant white press and governmental apparatus. Journalists Jennie Jarvie and Richard Fausett, on the front page of the *Los Angeles Times*, detailed the multiple venues used throughout black communities to spread the word about the Jena Six case.

Jasmyne Cannick—a blogger and black activist from Los Angeles... devoted much of her blogging to the case, and encouraged supporters to go to Thursday's protest or wear black in their hometowns....Cannick and other bloggers linked to an online petition that had more than 380,000 signatures by Thursday afternoon....Members of the social networking website Facebook formed "Free the Jena 6" groups. On the video site YouTube, users posted snippets of news broadcasts and footage from local rallies in support of the defendants. Some delivered homemade protest raps....In the radio industry, Thursday's protest was seen as a sign of the growing influence of black talk show hosts....That power has been evident in Atlanta, where radio station WAMJ-FM (102.5) delivers hours of black-oriented talk radio programming. Derek Harper, the station's program director, said that in the last month, most of the station's syndicated talkers—including Steve Harvey, Al Sharpton, Michael Baisden and Warren Ballentine— had picked up on the story and made it a major issue....Ballentine was among a number of radio personalities broadcasting live from Jena on Thursday. He said he had been rallying black people around the issue since learning about it in June.

On September 14, the state appeals court overturned Bell's conviction on the grounds that he should have been tried as a minor.[8] In spite of this positive development, organizers decided to go forward with their planned demonstration. And so on September 20, demonstrators descended on Jena, Louisiana—population fewer than 3,000—to protest the injustice doled out to the Jena Six. Individuals and groups came by bus, car, train, and plane to let the world know that some in black communities would not stand idly by as justice was unequally allocated yet again between black and white people, this time black and white young men. Rallies were held simultaneously by different groups in different parts of this small town. Speakers included the familiar, such as reverends Al Sharpton and Jesse Jackson; the anointed, such as Martin Luther King III; and members of the hip-hop community, such as Mos Def and Salt-N-Pepa. Some who could not make it to Jena wore T-shirts, armbands, and hats in their schools, workplaces, and neighborhoods to demonstrate their support. Across the country, black people—overwhelmingly, young black people—stood up and made themselves visible in support of the Jena Six and all black people who have experienced injustice through the criminal justice system.

Reporting on the Jena Six mobilization provided journalists an opportunity to wax poetic (again) about the civil rights movement and the possibility of a new movement among black youth. Reverend Sharpton called the mobilization "the beginning of the twenty-first-century civil rights movement."[9] National Public Radio interviewed Tina Cheatham, age 24, who said she planned to attend the mobilization because she believed "it was a good chance to be part of something historic since I wasn't around for the civil rights movement. This is kind of the twenty-first-century version of it."[10] For many in black communities, mobilization around the Jena Six reignited the hope that black politics—as it is often imagined and conceptualized: that is, extrasystemic, collective, movement politics—is still alive among the younger generation of black Americans. Ironically, despite data indicating that young black Americans spurred an increase in youth voting in the 2004 presidential elections and in 2008 had the highest turnout of young people among any ethnic or racial group since 1972, when talking about politics, it is the spectacle of mass mobilization that seems to hold the imagination of both young and old in black communities.

One can understand the allure of the idea of a new civil rights movement in the twenty-first century, given the mythic proportions that the civil rights movement of the 1940s, 1950s, and 1960s has taken on, not only in black communities but in the American narrative of politics, race, and progress. In contrast to many of the uninspiring politicians of today, who can deny the attraction of a charismatic leader able to galvanize a country and mobilize both those most in need and those most entrenched in a white supremacist system? I understand the desire to believe that we can replace the mundane politics of voting, interest groups, policy debates, corrupt politicians, and congressional gridlock with a spirited, if not spiritual, collective mobilization of "the people," steeped in moral fortitude and unconventional political tactics and intent on winning over individuals, not just votes. But while many yearn for a new civil rights movement, black youth are engaged in a different form of politics at the beginning of the twenty-first century.

In this chapter I explore the range of politics in which black youth engage when they are active in politics at all. While the rallies, petitions, mass e-mails, blogs, T-shirts, and general organizing around the Jena Six remind us that young black people and the larger black community still have the ability to produce mass mobilization *events*—albeit different in longevity, sustainability, and impact from the idealized *social movements* of the fifties, sixties, and seventies—the multifaceted nature of the mobilization around the Jena Six is more indicative of the politics of this generation of black youth. Instead of looking at the end result of the mobilization in Jena, looking at the processes of communication and information dispersal that generated the mobilization may yield more significant insights into the nature of black politics in the twenty-first century. Instead of looking for the next group of young black people who will stage a boycott, the civil rights generation would do better to look at the significant numbers of young black people engaging in "buycotts"—making consumer purchases based in part on the social values and employment practices of a company.

Along with the glimpse into the new black politics of the twenty-first century that the mobilization surrounding the Jena Six provides, much of the data suggest that the evolving political practices of this generation of black youth and young adults will not emulate the civil rights movement. Instead, the political activity of this generation will probably be more solitary, as people engage in collective efforts largely through the use of technology and around event-specific activities. Furthermore, while a previous generation most often targeted the government for needed change, demanding legislative action to improve their lives, this generation may be just as willing to target corporations, based on their perception that the government is largely inept and the real power to change people's lives is rooted in the market, not the state.

While detailing the number of youth engaged in certain political behaviors is a fairly straightforward task, understanding what such actions or inactivity means is more complicated. As in the case of the Jena Six, the details matter and are often debated. For example, it has been disputed that the tree at the center of the Jena Six controversy was designated only for whites or even that it was known as "the white tree." Similarly, it seems that the punishment meted out to the white students who placed the nooses on the tree was more than three days of in-class suspension. Furthermore, prior to his sentencing for the Barker attack, Bell was returned to a juvenile facility after he was found to have violated the terms of his probation agreement on two other nonrelated convictions. Eventually, he pled guilty to a reduced charge of battery in the Barker case, agreeing to testify against the other five members of the Jena Six, and received an 18-month prison sentence. The other five defendants—Carwin Jones, Jesse Ray Beard, Robert Bailey, Bryant Purvis, and Theodore Shaw—all pled no contest to the charge of simple battery, a misdemeanor. Four of the five received a sentence of seven days of unsupervised probation and a fine of $500. Shaw's fine was waived because of the seven months in jail he served.[11]

None of these details negates the fundamental claim that punishment or justice was unequally assigned on the basis of race in the case of the Jena Six. They do, however, make distinctions between the innocent and the guilty a bit grayer. I suspect we will find the same gray areas when trying to decide whether black youth today exert a different politics than young people from other racial and ethnic groups. The murkiness of our exploration should not detract from the fundamental importance of giving voice to the political decisions and actions of black youth in the twenty-first century, especially if we are to grapple with the future of our democracy.

In chapter 4, not surprisingly, we found that black youth tend to exhibit intense feelings of alienation along a number of dimensions. Left unexplored was the impact of alienation, along with any number of other factors, on the political behavior of black youth. In fact, we have no real sense whether the political engagement of black youth varies significantly from that of other youth from different racial and ethnic communities. As in previous chapters, we use data from the Black Youth Project to assess the participation patterns of white, Latino, and black young people. In addition, in this chapter we supplement our analyses by using data collected in 2008 and 2009 through the MCPCE Study, as detailed in chapter 1.[12]

Throughout this chapter, we will take a closer look at the participation patterns of black and other youth. We will try to tease out which factors encourage and which inhibit the participation of black youth. We will also explore how young black Americans describe in their own words the prospect of political participation in the United States. Many of our respondents believed that politics has little direct bearing on the overall quality of their lives and had little faith in its ability to represent and respond to the interests of all Americans, even after the election of President Obama. However, in contrast to the feelings of political alienation detailed in the last chapter, young black Americans reported being very proud and excited about participating in the election of the nation's first black president.

In a focus group held in February 2009 with black youth aged 18–24 in Chicago, one young woman explained that she had voted in 2008 because she had wanted to be part of history.[13] And while the shared feelings of elation at President Obama's election were evident among nearly all the young people in the room, there was also a shared understanding of the limited impact of the Obama presidency on the everyday reality of their lives. The symbolic potential of President Obama was indisputable among the group; they believed that his life story had the power to motivate young black Americans. What was up for debate, at least among this group of young people, was his political power and possibly personal will to dramatically change the daily lived experience of black youth, especially those more vulnerable. This distrust of political officials and, at times, the political process makes exiting from political participation or pursuing what I call "the politics of invisibility" an attractive option for some young black Americans—a process we will explore in the final pages of this chapter.

VOTING PRIOR TO OBAMA

On July 1, 1971, with the ratification of the Twenty-Sixth Amendment to the Constitution, 18-year-old citizens won the right to vote. The movement to lower the voting age from 21 to 18 was thought by many to be the most effective way to attack the disparity in the higher rates of participation among older Americans compared to those in their twenties, to infuse the political process with an energized and educated voting bloc, and to bring into the fold some younger Americans who had secured their political voice outside the system through protests and social movements. This lowering of the voting age was also facilitated by the reality that 18-year-olds were expected to serve their country by traveling to Vietnam and fighting in a war that many questioned, that some disapproved of, and in which too many died. So in 1972, 18-year-olds were allowed to vote for the first time, and in that election—between George McGovern and Richard Nixon—50 percent of young people aged 18–24 turned out to vote, overwhelmingly for McGovern, who lost.[14] Ironically, while the 50 percent turnout rate in 1972 was considered the gold standard in youth turnout until the 2008 presidential election, at the time it was disappointing to many who had expected the turnout rate of young people to match the turnout rate of those older than 35, which ranged from 64 to 71 percent.[15]

It is important to note that although the average turnout for young people aged 18–24 in 1972 was 50 percent, there were significant racial disparities in voting among this population. In 1972, 52 percent of white youth voted, compared to only 35 percent of black youth and 31 percent of Latino youth.[16] Since that high point in "youth" voting, there has been a fairly steady decline, with turnout percentages among this population ranging from the low forties to the low thirties until they rose in 2004 and 2008.[17] Interestingly, the decline has been most steep among young white voters, with the gap in voting between black and white young adults shrinking since 1984, when Jesse Jackson ran for the Democratic nomination, mobilizing black and Latino youth to get to the polls.

Despite the general decline, there have been upswings in youth turnout. The election of Bill Clinton was facilitated in part by the fact that 43 percent of 18- to 24-year-olds voted. However, most of that surge was driven by an 8-percentage-point increase in voting among white youth, up from 37 percent in 1988 to 45 percent in 1992. In contrast, black and Latino youth in 1992 increased their turnout only by 1–2 percent above that of 1988, as shown in table 5.1. Thus, contrary to the narrative that 1992 was a high point for youth voting, it was actually only a high point for white youth voting and marked the reemergence of racial disparities in voting among blacks, whites, and Latinos that had trended downward since 1984.

There is a critical lesson to be gleaned from the historical data on voting among young people: the danger of representing the experience of white Americans as the normative experience for all groups. In our brief examination of voting patterns among young people aged 18–24, it is apparent that white, black, and Latino youth have traveled different voting trajectories. On one hand, starting strong in 1972, white youth have experienced a significant and relatively consistent

TABLE 5.1   U.S. Census Bureau, Reported Voting, 18- to 24-Year-Olds

Election year	Black youth (%)	White youth (%)	Latino youth (%)
1972	34.7	51.9	30.9
1976	27.9	44.7	21.8
1980	30.1	41.8	15.9
1984	40.6	41.6	21.9
1988	35.0	37.0	16.8
1992	36.6	45.4	17.6
1996	32.4	36.9	15.1
2000	33.9	37.2	15.4
2004	44.0/47.0*	48.5/49.8*	20.4/33.0*
2008	52.3/55.4*	48.3/49.4*	27.4/38.8*

Percentage of citizens ages 18 to 24 who voted. Percentage of white non-Hispanic 18- to 24-year-olds who reported voting is included in table 1996 onward. Data for whites prior to 1996 represent all whites, including those of Hispanic origin.
Source: U.S. Census Bureau, Current Population Survey, Reported Voting and Registration by Race, Hispanic Origin, Sex, and Age Groups: November 1964 to 2008

decline in their turnout at the polls up to 2004, with the exception of 1992. The decreases in black youths' voting have been less steep, in part because their beginning level of participation was not as high as that of white youth. Moreover, black youths' increases in voting power have been visible across the years, especially during the 1984, 2004, and 2008 presidential elections. The voting patterns of Latino youth have shared characteristics with both black and white youth with a relatively consistent decrease in turnout, although less dramatic than that of white youth, and with a bit of a turnaround in 1984 and again in 2004 and 2008, similar to the trajectory for black youth.

In addition to flexing their voting power recently, black and Latino youth have also expanded in overall numbers. They now comprise a larger percentage of the youth population. In 1972, white youth aged 18–24 made up 87 percent of all young people in that age range in the United States. By 2004, they accounted for only 64 percent of individuals aged 18–24. So if we are to tell a nuanced and complete story of youth voting participation in this country, not just white youth participation, then it must be rooted in the specific histories of different racial and ethnic groups that shape their willingness and ability to participate in the political process. For example, while 1972 was a watershed for youth voting, it came only seven years after the passage of the Voting Rights Act, in 1965, which generated the most dramatic change in black voting registration and turnout since Reconstruction. As late as 1962, less than 30 percent—28.8 percent—of the black voting-age population in the South was registered to vote. Three years after the passage of the act, the percentage of the black voting-age population in the South who were registered to vote doubled and approached nearly 60 percent—at 58.7 percent.[18]

A similar, though more modest, increase in black registration and voting occurred in 1984 during Jesse Jackson's campaign for the Democratic nomination for president. Specifically, in 1984, the number of blacks aged 18–24 who turned out increased by 10 percentage points, jumping from 30 percent in 1980 to 40.6 percent in 1984. Research suggests that the strong feelings of black Americans against Reagan and for Jackson, as well as the massive registration and mobilization drives that numerous organizations mounted, helped produce the increased registration and turnout among African Americans and African-American youth during this period.[19] The bottom-line lesson of this discussion is that without attention to the specifics of a group's history and current lived experience, we cannot accurately tell the story of not only black politics but American politics.

In the coverage of the 2004 presidential race, journalists and scholars again bemoaned the declining engagement of young people in the political process. Possibly concerned with the perceived illegitimacy of a political system with declining participation, especially among the young, pundits found it easy to produce commentary in newspapers and blogs about the disappearance of the youth vote. This alarm seemed appropriate when studying the overall voting trends of young people, especially young whites. Ironically, the increase in turnout among young black voters would help to change the story of the declining "youth vote."[20]

As is evident in table 5.2, in 2004 young people went to the polls in record numbers, with 42 percent of young people casting a ballot—numbers not seen since the 1984 and 1992 presidential elections. Not only did young people show up at the polls, they also recorded the greatest increase in voters among any age group. The turnout of young adults aged 18–24 increased from 32 percent in 2000 to 42 percent in 2004.[21] Important for this discussion is the fact that in 2004, the percentage of black, white, and Latino youth increased among those who reported voting, a trend that continued for blacks and Latinos into 2008's historic presidential election.[22] In 2004, 44 percent of black youth and 47 percent of black citizens aged 18–24 turned out to vote. Only slightly larger percentages of voting among white youth

TABLE 5.2   U.S. Census Bureau, Reported Voting, 2000 and 2004,
18- to 24-Year-Olds

Individuals by race/ethnic group	2000 (%)	2004 (%)
Total youth	32.3	41.9/46.7*
White, non-Hispanic	37.0	48.5/49.8*
Black	33.9	44.0/47.0*
Latino	15.4	20.4/33.0*
Asian	15.9	23.4/34.2*

Percentage of citizens ages 18 to 24 who voted. Data for whites represent percentage of white non-Hispanics ages 18 to 24 who reported voting.
Source: U.S. Census Bureau, Current Population Survey, Reported Voting and Registration by Race, Hispanic Origin, Sex, and Age Groups: November 1964 to 2008

were evident that year, with 49 percent of white youth and 50 percent of young white citizens aged 18–24 going to the polls. Both groups experienced a jump in participation of at least 10 percentage points between 2000 and 2004. Approximately 20 percent of Latino youth and 33 percent of Latino citizens aged 18–24 voted in 2004, up 5 percent from 15 percent of all Latino youth in 2000.[23] Sixteen percent of Asian youth voted in 2000; this group also staged an increase in their voting percentage in 2004, with 23 percent of Asian youth and 34 percent of young Asian citizens aged 18–24 voting. The figures for both Latino and Asian youth no doubt represent the specific challenges these groups face regarding formal representation.[24]

Table 5.3 confirms that data from the Black Youth Project generally correspond to the figures reported from the Census Bureau and other

TABLE 5.3   Youth Voting, U.S. Census and Black Youth
Project Comparison

Race/ethnic group	Black Youth Project, 2004, percentage who reported voting, ages 18–24 (%)	U.S. Census Bureau, 2004, percentage who reported voting, ages 18–24 (%)
White youth	50.0	48.5/ 49.8*
Black youth	40.0	44.0 / 47.0*
Latino youth	23.0	20.4 / 33.0*

Percentage of citizens ages 18 to 24 who voted. Data for whites represent percentage of white non-Hispanics ages 18 to 24 who reported voting.
Source: U.S. Census Bureau, Current Population Survey, Reported Voting and Registration by Race, Hispanic Origin, Sex, and Age Groups: November 1964 to 2008

TABLE 5.4   Sex Gap in Youth Voting in 2004

Race/ethnic group and gender	Black Youth Project reported voting (%)
Black females	47
Black males	30
White females	56
White males	45
Latina females	20
Latino males	26

Source: The Black Youth Project

surveys of youth voting in the 2004 presidential election, although the gap between black and white youth voters is higher in the Black Youth Project data than reported in the census data.[25] Approximately 50 percent of white respondents ages 18–25 reported voting in the 2004 election. Among black respondents, 40 percent said they voted, with 23 percent of Latinos indicating they did so. As is the trend, females voted at higher rates than males among black and white respondents, as demonstrated in table 5.4. In contrast, Latinas reported voting at lower rates than young Latino males.

Of course, understanding trends in turnout is important for the larger context of measuring "the" youth vote, but ultimately much of our interest is devoted to the following question: For whom did they vote? Not surprising, data from the Black Youth Project detailed in table 5.5 indicate that 90 percent of black youth who voted in 2004 cast a ballot for John Kerry. Only 3 percent reported voting for George Bush. Another 4 percent of young black adults said they voted for someone other than the two major candidates, with a final 3 percent refusing to share their vote choice.

Interestingly, while gender seemed to make little difference in vote choice among black youth, with approximately 90 percent of young black males and females casting a ballot for Kerry, age did show marked differences. Specifically, 94 percent of black voters aged 18–21 voted for Kerry, while 84 percent of black adults ages 22–25 indicated they voted for Kerry. Significantly, 7 percent of black 22- to 25-year-olds said they voted for someone other than Bush or Kerry, compared to 1 percent of 18- to 21-year-old black voters. While black youth turned out overwhelmingly for Kerry, the increase in voting for a third candidate among black youth voters age 22–25 might suggest increased skepticism toward the idea that candidates from either major party, the Democrats or the Republicans, will truly address the issues confronting black communities.

TABLE 5.5   Youth Vote in 2004 Presidential Election

2004 vote choice by race/ethnic group	John Kerry (%)	George Bush (%)	Other (%)	Refused to share vote choice (%)
Black youth	90	3	4	3
Latino youth	74	19	3	4
White youth	49	45	3	3

Source: The Black Youth Project

Among Latino youth voters, a significant majority, 74 percent, indicated they voted for John Kerry, with 19 percent voting for Bush, 4 percent refusing to divulge for whom they voted, and 3 percent indicating they voted for someone else. There were disparities in the Latino vote of both age and gender. Among young Latino men, 79 percent voted for Kerry and 19 percent for Bush. Sixty-five percent of young Latinas reported voting for Kerry, with 20 percent voting for Bush and another 12 percent refusing to say for whom they voted. We also find age discrepancies in voting among Latinos, but in the opposite direction identified for blacks, with more 22- to 25-year-old Latinos voting for Kerry than did those aged 18–21. Eighty-four percent of Latinos aged 22–25 voted for Kerry, compared to 63 percent of those aged 18–21. Of those who voted for Bush, 9 percent of Latinos aged 22–25 and 30 percent of those aged 18–21 said they made such a choice.

Young white voters are the only group in which we see a nearly even division in vote choice. Forty-nine percent of young white voters indicated they voted for John Kerry, while 45 percent said they voted for George Bush. Another 3 percent voted for someone else. The split in candidate choice is also evident when we look at young white male and female voters. Among young white women in our sample, 47 percent voted for George Bush and 44 percent voted for Kerry. This distribution is different among young white men, with 41 percent voting for Bush and 55 percent saying they voted for Kerry. Age also makes visible a significant division in vote choice, with 40 percent of 18- to 21-year-old white voters voting for Bush and 55 percent voting for Kerry, while 48 percent of 22- to 25-year-old white voters cast their ballot for Bush, compared to 45 percent for Kerry.

The comparisons of vote choice are important, but it is also important to explore the factors that were related to young blacks going to the polls. If one remembers the controversy surrounding the 2000 election—with the Supreme Court's ruling on hanging chads helping to determine the election of the president of the United States, as well as the claims of vote suppression and irregularities among black voters, especially in Florida—we have to ask ourselves: Who would take the time to vote in 2004? The answer to this question is not that surprising. Specifically, those young black Americans who went to the polls were mobilized by an infrastructure targeting young people, energized by their disdain for George Bush and his administration, and socialized by parents who had taken an interest in politics over the years.

Using the same statistical technique discussed in earlier chapters, an ordered probit, I explore what factors correspond with young black adults being more or less likely to report going to the polls in the 2004 election. Some of the variables I examine in this analysis have been identified in earlier studies as influencing voting turnout. Here I am talking about characteristics such as a person's education. We know from previous studies that individuals with more formal education are more likely to vote.[26] Research suggests that individuals with more education have more information about the election. They also feel more comfortable voting, believing that they have the knowledge and skills to participate. In addition to education, I include other traditional variables in this analysis such as sex, age, family SES, political efficacy, parents' interest and participation in electoral politics, immigration status, and the intensity of one's feelings toward the political parties. Finally, in terms of traditional variables, I include in the model a measure of whether people are engaged in religious activities such as attending meetings at their place of worship. Researchers have found that religious institutions can teach individuals the skills they need to feel confident in their ability to vote. Scholars such as Fred Harris have argued that black churches, in particular, can be an important source of information about an election as well as a center for mobilizing people to go to the polls.[27]

In addition to these more traditional characteristics thought to influence whether someone votes, I account for a number of factors that are tied to the lived experience of black youth. For example, the model contains a measure of neighborhood SES, spurred by the belief that in neighborhoods with fewer resources available for getting people to the polls, individuals are less likely to vote.[28] The presence of a sense of linked fate—the belief by a black person that he or she is directly affected by what happens to most black people—has been shown by political scientist Michael C. Dawson to be an important variable in predicting and understanding black political participation and is therefore included in this analysis.[29] Finally, I also include in this model the alienation scale discussed in chapter 4. Again, I want to know whether young people who express greater levels of political alienation in any of the three dimensions detailed in chapter 4 are less likely to vote.

THE FINDINGS: VOTING 2004

Ironically, none of the variables thought to be rooted in the lived experience of young black people had any relationship (statistically) to their decision to vote, at least not in 2004. Instead, it was the traditional factors of sex, age, parents' electoral interest and participation, immigrant status, political efficacy, and feelings about the political parties that seemed most closely related to the decision to vote among young black people. Interestingly, one dimension of political alienation was a significant factor associated with young black Americans who voted in 2004. Specifically, those individuals who felt more connected to the larger political community were also more likely to report voting. Noticeably missing from those factors thought to impact black political participation were a sense of linked fate, family SES, and religious activity. When we explore in greater depth the factors that were shown to be statistically linked to the likelihood of a young black person going to the polls, we unveil some interesting findings:[30]

- Young black women were 14 percent *more likely* to vote in 2004 than young black men.
- Older black youth in our sample, those who were aged 25, were 33 percent *more likely* to vote in 2004 than those black youth who were 18 and just lately eligible to vote.
- Young black Americans who were not born in the United States and who had parents and/or grandparents who were not born in the United States were 25 percent *less likely* to vote than young black Americans who were born in the United States and whose parents and grandparents were also.
- Black youth who registered the highest levels of political efficacy were 37 percent *more likely* to vote than those who registered the lowest levels.
- Black youth who felt like full and equal citizens were 22 percent *more likely* to vote than those who felt the least connected and included in the larger political community.
- Black youth who held much stronger feelings for the Democratic versus the Republican Party were 30 percent *more likely* to vote than those black youth who held similar feelings toward both parties.

The factors associated with whether white and Latino youth vote are not that different from those found to be significant for black youth. Among white youth, age and political efficacy were important. Again, white respondents who were older and those with greater feelings of political efficacy were more likely to vote. Interestingly, those white youth who were more active in their religious institutions were also more likely to vote. In terms of political alienation, those white youth who held more disdain for public officials or registered higher on the government-orientation dimension of political alienation were less likely to vote. Latino respondents more closely mirrored black youth, with older Latino youth and those with stronger feelings for the Democratic Party more likely to show up at the polls. In addition, those Latino youth who felt like full and equal citizens were more likely to vote in 2004 than those who felt less connected to the political community.

VOTING IN 2008

In 2004, the country experienced record turnouts, especially among black and Latino young people. Unfortunately, as was also the case in 2000, the election was marred by controversy. Despite registering the highest turnout for a presidential election since 1992, the election process in 2004 ended with accusations of vote fraud and voter suppression, highlighting, in particular, voting irregularities in the state of Ohio. In 2000, Americans watched with disbelief as the fiasco in Florida unfolded, with high-priced lawyers arguing over chads as a means to decide the election of the president of the United States. For many people, especially young black Americans, the reports of purged voting rolls that disqualified registered African-American voters confirmed that fundamental flaws still existed in the practice of democracy in the United States. In response to these democratic troubles, numerous scholars, pundits, and average Americans pondered whether the controversies surrounding the 2000 and 2004 presidential elections, in conjunction with the low approval ratings for President Bush, would lead in 2008 to a dramatic decline not only in voting but also in young people's general confidence in the fairness and legitimacy of the political system.

Almost as if it was dictated by the election gods, the 2008 primary season proved to be the antidote needed for the ailing democratic process so starkly visible in 2000 and 2004. With the presidential candidacies of Barack Obama and Hillary Clinton and the vice-presidential nomination of Sarah Palin, the country was invited to participate in a historic race for the White House. And participate we did. With unsurpassed turnouts for primary voting recorded in numerous states and record turnouts among young black Americans, some have suggested that in 2008, we witnessed the reinvigoration of participation, civic engagement, and trust in government, especially among the younger generation. Interest and participation in the primary races for the presidential nomination and in the general election spanned age, race, gender, and, to some degree, class. Across the country and around the world, people watched with anticipation for the uprising of democracy from below. And most exhilarating for many was the introduction of record numbers of new voters, many of them younger Americans, coming to the process with a restored belief that they could reclaim their government and their futures.

Numerous sources indicate that black Americans and specifically black youth went to the polls in record numbers in 2008. While the percentage of Americans reporting that they voted did not change significantly between 2004 and 2008, there was an important increase in the number of black Americans who cast a ballot in 2008: from 60 percent in 2004 to 65 percent in 2008. This increase resulted in about two million additional black voters in 2008.[31] Reports from CIRCLE and the U.S. Bureau of the Census suggest that the turnout of youth aged 18–29 for the 2008 election was "one of the highest recorded."[32] More specifically for our purposes, the data from the census in table 5.1 indicate that 52 percent of black youth and 55 percent of black citizens aged 18–24 voted in the election.[33] This is the highest turnout among 18- to 24-year-olds of any racial or ethnic group since the passage of the Twenty-Sixth Amendment granting 18-year-olds the right to vote. In addition, it marks the first time a majority of black youth participated in any national election. Young black women aged 18–24 reported voting at higher rates than young black men. Sixty percent of black female citizens and 57 percent of black females aged 18–24 voted in 2008. Among men aged 18–24, 51 percent of citizens and 48 percent of all black males voted.[34]

In addition to the historic turnout among African-American youth, young Latinos and Asians also demonstrated significant increases in their rates of turnout between 2004 and 2008, although the increase was greater between 2000 and 2004 than between 2004 and 2008. The same is true of black youth. Ironically, white youth did not increase their rates of turnout between 2004 and 2008. And according to a CIRCLE report, Native American youth "comprised the only group that experienced significant declines since 2004, and now have the lowest turnout percentage in that age category."

A review of the data from the second wave of the MCPCE Study provides some surprising findings. First, about 81 percent of black youth aged 18–30 in our sample reported voting in the 2008 presidential election. In contrast, the data from the U.S. Census indicate that 55 percent of black youth voted in 2008. Thus, either our sample does not represent the voting patterns of young black Americans aged 18–30 or a number of our respondents have misrepresented whether they voted in 2008, something that is not unique to this study.[35] Either way, I suggest that readers evaluate our findings with prudence. These questionable numbers are, however, yet another important marker of the significance of the 2008 election and the candidacy of Barack Obama to young black Americans across the country. Overwhelmingly, the young black adults in our sample and across the country felt compelled to place themselves in the democratic process in 2008 even if they did not vote: many who did not participate engaged in their own reconstructed history, imagining themselves as taking part in this historic moment, uniting behind the Democratic nominee, this time a black nominee.

Since the MCPCE Study was not focused exclusively on black youth or young people broadly, they make up a smaller percentage of respondents in this database. Given the limits of our data in this area, we did not run an ordered probit analysis. Instead, we will explore some findings from a focus group with black youth in Chicago only weeks after the inauguration of President Obama.

THE FOCUS GROUP FINDINGS

The importance of this election to young black Americans was made clear in their turnout but also in how they talked about the act of voting in 2008 and what it meant to them. In the aforementioned focus group held in February 2009 with black youth aged 18–24 from Chicago, participants were asked how they felt about the election.[36] The group was diverse and included a range of young black people, including some who were in school, some who worked, some who were unemployed, and some with children. This was not a "representative" sample of young black people, and no attempt should be made to generalize from their comments. They do, however, represent a group of young blacks willing to provide insight into their thoughts about the 2008 election and President Obama.

Many of the young people in the room talked about wanting to be part of a historic election and wanting to participate in the one way they knew they could—by voting. Explaining the motive for voting, one person said, "I wanted to be a part of history." Another added,

"I voted because it was my first time voting and I wanted to make a difference." One participant explained the importance of the election to him as follows,

> I think it means that anything is possible, that even as recently as five years ago nobody could believe that we would have a black president. Now we have a black president, and he was elected not just because he was able to get black people to vote for him, but he was able to get white people to vote for him. He was able to run on his platform of change and how things are going to be different from the way they were eight years ago and how people didn't trust the government. Now people may be able to trust their government again because they have a president that's more relatable to them—somebody who's a little bit younger, somebody who understands the culture, music, technology, and everything else.

Other members of the focus group emphasized what they believed the election of President Obama meant to black youth. One person explained that President Obama made him feel connected to a government that in the past had alienated him: "I just felt really disconnected from the government. I just felt like everything they were saying was a foreign language to me. Now that I've had a reason to pay attention to politics and stuff like that, I feel like a lot of what I've been hearing actually speaks to me directly, and I can understand it. It's more on a personal level, a more intimate level now than it was before." Another participant viewed Obama's election as a door opening for black youth: "For once, I feel like Obama opened up a lot of doors for young black people. They look at him like, well, if he did it...it makes a lot of young people want to go back to school. We think about it. Everybody's looking for a change nowadays, so hopefully it just speaks to them and they do what they got to do." Another participant added later, "Like Obama, yeah, he opened that door, but that don't mean nothing. Are we going to walk through it, that's the question."

At the same time that these young people celebrated the election of the country's first black president, they also made clear distinctions about what they believed to be the limits of his victory on their lives. For example, when they were asked if they thought their interactions with the police would change under the Obama administration, most in the room laughed and said no. One respondent said, "Now that we have a black president, white cops are going to be banging them little black boys because they don't like him. Racism is strong!" Another respondent explained that controlling the police and their interactions with black youth was outside the reach of what Obama could do. "I don't think it will change, because Obama can't go to the police station and say, 'You all need to change.' That's something they've been raised with. They're not going to stop. It's not like he's going to sit in the station with them or [ride] in the cars. He can't do all that. Whatever they can get away with, that's what they're going to do."

Whether the topic was violence in their neighborhoods, interactions with the police, or the prospect of getting a job, generally the young people in the room cautioned that people should not expect President Obama to create the change in their lives that they all hoped for. As one young woman explained, "Obama is only one person of many. He's not the only person to create a deep change, and people just talk like Obama is the savior." Another respondent explained that black youth were not equal citizens because money and wealth still made getting ahead easier.

> I know that, like, in terms of opportunities, in terms of, like, getting high-paying jobs and putting yourself in a situation to be successful and all of that, a lot of people who are in those high positions are there because they were rich and they were born rich or because of nepotism, because their parents or their grandparents or somebody was in high places and that's how they hired them. Or because they knew people or because if you're black or if you're a minority and those people who have those jobs that you want, you know, they don't understand, and they're not going to hire you because you're different, and that's not equal.

The young people in the room were also quick to recenter the discussion about change away from the national level to city politics, where they hold little hope of any change. One respondent explained why none of the respondents mentioned violence as an issue that government could address.

> I just think that no one on...no one really cares on a more governmental level....No one cares. Most of the, as far as the city of Chicago is concerned, most of the money and emphasis is being put on the more affluent neighborhoods and more like the North Side neighborhoods, like the Wrigleyvilles and the Andersonvilles and Lincoln Park neighborhoods that have already been flourishing for years that are more than well developed and have a good business flow and good money flow throughout the neighborhood. And that's pretty much where all the emphasis is being kept. But you go outside of those neighborhoods and it's like a whole other world. I guess as far as politics in Chicago is

concerned and how things are run in the city of Chicago, nobody cares about that, the neighborhoods, aside from those that I just named and others that are affluent and well developed.

I want to emphasize that these young people were very clear about the symbolic importance of having a black president as well as the reality of how much (or how little) his presence in the White House would change their lives. Signs of this insight are also found in the MCPCE data. For example, as we discussed in chapter 4, on the question "Do you agree with the statement 'Generally I feel like a full and equal citizen in this country with all the rights and protections that other people have'?" we find a substantial split in the level of inclusion that black and white youth feel, with 42 percent of black youth agreeing with the statement compared to 66 percent of white youth. A similar split was evident between Asian and Latino respondents, with 63 percent of Asian young adults agreeing with the statement, compared to only 43 percent of Latino young adults. Thus, days before the country was poised to elect its first black president, not only was there a sizeable gap in how fully included in the political community black and Latino youth felt compared to white and Asian young people, there was also a significant reduction in the number of youth generally who felt included in the political community from data gathered through the Black Youth Project in 2005.

BEYOND VOTING

While many are offering the increased voting of black youth in 2008 as a sign that our democracy is thriving across racial, ethnic, and generational groups, as I suggested at the beginning of this chapter, other forms of political participation matter and must also be examined. If we begin to look beyond voting at other traditional venues for political expression, we notice very quickly a disturbing pattern: the absence of not only black youth but all youth from these activities. Data from the Black Youth Project indicate that the majority of youth across racial groups believed they had the skills and knowledge to participate in politics, that their participation could make a difference, and that by working together, people in their neighborhood could solve many of their problems. But despite such optimism and confidence, very few young people reported engaging in political acts in the twelve months prior to completing the Black Youth Project survey in 2005. In fact, in the twelve months prior to taking the survey, less than 20 percent of young people from any surveyed racial or ethnic group had participated in traditional political acts, which included contacting a public official or agency; attending a protest meeting, demonstration, or sit-in; participating in a boycott; joining a political group; giving money to a candidate, party, or political issue; working or volunteering on a political campaign or for a candidate or a political party; working with people in one's neighborhood on a political issue or problem; or writing an article or letter to the editor about a political issue or problem. The general trend was one of nonparticipation.

The upside is that young people in general and young black Americans in particular are engaged in some political and civic acts. For example, 25 percent of black youth reported participating in a "buycott." Sixty-six percent reported that they talked with family and friends about politics. Forty-eight percent of black youth said that they engaged in organized volunteer or community service in the twelve months prior to completing the survey in 2005. Thirty-eight percent said they were a member of an organized group, such as one run through school, church, or the park system, and 45 percent of those who identified as having a religion reported that they attended religious service at least once a week. In all these endeavors, however, except attending religious service, black youth either trailed or were at best equal to white youth in their participation.

Table 5.6 shows the rates of participation for what I call traditional political activities. When asked in 2005 if they had contacted a public official or agency in the last twelve months, only 8 percent of black youth answered affirmatively, compared to 19 percent of white youth and 8 percent of Latino youth. When asked if they had given money to a candidate, party, or political issue, only 10 percent of black youth said yes. This time they were in good company, since only 11 percent of white youth and Latino youth indicated they had engaged in such an activity. The numbers are just about the same when the question was about working or volunteering on a political campaign, for a candidate, or for a party. Only 10 percent of black youth, 11 percent of white youth, and 8 percent of Latino youth had made such commitments. When asked if they had been active in or joined a political group, the young black people in our study again indicated little interest in such activities. Only 9 percent of black youth, 13 percent of Latino youth, and 14 percent of white youth were part of a political group. The numbers dropped even lower when they were asked if they had written an article or letter to the editor about a political issue or problem. Five percent

TABLE 5.6   Traditional Political Avctivities, Black Youth Preject, 15- to
25-Year-Olds

Traditional political acts	Black youth (%)	White youth (%)	Latino youth (%)
Contacted a public official	8	19	8
Given money to a candidate	10	11	11
Worked or volunteered on a political campaign, for a candidate, or for a party	10	11	8
Was active in or joined a political group	9	14	13
Wrote an article or letter to the editor about a political issue or problem	5	7	6
Worked with people in the neighborhood on a political issue or problem	12	17	11
Talked with family or friends about a political issue, party, or candidate	66	84	66

Source: The Black Youth Project

of black youth, 7 percent of white youth, and 6 percent of Latino youth were active in these areas.

The rates of participation begin to increase when the time demands for such activities decrease or the reward seems more concrete and direct. For example, when asked if they worked with people in their neighborhood on a political issue or problem, 12 percent of black youth, that is, one out of eight, said yes. Similarly, 17 percent of white youth, or one out of six, said yes, with 11 percent of Latino youth indicating they had worked with their neighbors. By far the most popular form of political engagement was political talk. Sixty-six percent of black and Latino youth and 84 percent of white youth said they talked with family or friends about a political issue, party, or candidate.

Data from the 2006 National Civic and Political Health Survey conducted by the Center for Information and Research on Civic Learning and Engagement (CIRCLE) replicate the low participatory numbers detailed above.[37] The center found that only 11 percent of their respondents aged 15–25 had contacted an official, only 7 percent had donated money to a candidate or party, only 2 percent regularly volunteered for a political candidate or group, and only 7 percent had contacted the print media. Sixteen percent of their respondents indicated they were a member of a group involved in politics, and

35 percent tried to persuade others in an election, a narrower indicator of our political-talk question. Thus, like the respondents from the Black Youth Project survey, the participants in the CIRCLE 2006 National Civic and Political Health Survey were also generally anemic when it came to traditional methods of political engagement.

It is important to put these responses in a useful context before we write off all young people as largely apolitical. First, the data from the Black Youth Project were collected during what might be considered a dormant political time, after the 2004 presidential season and before the 2006 midterm elections were in full swing. More recent data, as I discuss below, suggest that in 2008 young people were more engaged politically, especially in those activities that seemed directly connected to the 2008 presidential election. Second, if we examine other data sets, we find that while young people are especially allergic to participation through traditional forms of political expression, there has been continuous and declining activity among those older than age 30 in the same political activities.[38] In a society with an expanding entertainment industry—an increasing number of cable channels, high-definition DVDs, twenty-four-hour news cycles, and numerous other distractions from politics—there are not a lot of people, young or old, who are interested in engaging in old-time politics beyond talking to friends and possibly voting...if the line outside the polling area isn't too long and it isn't raining (or snowing). The domination of the "traditionalists" in American politics—those who walked the precinct, volunteered at the phone bank, wrote their public official a letter of complaint, or joined a political group—seemed to be coming to an end, at least before the 2008 election.

As noted above, black youth and all youth have seemingly decided not to engage in many of the activities traditionally associated with American politics, at least in its idealized form. Even when we examine the participation rates of young people aged 18–30 only weeks before the 2008 election, we find a pattern similar to that identified in the Black Youth Project data, namely, low levels of political engagement outside of voting. Only in a few areas directly tied to the election do we find healthy rates of participation, especially among black youth. For example, 42 percent of black youth reported wearing a campaign button or having a political sticker or sign in their window, compared to 17 percent of white youth, 18 percent of Latino youth, and 20 percent of Asian youth. Similarly, 16 percent of young black adults reported going door to door, making phone calls, or collecting signatures for the election, compared to 7 percent of white youth, 8 percent of Latino young adults, and 13 percent of Asian youth. While young black adults were clearly energized by this election, much of the data in table 5.7 suggest that their excitement did not spill over into other areas of political activity.

TABLE 5.7   Traditional Political Activities, MCPCE Project, 18- to 30-Year-Olds

Traditional political acts	Black youth (%)	White youth (%)	Latino youth (%)	Asian-American youth (%)
Contacted a public official (8)	8	10	2	17
Given money to a candidate (6)	12	6	3	17
Worked or volunteered on a political campaign, for a candidate, or for a party (7)	10	7	2	13
Was active or joined a political group (17)	8	7	2	11
Wrote an article or letter to the editor about a political issue or problem (11)	7	5	5	12
Worked with people in the neighborhood on a political issue or problem (22)	5	5	8	8
Talked with family or friends about a political issue, party, or candidate (21)	69	77	65	65
Called a radio show (12)	8	.09	6	7
Attended meetings, rallies, speeches, or dinners in support of a candidate (4)	14	11	10	13
Had a campaign button, political sticker, or sign in your window (5)	42	17	18	20
Attended a meeting of a local government board or council (9)	5	8	3	10
Signed a paper petition (10)	11	3	6	15
Tried to involve others in election, including going door to door, making phone calls, collecting signatures, and passing out literature (14)	16	7	8	13

Source: 2008 Mobilization, Change, and Political and Civic Engagement

TABLE 5.8　Digital Democrats, Black Youth Project, 15- to 25-Year-Olds

Political acts of Digital Democrats	Black youth (%)	White youth (%)	Latino youth (%)
Wrote a blog or sent an e-mail	15	21	18
Signed a paper or e-mail petition	16	28	19
Engaged in buycotting	25	23	20

Source: The Black Youth Project

Luckily for us all, the world has evolved, especially in terms of technology. New methods of political engagement have developed via the Web, making for easy access and dissemination. The data from the Black Youth Project suggest that in 2005, young adults were more interested in expressing their political views through these new forms of political expression than the older ones just discussed. These activities included writing blogs, sending e-mail petitions, sending an e-mail in support of a cause, and buycotting. It seems that more young people are engaged in such activities in part because of the ease of participation, in part because of the solitary nature of such acts—they do not require the direct coordination of large or small groups—and in part because these activities allow young people to be engaged where they are, on their computers and their cell phones.

These *digital Democrats*, as I call them, seem more willing to participate when a computer or the Web is part of the scheme, as is evident in table 5.8. When we asked young people if they had sent an e-mail or written a blog about a political issue, candidate, or party, 15 percent of black youth, 21 percent of white youth, and 18 percent of Latino youth said yes. When asked if they had signed a paper or e-mail petition, 16 percent of black youth, 28 percent of white youth, and 19 percent of Latino youth concurred. Finally, when we asked if they had engaged in buycotting, 25 percent of black youth, 23 percent of white youth and 20 percent of Latino youth reported doing so. Again, data from CIRCLE's 2006 report on the civic and political health of the nation confirm the move toward the internet when it comes to youth participation. Sixteen percent of their respondents signed an e-mail petition, while 29 percent buycotted.

The use of the Web by young people across racial and ethnic groups to watch campaign speeches, debates, and political commercials was especially evident in the MCPCE Study data reported in table 5.9.

TABLE 5.9   Digital Democrats, MCPCE Project, 18- to 30-Year-Olds

Political acts of digital Democrats	Black youth (%)	White youth (%)	Latino youth (%)	Asian-American youth (%)
Engaged in buycotting (16)	5	10	7	15
E-mailed the editor or manager of a newspaper, television station, or Web site about a political issue or candidate (20)	9	1	3	10
Got campaign/candidate information from Facebook/ MySpace (30)	23	19	17	25
Used YouTube or campaign Web site to see candidate debates, interviews with candidates, campaign commercials, or a candidate's speech or announcement (31)	31	34	23	40
Written a blog about a political issue, candidate, or political party (19)	11	3	6	15
Written or forwarded an e-mail, signed an e-mail petition, or posted a comment to a blog about a political issue, candidate, or party (18)	32	22	10	19

Source: 2008 Mobilization, Change, and Political and Civic Engagement

Significant numbers of young people are using YouTube and social networking sites to gather information about politics. Thirty-one percent of young black adults, along with 34 percent of white youth, 23 percent of Latinos, and 40 percent of Asian young people, report using YouTube or a campaign Web site to follow the candidates in 2008. Similarly, 23 percent of blacks aged 18–30, 19 percent of whites, 17 percent of Latinos, and 25 percent of Asians received campaign or candidate information from Facebook or MySpace. The data necessitate that any future discussion of the politics of black youth be especially attentive to the force of technology and how the differential access to new media across racial, gender, and class groupings might inhibit democratic participation for some groups. Interestingly, however, reported increase use of the Web and new media for political participation was largely confined to activities related to the traditional domain of electoral politics in 2008. It seems that the 2008 presidential election captured the political imagination and energy of all young people, especially black youth.

Finally, there is the question of participation in extrasystemic forms of political engagement such as protest meetings, demonstrations, and boycotts. As noted, for many who grew up during the civil rights movement, these methods of engagement came to define black politics and black youth politics at that time. It was young people who sat at the lunch counters and refused to move in the presence of threatened and real violence. It was young people who filled the jails in southern cities, unwilling to be deterred by arrest, water hoses, and attack dogs. It was young people who organized through the Student Nonviolent Coordinating Committee, the Congress of Racial Equality, the Black Panther Party, and the Combahee River Collective to fight for the liberation of black people. It was young black children—the four girls killed at Ebenezer Baptist Church and Emmett Till, killed in Money, Mississippi—who came to symbolize the ultimate sacrifice blacks would be forced to make in the struggle for legal and social equality. It was young leaders like Martin Luther King Jr., John Lewis, Jesse Jackson, Angela Davis, Kathleen Cleaver, and Elaine Brown who would shoulder some of the burden and gain much of the media attention as they recruited, mobilized, and in some cases revolutionized generations of young black activists.

To those of the baby boomer generation who have come to control the leadership of black politics and many of the traditional, indigenous communication vehicles through which a black perspective is offered, the era of the civil rights movement was the best of times. Today, for many older black Americans, it seems that traditional electoral power has proven to corrupt if not black politics at least some black politicians. They have witnessed, for example, the fall of Detroit's "hip-hop mayor," Kwame Kilpatrick; D.C.'s former mayor Marion Berry; and more recently, former Louisiana representative William Jefferson, whose freezer was found stuffed with money.[39] For an older generation of black people and for many young people also, the mobilization in support of the Jena Six was more important than the increase in voting among young black adults in 2004 and 2008. While voting often allows us to have a say in a choice between the lesser of two evils, social movements, demonstrations, and sit-ins hold the promise of serious reallocation of resources and power—at least, that is the dream.

As we might expect, young black people have not bought into that dream, or if they have, it is just that, a dream. Very few are what I might call "movement activists." The data in table 5.10 demonstrate this fact.

TABLE 5.10 Movement Activists, Black Youth Project, 15- to 25-Year-Olds

Movement political acts	Black youth (%)	White youth (%)	Latino youth (%)
Attended protest meeting, demonstration, or sit-in	8	9	7
Boycotted	2	6	4

Source: The Black Youth Project

When asked if they attended a protest meeting, demonstration, or sit-in, only 8 percent of the black youth in the Black Youth Project responded affirmatively. Nine percent of white youth and 7 percent of Latinos had engaged in these extrasystemic acts of defiance. Similarly, when asked if they had participated in a boycott, only 2 percent of black youth, 6 percent of white youth, and 4 percent of Latino youth had boycotted in the last 12 months.

The same movement anemia was found among young people aged 18–30 in the MCPCE Study of 2008, with only 7 percent of black youth, 5 percent of white youth, 6 percent of Latino youth, and 10 percent of Asian youth saying that they had attended a protest meeting, demonstration, or sit-in.

Again, some context is called for. Specifically, everything suggests that the massive mobilization concerning immigration that occurred across the country in 2006 was heavily populated by young Latinos, so we would expect their participation in a movement numbers to be higher in 2006. None of our questions about movement activities included the time period of the immigration mobilization. This is, I believe, one reason for the sharp discrepancy between our numbers and those reported by CIRCLE in 2006. The researchers at CIRCLE found that 30 percent of their respondents aged 15–25 indicated that they had participated in a boycott, and 11 percent said they had protested.

Before exploring the broader political participation of youth in 2008, I would be remiss not to briefly evaluate the civic engagement of our respondents. Civic activity has gained greater visibility both in the media and in academic disciplines such as political science in recent years, as many have hoped that the declining rates of formal and institutionalized political participation across the generations would be replaced by expanded activity in the civic realm. The focus on civic engagement was also undoubtedly generated by the success of political scientist Robert Putnam's work on decline in the United States of civic or neighborhood and community-based activities.[40] Putnam thoroughly makes the case that civic participation—our participation in bowling leagues, church groups, and community organizations—has been dropping across age groups.

While overall civic activity may have been decreasing, compared to traditional forms of political participation, civic engagement is a gold mine. Black Youth Project data indicate that civic engagement is an area in which we do find more activity among young people (table 5.1). Asked if they were a member of an organized group, 38 percent of black youth, 47 percent of white youth, and 33 percent of Latino youth said yes. When asked if they had engaged in organized volunteer or community service, again we see a high return, with 48 percent of black youth, 62 percent of white youth, and 54 percent of Latino youth answering yes. While the general trend here is greater rates of participation among all groups than that indicated for explicitly political activities, our data stand in opposition to the CIRCLE data that show black youth as more civically engaged. To the contrary, black youth in our sample lag behind white youth by 9 to 14 percentage points, depending on the activity. There is one area of civic engagement in which black youth lead the way—religious activity. When asked about activity at their places of worship, black youth who identify as having a current religion far exceed their white counterparts.

Forty-five percent of black youth who had a religion with which they identified said that they attended religious service at least once a week, compared to 40 percent of religion-identified Latino youth and 35 percent of similarly situated white youth.[41] There appeared to be a

TABLE 5.11   Civic Engagers: Black Youth Project, 15- to 25-Year-Olds

Civic engagers	Black youth (%)	White youth (%)	Latino youth (%)
Member of an organized group	38	47	33
Engaged in organized volunteer or community-service work	48	62	54
Attended religious service at least once a week*	45	35	40
Served on a committee, organized a meeting, helped with special project at place of worship at least once or twice a month*	37	33	28

*Note: Percentages are for those respondents who indicated that they had a current religion, not all respondents.
Source: The Black Youth Project

TABLE 5.12 Civic Engagers, MCPCE Study, 18- to 30-Year-Olds

Civic engagers	Black youth (%)	White youth (%)	Latino youth (%)	Asian American youth (%)
Member of an organized group	21	34	16	33
Engaged in organized volunteer or community-service work	24	27	23	24

Source: 2008 Mobilization, Change, and Political and Civic Engagement

significant sex gap in rates of attendance only among black youth, with 49 percent of young black women attending service at least once a week, compared to 40 percent of young black men. Finally, when asked about their participation in civic activities at their religious institutions, such as serving on a committee, organizing a meeting, or giving time to a special project, the numbers dropped. Specifically, 37 percent of black youth indicated they participated in such activities at least once or twice a month. Thirty-three percent of white youth and 28 percent of Latino youth similarly were active once or twice a month. Again, the most significant gender difference in such participation was found among black youth, with 30 percent of young black men saying they engaged in such activities at least once a month and 43 percent of young black women saying they participated in these activities. Interestingly, the numbers in table 5.12 suggest that the percentage of young people engaged in civic activity in 2008 was lower than that found in the Black Youth Project data but still higher than that registered for most other forms of political engagement. It might be, as we found earlier, that MCPCE respondents, if involved at all in 2008, were preoccupied with activities related to the election.

FINDINGS ON DIGITAL DEMOCRATS

Having reviewed the general participation patterns of black youth, I want to return once again to the digital Democrats in our Black Youth Project data to get a sense of the factors corresponding with their participation.[42] Interestingly, it is through this set of analyses that a number of the variables that previous scholars suggest should influence participation start to show up. For example, when trying to explain which young blacks are more likely to send an e-mail or blog about a political issue, three factors stand out: age, whether one is in an organization or group, and one's level of political efficacy. As one gets older—that is, moves toward 25—one is less likely to send an e-mail or write a blog. One possible reason for this might be that 18- and 19-year-olds are in school or have more time to engage in such activity.

- A 25-year-old black adult is 11 percent *less likely* to send an e-mail or write a blog than an 18-year-old.

Similarly, those young people who are in an organization or group are more likely to send an e-mail or write a blog. In this case, it could be that being part of an organization provides you with the information that would incite participation. In addition, being a member of a group may mean you are part of a network that communicates through e-mails.

- A young black person who is in an organization or group is 7 percent *more likely* to send an e-mail or write a blog than a similarly situated black youth with no organizational or group ties.

Finally, as we have found previously, those young people who feel more politically efficacious are also more likely to send an e-mail or write a blog.

- Black youth with the highest levels of political efficacy are 15 percent *more likely* than those with the lowest levels of political efficacy to send an e-mail or write a blog.

Among young white respondents, factors such as age, family SES, immigrant status, and political efficacy were found to be significant. Latino youth were more likely to write a blog or send an e-mail if they were involved in a group or organization. They were less likely to do so the higher they scored on the dimension of political alienation that measured one's belief in equal opportunity in the United States.

The other political act that I want to explore in this section is buycotting. Some young people will only buy products from environmentally conscious companies; others, especially black youth, may make a decision to only buy products from black-owned companies. As shown in table 5.8, 25 percent of black youth from the Black Youth Project said they had participated in buycotting. When we examine the factors that might influence such participation, a number of variables emerge as important. Specifically, age, family SES, whether one is in school or a member of an organization, as well as feelings about the equal opportunity dimension of our political alienation scale all are statistically significant.

- A young black person aged 25 is 12 percent *more likely* to engage in a buycott than someone aged 18.

This finding might result from the fact that at 25, a person may have more discretionary income, may be making his or her own decisions about what to purchase, or may be more aware of the reputations of companies producing goods he or she is interested in purchasing.

Family SES was similarly shown to be significant, with higher family SES increasing the probability of engaging in a buycott. Again, this group of young people might have access to numerous resources associated with buycotting, the most important being income and information.

- Black youth with the highest levels of family SES are 18 percent *more likely* to engage in a buycott than those black youth with the lowest levels of family SES.

As we found when examining factors that shaped whether one sent an e-mail or wrote a blog, being in an organization or group leads to a greater probability of buycotting. In this analysis, being in school also facilitates buycotting. In both cases, we can imagine that black youth who are in school or members of organizations may be receiving information about formally organized buycotts or generally may be the type of young people who get involved in activities thought to make a difference.

- Black youth in a group or organization are 7 percent *more likely* to buycott than those who are not members.
- Black youth who are in school are also 7 percent *more likely* to engage in buycotting.

Finally, black youth who are less likely to agree that in the United States everyone has an equal chance to succeed are also less likely to engage in buycotting. We might imagine that those young people who are skeptical of the promise of equal opportunity are also more skeptical of the impact of buycotting as a political practice.

- Black youth who scored higher on the opportunity dimension of the political alienation scale were 11 percent *less likely* to engage in a buycott than those who scored lower on this dimension.

Among our white respondents, family SES was shown to be significant, as was political efficacy and the opportunity dimension of the political alienation scale. More variables emerged as important among Latino respondents. Like blacks, the opportunity dimension, family SES, age, and whether one is in school and a member of a group or organization were all statistically significant in determining whether Latino youth buycotted. Not surprisingly, immigrant status led to decreased involvement in buycotting among Latino youth.

While the notion of increased political participation on and through the Web is important to note, we also must remember that young people engage in a range of activities that they might consider political although they are not understood that way by the general public. Student researchers on the Black Youth Project repeatedly made the case that listening to rap music, engaging in spoken word, or even forming a book group might be considered political by some young people. To find out if their assertions were true, we asked the open-ended question on our survey "Are there ways that you participate in politics that I have not mentioned?" Only a small number of respondents answered yes: 5 percent of black youth, 8 percent of white youth, and 7 percent of Latino youth.

The activities they considered political were both surprising and illuminating. They included hosting a cable-access television show that discussed politics, serving in the military or participating in the Junior ROTC, calling a radio show to talk with the governor, fighting for more skateboard areas at the local park, holding up a political sign during a rally, watching CNN regularly, and discussing politics in online chatrooms. However, most of the responses centered on school activities that the respondents believed don't count as politics but should. These included participating in school debates and forums, attending political conferences at schools, serving in internships, planning and participating in mock elections, writing for the school newspaper, and serving on student governments. Somewhere in these answers we see the gray area in what is political versus civic engagement, what is political activity versus political learning, and what is politics versus everything else. These answers also reveal a broadening, even tearing down, of the boundaries between the political and personal that feminists have been discussing for the last forty years. Politics, it seems, is everywhere and nowhere, especially among the young. There are, however, some young people who engage in what I call a *politics of invisibility*. These young people see politics nowhere in their lives, or they consciously avoid it because they regard it as ineffectual and repressive politics. I turn to them now.

THE POLITICS OF INVISIBILITY

In their now classic book *Voice and Equality*, Verba, Schlozman, and Brady begin by writing that "citizen participation is at the heart of democracy....Through their activity citizens in a democracy seek to control who will hold public office and to influence what the government does. Political participation provides the mechanism by which citizens can communicate information about their interests, preferences and needs and generate pressure to respond." It was just such a premise that motivated thousands of black Americans to travel to Jena, Louisiana, in 2007. Similarly, it was the promise and possibility of having their voices heard and of deciding on a president that led to the increase in youth voting in both 2004 and 2008, especially among black Americans. And it is the agreement that at the heart of our governing process, individuals will have the freedom, resources, and opportunity to influence the government and shape their lives that makes the numbers of young Americans who not only stay away from the polls but refuse to engage in any type of political activity so alarming.

As we rightly celebrate the entry of young people in record numbers into the political process, as witnessed by the turnout among young black Americans in 2008, I want to also call attention to those young people who continue to be politically disengaged—a phenomenon I call the politics of invisibility. Specifically, I am referring to the significant numbers of young Americans who are nowhere to be found in the political arena. These are individuals who have engaged in none of the aforementioned acts of political engagement meant to influence the government and its policies. The list of possible political activities in the Black Youth Project data set includes twelve such acts:

1. voting
2. contacting a public official or agency
3. giving money to a candidate, party, or political issue
4. working or volunteering for a campaign or party
5. joining or being active in a political group
6. writing an article or letter to the editor
7. working with people in one's neighborhood on a political issue
8. attending a protest meeting, demonstration, or sit-in
9. boycotting
10. writing and sending an e-mail or blog about a political issue, candidate, or party

11. signing a paper or e-mail petition
12. buycotting

Table 5.13 details the percentages of black, white, and Latino youth who engaged in zero to five of these activities. The table stops at five activities because when we reach that amount we have accounted for more than 90 percent of youth participation across racial and ethnic groups.

Let's start with the basic numbers. Among white respondents to the Black Youth Project survey, nearly 25 percent indicated that they did not engage in any of the acts mentioned in our long list of possible political activities. With black youth, we approach almost one out of every three—29 percent—reporting that they are largely invisible in the political realm. Unfortunately, our Latino participants outpaced both black and white youth in being missing when it comes to political engagement. Forty-three percent of them had not participated in even one political act mentioned in the survey.

Have the numbers reported in table 5.13 changed since 2005? Specifically, did the record turnout among most groups of young people in the 2008 election increase the number of youth active in the political realm? The numbers represented in table 5.14 are drawn from the political activity of those aged 18–30 in the MCPCE Study. In this case, we asked young people how many of 18 political acts they had engaged in during the last year, providing even more possibilities for political activism than were assessed in 2005. These activities were as follows:

TABLE 5.13   Rates of Participation, Black Youth Project, 15- to 25-Year-Olds

Number of political acts	Black youth (%)	White youth (%)	Latino youth (%)
0 political acts	29.1	24.2	43
1 political act	32.5	25.1	21.3
2 political acts	17.5	16.3	14.2
3 political acts	9.9	12.6	9.4
4 political acts	4.7	7.4	3.8
5 political acts	1.9	4.8	3.8
Total of youth represented in 0 to 5 political acts	95.6	90.4	95.5

Source: The Black Youth Project

1. contacting a public official
2. giving money to a candidate
3. working or volunteering on a political campaign, for a candidate, or for a party
4. being active in or joining a political group
5. writing an article or letter to the editor about a political issue or problem
6. working with people in the neighborhood on a political issue or problem
7. calling a radio show
8. attending meetings, rallies, speeches, or dinners in support of a candidate
9. wearing a campaign button or placing a political sticker or sign in your window
10. attending a meeting of a local government board or council
11. signing a paper petition
12. trying to involve others in an election, including going door to door, making phone calls, collecting signatures, and passing out literature
13. engaging in buycotting
14. e-mailing an editor or manager of a newspaper, television station, or Web site
15. writing a blog about a political issue, candidate, or political party
16. writing or forwarding an e-mail, signing an e-mail petition, or posting a comment to a blog about a political issue, candidate, or party
17. attending a protest meeting, demonstration, or sit-in
18. voting

Interestingly, we found that the percentage of young people aged 18–30 reporting that they had engaged in none of the political acts mentioned above decreased markedly for white and black respondents, while the rates for Latinos decreased only slightly. As is evident in table 5.14, among the respondents aged 18–30 in the MCPCE Study, 18.4 percent of whites, 11.7 percent of blacks, 35.2 percent of Asians, and 40.9 percent of Latinos engaged in no political acts in the twelve months prior to the 2008 election. Unfortunately, we do not have data on Asian young people from the Black Youth Project survey to use in comparison. While much of the decrease in 2008 in those who were previously politically invisible has to do with their actual (and

TABLE 5.14   Rates of Participation, MCPCE Study, 18- to 30-Year-Olds

Number of political acts	Black youth (%)	White youth (%)	Latino youth (%)	Asian American youth (%)
0 political acts	11.7	18.4	40.9	35.2
1 political act	23.1	40.2	26.0	36.9
2 political acts	24.7	16.4	14.6	6.8
3 political acts	7.6	6.1	9.3	5.1
4 political acts	10.6	6.1	2.6	7.2
5 political acts	5.8	3.8	1.1	0.0
Total of youth represented in 0 to 5 political acts	83.5	91.0	94.5	91.2

Source: 2008 Mobilization, Change, and Political and Civic Engagement

imagined) voting in the presidential election, as well as the additional modes of activism included on our expanded list, we also have to note that the number of black youth indicating that they engaged in four or five political acts was also higher in 2008 than in 2005. So it is possible that the excitement of the 2008 election facilitated even greater political activity beyond voting, in particular in those acts associated with the election.

Will the 2008 election serve as an outlier in the voting history of black youth, or will black youth continue to outpace their contemporaries in voting, if not in participation overall? Clearly, we do not know the answer. The data do suggest that given the right candidate, young people will come to the polls and pay attention to electoral politics. Furthermore, while we may see the decline of some traditional acts of participation, voting still seems to be a viable expression of political voice for young people as they develop new ways of using the Web to express their political opinions and get involved. Given what we have learned about the potential for increasing the political participation of black youth, the staggering rates of political invisibility among Latinos and Asians need to be addressed. Advocates and political organizations need to select and promote candidates that resonate with these young people. They need to push for the adoption of progressive immigration laws that will include more Latino and Asian youth and their families in the formal political community. Finally, Latino and Asian young people should be encouraged to actively participate in politics through messaging and programs that target them specifically.

FINDINGS: THE POLITICS OF INVISIBILITY

The last question I want to address concerns the young people who seem invisible when it comes to their political activity and political standing.[43] We use the data from the Black Youth Project for this analysis because that data set has more respondents in our age range and across racial groups. In addition, black youth registered lower levels of invisibility in 2008, and it is difficult at this point to distinguish whether these data are part of a new trend or are an outlier in the political history of black youth. The model for the Black Youth Project data replicates earlier models and includes the following variables: gender, age, family SES, education, parents' interest in politics, neighborhood SES, whether one is in school, whether one is a member of a group or organization, one's sense of linked fate, one's sense of political efficacy, intensity of feelings toward the political parties, and the three dimensions of political alienation. The findings from the analysis are fairly straightforward:[44]

- Black youth aged 25 are 16 percent *more likely* to participate in some form of political activity than those who are 15.
- Black youth whose parents are highly interested in politics are 14 percent *more likely* to be participants than those young black people whose parents show no interest in politics.
- Black youth who are in an organization or group are 8 percent *more likely* to be at least mildly politically active than those who are not affiliated.
- Black youth who feel that what happens to other black people will impact their lives a lot (linked fate) are 24 percent *more likely* to be participants than those who register no feelings of linked fate.
- Black youth who hold intensely positive feelings toward the Democratic Party are 23 percent *more likely* to be participants than those who are intensely aligned with the Republican Party.[45]

Again, more variables are statistically significant in our model exploring the differences between white participants and nonparticipants. The measure for age indicates that as white youth grow older, they are more likely to be participants. Similarly, as family SES increases, so does the probability that white youth will make themselves politically visible. Parental interest, political efficacy, and being a member of a group or organization all increase the likelihood of white youth participating in some form. Only more hostile feelings toward government officials decreases the probability of white youth participating. Among our Latino respondents, parental interest and being in an organization or group is related to greater participation in the political process. Feeling a part of the broader political community, one of the dimensions of my expanded political alienation concept, was also mildly statistically significant, increasing the probability of participating. Those young Latinas and Latinos who felt like full and equal citizens were also more likely to express their political views in some available manner.

These numbers provide a glimpse into the factors that are related to being a participant versus being someone who is largely invisible to the political officials who are responsible for our well-being. But we have yet to answer the question whether the politics of invisibility is an active strategy on the part of some black youth to make themselves invisible to government authorities whom they believe are interested only in identifying, regulating, controlling, and possibly incarcerating them. Unfortunately, I do not have definitive evidence with which to answer this question, but some of the comments of our focus group participants provide some clues. A number of respondents talked about the need to change their behavior or "say a little few words and try not to say something out of pocket" when interacting with caseworkers, teachers, and other authorities like the police. One male participant explained that "in the streets when I'm moving around, I don't draw attention to myself so the police or whoever don't have a reason to look at me."

Many of the young black Americans who told us their stories through surveys, in-depth interviews, and focus groups have grown up with police cars patrolling their streets to make the community safe from youth like them. These young people have grown up with other black people holding the reins of authority in their cities and neighborhoods, as debilitated housing stock has expanded or gentrification has been allowed to displace their families and networks of support.[46] These young black people have watched friends and schoolmates get killed routinely, and the visible presence of police and metal detectors has come to define part of their school experience—what others call the militarization of urban schools. These young people have seen increasing numbers of family and friends arrested, sent to prisons and jails, and "domestically deported" out of their neighborhoods and their lives. Because of such experiences, these young people have decided that their best survival strategy is to be invisible to state, community, and often family authorities who appear to have done little to nothing to fundamentally provide the protection, opportunity, and support due any young person in our society, let alone to improve their condition. (I want to be clear that increasing numbers of black youth also experience excellent schools and are part of supportive families and resource-rich networks, but some of these young people also abstain from political engagement, labeling politics irrelevant to their lives.)

After reviewing the numerous in-depth interviews, focus groups, and surveys we have mounted with black youth during the last five years, I believe that significant numbers of black youth, at least prior to 2008, have used the limited agency available to them to stay under the radar. These young people have chosen a politics of invisibility, disengaging from all forms of politics and trying to remain invisible to officials who possibly could provide assistance but were more likely to impose greater surveillance and regulations on their lives. They have focused and relied on their local social worlds instead.

Of course, the danger of a politics of invisibility is that the voices of young black Americans, especially those who are most marginal—and whose voices are very critical in a representative system that is based on the articulation of wants and needs by the populace—are muted. Without black youth and their advocates being willing and able to tell their stories, communicate their perspectives, and detail a political agenda that addresses their wants and desires, we are left with silent black bodies of these vulnerable and marginalized young people being deployed to support the very rhetoric that seeks to criminalize, victimize, pathologize, and quarantine them.

The promising news is that in 2008, more black youth refused to be silent. In record numbers, they voted, worked on campaigns, and intensely followed Barack Obama's battle to win the White House. Understanding the symbolic importance of Obama's victory for black people, as well as the possibly limited impact he would have on their daily lived experience, at least immediately, many young black people still engaged in a reimagining of what might be possible in the United States. Now their president is black, but what will that mean for their future political participation? Will the election of Barack Obama signal the end of black politics, as some have suggested, and the full and equal incorporation of young black Americans into the larger political community of this country? Or is the election of Obama a new stage in an old racial order, in which class is now more visible as a factor defining the boundaries of success, progress, and respectability in black communities?

Appendix

2004 Youth Vote, 18–25 Year Olds

2004 Youth Vote	White (SE)	Black (SE)	Latino (SE)	First difference	Max difference
Gender	.10	.37**	.03	.06	.14
	(.18)	(.15)	(.23)		
Age	.22***	.12***	.11*	.19	.33
	(.04)	(.03)	(.06)		
Family SES	.01	−.00	.03	–	–
	(.03)	(.02)	(.03)		
Immigrant status	.17	−.26**	.02	−.25	−.28
	(.03)	(.11)	(.12)		
Education	−.06	.01	−.12	–	–
	(.05)	(.00)	(.07)		
Parent vote	−.15	−.01*	−.00	−.32	−.33
	(.08)	(.00)	(.01)		
Neighborhood SES	−.00	−.00	.00	–	–
	(.00)	(.00)	(.00)		
Religious activity	.09*	.01	.03	–	–
	(.04)	(.04)	(.07)		
In school	.14	−.06	−.22	–	–
	(.20)	(.16)	(.29)		
Part of a group or organization	−.05	−.06	.29	–	–
	(.18)	(.17)	(.28)		
Linked fate	−.03	.10	.02	–	–
	(.09)	(.07)	(.12)		
Political efficacy	.59***	.33**	.27	.14	.37
	(.14)	(.11)	(.17)		
Political community	.10	.13*	.29*	.10	.22
	(.09)	(.07)	(.13)		
Equal opportunity	−.05	.07	−.02	–	–
	(.08)	(.07)	(.09)		
Government orientation	−.18*	−.02	−.08	–	–
	(.08)	(.06)	(.10)		
Party feeling	.00	.00*	.01***	.11	.30
	(.00)	(.00)	(.01)		
Sample size	281	358	169		

Note: Data is imputed.
* *Denotes statistical significance at .05 level.*
** *Denotes statistical significance at .01 level.*
*** *Denotes statistical significance at .001 level.*
Source: The Black Youth Project

TABLE A5.2   2008 Youth Vote, 18–25-Year-Olds

2008 Youth vote	White (SE)	Black (SE)	Latino (SE)	First difference	Max difference
Gender	.55*	−.27	.33	–	–
	(.23)	(.33)	(.23)		
Age	.03	.12**	−.05	.07	.35
	(.03)	(.04)	(.03)		
Family SES	.06*	.00	.04	–	–
	(.03)	(.03)	(.03)		
Education	.17*	.22*	.31***	.08	.15
	(.08)	(.11)	(.06)		
Linked fate	–	−.07	−.17	–	–
	–	(.12)	(.09)		
Political efficacy	.41***	.24	.16	–	–
	(.08)	(.16)	(.10)		
Party identification	.02	.16	−.04	–	–
	(.06)	(.13)	(.06)		
Sample size	173	149	195		

Note: Data is imputed.
* Denotes statistical significance at .05 level.
** Denotes statistical significance at .01 level.
*** Denotes statistical significance at .001 level.
Source: The Black Youth Project

TABLE A5.3   Determinants of Having Written a Blog or Sent an E-mail

Wrote a blog or sent an e-mail	White (SE)	Black (SE)	Latino (SE)	First difference	Max difference
Gender	−.09	−.10	−.09	–	–
	(.13)	(.13)	(.18)		
Age	−.06**	−.05*	.00	−.05	−.11
	(.02)	(.03)	(.03)		
Family SES	.05**	.03	.02	–	–
	(.02)	(.02)	(.02)		
Immigrant status	.21*	.13	.12	–	–
	(.11)	(.10)	(.08)		
Education	.03	.06	.03	–	–
	(.04)	(.04)	(.06)		
In school	−.01	.33	.32	–	–
	(.19)	(.19)	(.26)		
Part of a group or organization	.23	.32*	.37*	.05	.07
	(.13)	(.13)	(.19)		
Linked fate	.03	.06	.10	–	–
	(.07)	(.07)	(.09)		
Political efficacy	.41***	.26**	.23	.07	.15
	(.11)	(.10)	(.14)		
Political community	.11	.02	.11	–	–

		(.07)	(.06)	(.09)		
Equal opportunity		−.02	−.07	−.17*	-	-
		(.06)	(.06)	(.07)		
Government orientation		−.10	−.07	−.00	-	-
		(.05)	(.05)	(.07)		
Sample size		559	625	308		

Note: Data is imputed.
* *Denotes statistical significance at .05 level.*
** *Denotes statistical significance at .01 level.*
*** *Denotes statistical significance at .001 level.*
Source: The Black Youth Project

TABLE A5.4   Determinants of Engagement in Buycotting

Engaged in Buycotting	White (SE)	Black (SE)	Latino (SE)	First difference	Max difference
Gender	.00	−.03	−.17	-	-
	(.12)	(.13)	(.18)		
Age	.01	.05*	.08*	.08	.12
	(.02)	(.02)	(.03)		
Family SES	.05***	.04*	.02**	.11	.18
	(.02)	(.02)	(.02)		
Immigrant status	.10	.12	−.21*	-	-
	(.10)	(.09)	(.10)		
Education	.01	−.00	.03	-	-
	(.03)	(.04)	(.07)		
In school	.28	.33*	.65*	.03	.07
	(.17)	(.17)	(.26)		
Part of a group or organization	.18	.26*	.42*	.05	.07
	(.13)	(.13)	(.19)		
Linked fate	−.10	.04	.12	-	-
	(.06)	(.06)	(.09)		
Political efficacy	.40***	.07	−.01	-	-
	(.10)	(.09)	(.14)		
Political community	−.01	.05	−.05	-	-
	(.07)	(.06)	(.09)		
Equal opportunity	−.23***	−.11*	−.22***	−.04	−.11
	(.06)	(.06)	(.07)		
Government orientation	−.04	−.04	.01	-	-
	(.05)	(.05)	(.07)		
Sample size	559	625	308		

Note: Data is imputed.
* *Denotes statistical significance at .05 level.*
** *Denotes statistical significance at .01 level.*
*** *Denotes statistical significance at .001 level.*
Source: The Black Youth Project

TABLE A5.5   Results for Politics of Invisibility

Politics of invisibility	White (SE)	Black (SE)	Latino (SE)	First difference	Max difference
Gender	.06	.06	.05	-	-
	(.15)	(.13)	(.18)		
Age	.11***	.05*	.06	.08	.16
	(.03)	(.03)	(.04)		
Family SES	.04	−.00	.00	-	-
	(.02)	(.02)	(.02)		
Education	−.05	.01	−.03	-	-
	(.04)	(.04)	(.05)		
Parent interest	.20*	.14*	.20*	.04	.14
	(.08)	(.06)	(.08)		
Neighborhood SES	−.00	−.00	.00	-	-
	(.00)	(.00)	(.00)		
Religious activity	.04	.02	.02	-	-
	(.04)	(.04)	(.05)		
In school	.35	−.01	.03	-	-
	(.22)	(.17)	(.26)		
Part of a group or organization	.36*	.24	.49*	-	-
	(.17)	(.14)	(.21)		
Linked fate	.00	.18**	.08	.07	.24
	(.08)	(.06)	(.09)		
Political efficacy	.44*	.10	.20	-	-
	(.13)	(.09)	(.15)		
Political community	.04	−.02	.16	-	-
	(.09)	(.06)	(.09)		
Equal opportunity	−.05	.01	−.05	-	-
	(.08)	(.06)	(.07)		
Government orientation	−.24***	.03	−.07	-	-
	(.08)	(.00)	(.08)		
Party feeling	.00	.00*	.00	.07	.24
	(.00)	(.00)	(.00)		
Sample size	457	553	257		

Note: Data is imputed.
* *Denotes statistical significance at .05 level.*
** *Denotes statistical significance at .01 level.*
*** *Denotes statistical significance at .001 level.*
Source: The Black Youth Project

CHAPTER 6

"My President Is Black"

Barack Obama and the Postracial Illusion

URING THE 2008 presidential campaign, *New York Times Magazine* ran a story with the provocative title, "Is Obama the End of Black Politics?" In the article, reporter Matt Bai explores whether there is generational tension among the black politicians who were elected during the civil rights era and the ones who were born during that era. Are older black elected officials and leaders pushing back against a generational shift in the politics of black communities that some argue will mean the end of what until now has been known as black politics? Bai writes, "for a lot of younger African-Americans, the resistance of the civil rights generation to Obama's candidacy signified the failure of their parents to come to terms, at the dusk of their lives, with the success of their own struggle—to embrace the idea that black politics might now be disappearing into American politics in the same way that the Irish and Italian machines long ago joined the political mainstream."[1]

I, like Bai, am interested in the changing nature of politics in this country with the election of our first African-American president, Barack Obama. I am especially interested in the question of generational tension and whether the new black politicians of today feel connected and accountable to black youth. As Bai points out in his article, a new group of black politicians has emerged who seem not to feel bound by the restrictive limits of black politics. This new generation of black officials and elites have their sights set not on conquering the domain reserved for them—the domain of leading black people—but are interested in having power over and in every aspect of American politics. This generation of black officials is represented as transcending race and signaling the emergence of a true postracial era. Despite the declarations from some pundits and politicians that racism and white supremacy is now over and that every child, no matter of what class, race, or gender, has the possibility of being president, I am a bit more skeptical about where we are as a nation on the issue of race, not to mention gender, class, and sexuality.[2]

In the pages that follow, I briefly explore the evolution of black politicians, focusing most of my attention on the emergence of a group of officials I will call third-wave black politicians, borrowing from and building on the work on black mayors of political scientist J. Philip Thompson III.[3] In his insightful book *Double Trouble*, Thompson examines what he calls the three waves of black mayors who have been elected to office since the 1965 Voting Rights Act. Although I share an interest in the evolution of black politicians since then, my focus is not exclusively on black mayors, but on a new generation of black officials that includes individuals such as Barack Obama, Deval Patrick, and Cory Booker. I am especially interested in what the candidacy and election of such politicians means for black youth and more generally the future of American politics. Are these third-wave black politicians willing and ready to push a political agenda intent on bettering the lives of young black Americans, especially those most vulnerable and marginalized? Or does the emergence and ascension of this wave of black politicians signal the end of black politics?

It is my contention, as it has been throughout the book, that far from signaling the end of black politics, the election of President Obama means that race and racism may be taking on a more prominent role in some political strategies. Ironically, while the Obama administration and other black officials are attempting to avoid discussions of race, members of the Republican Party and the Far Right have escalated their racial and racist talk and attacks. These contrasting trends have meant that racial discourse is increasingly being shaped by, or at least framed by, the right wing. And while a color-blind framework seems to be the accepted mode of thinking and talking about race today, the struggle to make race visible and visceral is now coming from the Right and not the Left. Thus, those public officials who might traditionally be mobilized to fight for and articulate a political agenda meant to, at the very least, improve the conditions and save the lives of young black Americans, are exceedingly reticent to make and defend an explicitly racialized agenda.

EVOLVING BLACK POLITICIANS

The First Wave

Voting and the election of black officials once again took center stage in the politics of black Americans with the passage of the 1965 Voting Rights Act. An increase in both registration and turnout among blacks occurred after 1965, due not only to the formal change in law and the Justice Department's sparing use of federal registrars in the South but also to factors such as the work of local and national activists who implemented massive voter registration drives through entities like the Voter Education Project. In fact, prior to the enactment of the Voting Rights Act, there was already substantial movement in the number of blacks registering to vote in the South, largely due to the actions of grassroots voting advocates.

The increase in black voters in the mid- to late sixties was pre-dated by the protest, in particular, of young black Americans through the civil rights movement. This combination of electoral interest and protest activity produced a period of very high voter turnout among black Americans and the resulting well-documented expansion in the number of blacks elected to office.[4] The mayoral election of Carl Stokes in Cleveland, Ohio, in 1967, followed by Richard Hatcher in Gary, Indiana, was the beginning of a period of significant expansion in the number of blacks being elected to public office. In line with Thompson, I call individuals elected during this early period "con-temporary first-wavers," well aware that the real first wave in black elected officials occurred during Reconstruction.[5] In the early history-making elections that occurred after the passage of the Voting Rights Act, blacks turned out in record numbers and voted overwhelmingly for black candidates. Blacks elected to office at the end of the civil rights movement traveled a far different path to office than did the Obama generation of black public officials. Early black mayors like Stokes and Hatcher, as well as black officials elected to the U.S. House, like John Conyers Jr. of Michigan (1965), Louis Stokes of Ohio (1969), William Lacy Clay of Missouri (1969), and Shirley Chisholm of New York (1969) were often the first blacks elected to their positions and would come to represent what many would call the civil rights generation of black elected officials.[6]

Black officials elected in the late 1960s and early 1970s usually won electoral contests in which race was a significant, if not primary, polarizing factor in the election. These elected officials were not interested in transcending or able to transcend race. Theirs was largely a racialized agenda, fighting for services, resources, and the dignity of their largely black constituencies. For example, a number of black mayors made police brutality and police residency laws hallmarks of their campaigns; others focused on increasing the number of blacks in state and local governments; others fought to increase the number of government contracts awarded to minority contractors.[7] Thus, far from avoiding or downplaying the significance of race to the country—a political strategy that was not available to black elected officials at that historical moment—their constituents expected these officials, many of whom came out of the civil rights movement and/or the black church, to make race central to their representational styles and agendas.

We should remember that most of these officials and their constituencies grew up and were intimately familiar with Jim Crow. Many were educated in historically black colleges and universities. They saw their duties as clearly linked to their localized black constituencies but also to a broader black agenda, a continuation of the civil rights movement and in some cases the Black Power movement. The establishment of the Congressional Black Caucus in 1969 is an example of the race agenda of this early post–civil rights movement cohort of elected black officials. Through the caucus, black elected officials "joined together to strengthen their efforts to address the legislative concerns of black and minority citizens."[8]

Even more radical, and different from the politics practiced today, was the participation of a number of prominent black elected officials in the National Black Political Convention, held in Gary, Indiana, in 1972. This convention was an attempt to build a unified political agenda and movement among black people. It is estimated that several thousand black Americans attended the event, including elected officials such as Carl Stokes, Louis Stokes, Walter E. Fauntroy, Ronald Dellums, and Barbara Jordan.[9] Having lived with the daily reminders of systemic racism in this country, first-wave black elected officials understood that statewide offices and predominately white districts were probably not available to them, so the focus of their agendas, their aspirations, and the roots of their power were clearly tied to their black constituencies.

Unfortunately, as blacks were increasingly elected as mayors and representatives they found themselves governing cities and representing districts that were suffering from massive white flight to the suburbs, the disappearance of their tax base, and the Reagan administration, which was intent on defunding social service and urban development programs. These elected officials, especially mayors, found themselves and their cities with little federal support and few mechanisms and resources to improve the condition of their black constituencies. Scholars such as Adolph Reed have written about the transformation of black elected officials from race leaders to politicians consumed with reelection (like all politicians). This transformation was often accompanied by compromises with downtown interests that were meant to stabilize a governing coalition, which in turn increasingly ignored the voices and needs of the black poor.[10]

Of course, given the continuing segregation experienced by blacks in urban cities and the crowding together of different classes of black people, the neglect of the black poor had spillover effects for the black middle class. As the neighborhoods and opportunities of the black poor were allowed to erode, so did the living conditions of the not-so-distant black middle class. Believing that their interests were being ignored, black constituencies, especially the middle class, became increasingly disenchanted with this first wave of black elected officials. They were decried by whites for fueling a divisive racial agenda that facilitated the exit of business and tax resources from their cities and by black constituencies for their inattentiveness to the agenda of black people. The result was the defeat (or retirement) of incumbents who were among the first wave of black mayors and representatives.

The Second Wave

Thompson argues that as first-wavers were exiting the political stage, a second wave of black mayors emerged.[11] He suggests that these new black officials, elected in the 1990s, were technocrats. They promised to manage cities, making them more efficient, safe, and enticing to businesses, whites, and middle-class residents. They did not avoid the issue of race, but it was not the hallmark of how they built their constituencies. A number of these mayors, such as Mike White in Cleveland and Dennis Archer in Detroit, garnered significant numbers of white votes in their bids to become mayors.

These second-wavers were well educated, often at predominately white institutions, who ran on platforms of securing public safety and infusions of more police, not the regulation of police brutality. These officials never established a firm base either within or outside of black communities, so their electability always seemed tenuous. What is important to note is the change in the agenda, as well as the constituency base that these representatives pursued and built. Often these mayors won an election by beating another black candidate closely identified with the civil rights generation of black elected officials. Second-wave black mayors also drew significant numbers of white voters beyond the liberal whites who supported first-wave politicians. Thompson notes that the accomplishments of the second wave of black mayors often centered on the building of a new athletic stadium in the downtown area, without the achievement of any significant and sustained changes in daily life, for particularly the lower middle class and the poor.[12] As had been the case for the first wave, it was the inability of the second wave of black officials to significantly alter the position of the poor or to buffer the middle class from spillover effects of living in and near poor communities that led to the downfall of many black mayors.

The story of second-wave black politicians is not confined to just black mayors. There also was a group of black officials elected from predominately white congressional districts or with significant white support for state offices. Republican congressmen J. C. Watts (Oklahoma) and Gary Franks (Connecticut) are examples of conservative black elected officials who ran on a platform of reduced government involvement in the lives of individuals and fewer government "handouts," a line of argument popular with conservative white voters. Similarly, there was a small group of black elected officials who pushed a more traditional democratic agenda who were elected to state offices and were also from predominately white congressional districts. Individuals such as H. Carl McCall, state comptroller for New York, and Carol Mosley Braun, the first African-American woman senator, were, as journalist Benjamin Wallace-Wells writes, "wholly conventional partisans, captains of ideologically unrocked boats; they won office by picking up loyal party voters—they crossed racial lines but not political ones and so ... generated no great national excitement."[13]

These individuals demonstrated that black officials could broaden their constituencies to include significant numbers of white voters, modeling new ways of building a base for the next generation of elected black officials like Barack Obama. Virginia's L. Douglas Wilder, the first black governor in the nation's history (1989), and Colin Powell, who was never elected to public office yet is understood as a national political leader, also modeled a different racial politics that would be adapted by third-wave black politicians. In both of these men we see not only the willingness of whites to support them but a rhetoric and political ideology that seems to stretch across the aisle. They were early uniters who actively downplayed the importance of race, valuing policy effectiveness over partisan attachment.

The Third Wave

I present here this brief and undoubtedly incomplete outline of the trajectory of black elected officials after the civil rights movement so that we might better understand what makes individuals like Barack Obama, Deval Patrick, Newark mayor Cory Booker, and other third-wave elected black officials unique, or at least different from previous "generations" of black elected officials. I am especially interested in trying to figure out how their differences from civil-rights-generation as well as second-wave black elected officials will impact the representation they can and will provide to black youth and the nation as we move through the twenty-first century.

These new politicians not only face a different political landscape than their predecessors did, they have built their political "machines" according to different assumptions. No longer is the legitimizing constituency for black officials only the black community. In the case of Obama and Patrick, the legitimizing constituency was and is white voters. It was white voters during the Iowa caucuses who "vouched" for Barack Obama when many black voters were either sitting quietly on the sidelines or throwing their support behind Hillary Clinton. Black voters, understanding the need to back a winner and believing that a black man would never be elected president in their lifetimes, withheld their support from Obama as they watched to see if the Clinton dynasty and infrastructure would rise again. Surprisingly, Clinton was defeated in Iowa and severely tested in New Hampshire by Obama. By the time of the South Carolina primary, significant numbers of black voters were moving into the Obama camp.

I recount this recent history to underscore the point that third-wavers are not exclusively—or even primarily—beholden to black communities as most black candidates have been in the past. They have galvanized crossracial segments of the population such as young people, building coalitional infrastructures like none witnessed before, especially in the electoral arena of black candidates. I am not suggesting that "the" black vote is no longer a substantial factor in the election of black candidates, including Obama's victory, but it did not propel him to victory in either 2004 or 2008.

Given that this new wave of candidates has built a significant segment of their electing constituency among white voters and that generally they are running against white candidates, they often find themselves employing a strategy around race that has at least two central components. First, they insist that they are running independent of or against race, even though they often have to deal with the racially historic nature of their candidacy. In 2008, it was hard to find an article on the presidential race that did not mention the historic nature of the election, yet the public was told repeatedly that Obama was not running to be a black president but instead to be a president who happened to be a black man.

Thus, an interesting dilemma that must be addressed in choosing to run against race is what to do with the historic nature of some of these elections—whether the candidate will be the first black president or the second black governor in the nation's history. I believe what these candidates do is reinterpret the historic nature of their race not as a beginning but as a marker of the end of racial divisions. What these candidates promise—at least to whites—is that if citizens unite to elect the first black (you fill in the blank), they will be writing a new, possibly final chapter in the public white supremacist history of this country, allowing all of us to move beyond racially divisive narratives of the nation, those narratives' corresponding obligations, and vocal opposition from people of color. Third-wavers, therefore, implicitly promise if not an end at least an answer to the racial talk and racial demands of people of color. When asked, for an article in *New York Times Magazine*, whether he thought "Obama's race would be a detriment, David Axelrod—Obama's trusted advisor and architect of his campaign—said, "I think that in a sense Barack is the personification of his own message for this country that we get past the things that divide us and focus on the things that unite us."[14]

If the promise of an end to the racial divide is what third-wavers symbolize to whites, one wonders why people of color support them. Perhaps it is because these candidates seem to represent and promise to people of color that they will challenge the racist work of the state, quietly dismantling policies that disproportionately and negatively affect people of color, especially middle-class people of color. Thus, people of color are willing to allow third-wavers to be silent on race so as to get elected, as long as there is a "wink, wink" agreement that once in office they will do the work of communities of color under the broad banner of helping the middle class.

The second component of the racial strategy of third-wavers is to use their racial status and the racial status of their authenticators—in Obama's case we might suggest that this is Michelle Obama—to locate themselves both inside and outside of black communities and black politics. Interestingly, it is their ease with and closeness to whiteness, without the danger of being read as wanting to be white, that has allowed third-wave politicians like Obama and Patrick to build constituencies including, but not limited to, black communities.

Many third-wavers are comfortable with whiteness in a way that is simultaneously reassuring to whites and not too threatening to blacks. Benjamin Wallace-Wells has written in an article on Cory Booker that for a small group of black politicians, "race has been an advantage because whites see in them confirmation that America, finally is working." They represent a racial success story—identity politics without bitterness, minimal demands from people of color, and only a few references to past inequality. These are largely black men ascending to the greatest heights of success and "proving" to the country and the world that race and racism are no longer significant problems in the United States. Wallace-Wells suggests that two institutions in particular, the military and elite universities, have been critical in producing these third-wave elected black officials who are thought to transcend race. I would add yet another important component to the list: their specific personal narratives and family structures.

By now we know Obama's story—a mixed-race kid with a white mother, raised in part by white grandparents, who struggled to find his blackness and then clinched his markers of blackness by becoming a community organizer, marrying Michelle Robinson, and attending Trinity United Church—to mention a few such indicators. Deval Patrick was born into poverty on the South Side of Chicago, was raised primarily by his mother, was given the opportunity to go to a private school, the Milton Military Academy, and then won admittance to Harvard University and Harvard Law School. In both of these examples, we find young men who at times were more immersed in dominant white culture than in black communities. It is the shared experience of being socialized through white institutions and sometimes white family members that signals to whites, as Wallace-Wells writes, that third-wavers "fully share in the culture and values of mainstream America" or, more specifically, mainstream white America.[15]

It is, however, their relationships with and connections to black friends and family members that allow third-wavers to solidify their support among racialized constituencies, especially black support in the Democratic Party. Through their speech cadence, cultural references, and family pictures, they signal to black communities "I am one of you." Nevertheless, because third-wavers are intent on personifying a blackness that is in step with the neoliberal discourse and values of "mainstream America" they are frequently willing to engage in a bit of racial bullying of the black poor or, as it is more gently described, a little public tough love and truth-telling directed at their own people so as to solidify their middle-class, crossracial persona. Using their racial insider status, third-wavers publicly reprimand black parents, black children, the black poor, and whoever else is available in black communities about their self-destructive behaviors—whether it is what they feed their children, their absence from the home, or their attitudes toward work. All of these topics, in relation to black people, candidate Obama willingly discussed while on the campaign trail.

But who is the real audience for such truth-telling? Is it a supportive and highly receptive internal black audience or the white public who hold similar ideas about "black" personal responsibility and welcomes black legitimization of their feelings? Most of these "discussions" of race by third-wavers are structured around the public scolding of, in particular, poor black people, who are portrayed as not holding up their end of the bargain for receiving full membership in the larger political community. What for Bill Clinton was his Sister Souljah moment is now the Bill Cosby moment for this new generation of black leaders.[16] They must demonstrate to white voters that they are willing to take on their own black community. They must prove that they are not *race* leaders but *raced* leaders, a title imposed but not embraced.

I am not suggesting that black leaders should be silent or silenced on the topic of how personal failures or limitations contribute to the difficult positioning of some in black communities. My twofold concern, instead, is (1) that these moments of racial truth-telling become the predominant way that race and more specifically black communities are explicitly and implicitly brought into the political discussion of the nation, and (2) that counterarguments about black poverty and the black poor, especially those that emphasize structural arguments, are silenced when "black authorities" like Obama—those who made it the "right way," those who are safe and to be trusted, those who "prove" that racism is no longer the systemic problem it was when Reverend

Jeremiah Wright Jr. was growing up—suggest that the struggles of black poor people stem primarily from their own pathologies.

In this and other ways, Obama, Patrick, and the new generation of elected black officials are traditional Democrats, not black Democrats. Their rhetoric is more reflective of the Democratic Leadership Council than of the first-wave members of the Congressional Black Caucus. We could think of them as Bill Clinton Democrats. In fact, during the last week of the campaign, while making a visit to Florida with former president Bill Clinton, candidate Obama praised Clinton for his restructuring of the Democratic Party (to the right) and for highlighting the role of personal responsibility in social change, reminding us all that government cannot and should not try to solve all of our problems.

What is especially interesting and sadly ironic is that the policies third-wavers often support are those any traditional left-of-center Democrat would support. However, they seek to distinguish themselves as uniters, and thus their rhetoric is one of political ideological independence. During Obama's campaign for the presidency, Axelrod underscored this idea of ideological independence among the third-wavers, describing Obama as someone who was "not wedded to any ideological frame or dogma." Rather, he was an "agent for change."[17] Since the political independence professed is not fully represented in the policies of third-wavers, it often shows up in their discussions of the role of government and their "willingness" to expand the role of personal responsibility in the governing system they prescribe. What most third-wavers fail to mention in their discourse on personal responsibility, of course, is the fact that self-reliance and personal responsibility among the upper and middle class is a less imposing directive when it can be bought and supported through nannies, private schools, dinners at restaurants, tutors, and greater access to leisure time and disposable income. Thus the target of third-wave personal responsibility lectures is most often the poor—usually the black poor.

Since third-wavers are not "wedded" to a specific ideological perspective, they are allowed to dream big. As third-wavers declare their ideological independence, they also seek to expand their constituencies. Often, these politicians are not content to win from a traditional democratic base but hope to expand their constituency to include Democrats, Republicans, and independents. Their focus is not on just representing black people, black youth, or even the Left. They are engaged in a process of "remixing democracy," reimagining America, making claims on leadership for the country and, in Obama's case, the world. Wallace-Wells notes that "an underlying message of the [Obama] campaign is that African-American candidates can symbolically represent the future." Symbolic precursors to the pending demographic changes in the United States, third-wavers are poised to provide leadership for the racially remixed nation.

This focus on remixing American politics is emblematic of the last characteristic I want to highlight of third-wavers: their focus not only on the policies they will deliver but, just as important, the psychological transformation—the production of hope and the ability to "dream America again"—that they will provide. Deval Patrick stated in his acceptance speech after being elected governor of Massachusetts in November 2006 that his election was "not a victory just for me, this was not a victory just for Democrats; this was a victory for hope." Cory Booker, in remarks he delivered at the Harvard Business School Club of New York in June 2008, stated, "Change does not come on the wheels of inevitability. We need every day to choose America again.... It is time to dream America again." This new generation of hopemongers repeatedly characterize themselves as uniters, as political inspirers above the fray, as individuals who are not beholden to any one community, social location, or political identity but are able and willing to reach across the aisle, across communities, across races to reimagine and remix our political community.

The idea that the campaign is not about them but some larger entity—the people, the grassroots—is closely linked to the framing of their politics as not just politics, especially old traditional politics, but a movement for change. This was the framing of both the Patrick and the Obama campaigns. Third-wavers embed their campaigns and their elections in the notion that these are movements outside of traditional electoral politics for fundamental change in the country. The basis of the movement is not about them but about their followers and workers. Democratic media consultant David Eichenbaum explained that "what they were able to do in the Patrick campaign was similar to what they've been able to do with Obama. The campaign managed to energize the grass roots, but there was a sense of idealism and hope and being able to break that historic barrier that was very unifying and reached out beyond liberals or the base. It became a movement that took on a life of its own."[18]

The question now remains: What does the emergence of this group of third-wavers, and Obama specifically, mean for black youth, a group that holds a special status and significance when thinking about the future of American politics? There is no denying that the Obama candidacy brought people, in particular young black people, into the political system who had never participated before. But will these young people remain engaged? Will they change their ideas about the government and become less suspicious and more trusting of the state? Will they be able to hold the Obama presidency accountable to the needs of their communities? Furthermore, as third-wavers remix and reimagine American politics, who will stand at its core? How will young black Americans who have been marginalized throughout the history of this country figure into the future of American politics? Does the thinking of young blacks align with that of President Obama and other third-wavers on the topic of race? Do young black Americans also represent the "end of black politics"? Examining the thoughts and beliefs of young black Americans about race will allow us to measure the general progress we have made in broadening the political community to fully include, as equal members, black people and black youth.

Black Youth in the Age of Obama

As third-wave black officials like Obama change the political landscape, decentering race as the primary organizing unit for their campaigns and their politics, promising to change politics forever, and encouraging young people to reengage in the political process, I am interested in whether young black people are moving in the same direction. One way to answer some of my questions is to look at the attitudes of black youth since Obama was elected to office in November 2008 and compare them to some of the statements he has made about race and racism in this country. To assess the attitudes of black youth, I will turn again to data from the MCPCE Study. However, before I explore the attitudes of young Black Americans, I will look briefly at some of Obama's statements on the topic of race.

President Obama and Race

To explore President Obama's discourse on race, I will briefly examine two prominent speeches he has given: his 2004 National Democratic Convention speech and his "More Perfect Union" speech, given on the campaign trail in response to attacks relating to his former minister the Reverend Jeremiah Wright Jr. In both of these speeches President Obama provided both implicit and explicit messages about his positioning on the topic of race and the fluidity of his thinking under the political circumstances surrounding his statements.

Most would agree that it was President Obama's speech at the 2004 Democratic National Convention that first ignited national attention and excitement about this young state senator from Illinois who was vying for a seat in the U.S. Senate. Entering the stage as a relative unknown to all but the Democratic faithful and the residents of Illinois, Obama left the stage a rising star within the Democratic Party and someone sure to be on the national scene for some time to come. Despite his having given what was generally agreed to have been one of the best convention speeches in modern times, few thought that in four short years the speaker at that podium would win an election as the forty-fourth president of the United States. Given the importance of this speech in resetting his political trajectory, it is important that we explore what the speech tells us about the racial politics of then state senator Obama.

One of the first interesting things to realize about the 2004 speech is that Obama never positions himself as black or African American. Instead, he begins his speech in an autobiographical tone, telling the audience about his parents and grandparents, his father from Kenya, and his mother from Kansas. Throughout the speech, it is his class positioning, his personification of the American dream, and his attention to middle-class concerns that take center stage. He says about his father and grandfather: "My father was a foreign student, born and raised in a small village in Kenya. He grew up herding goats, went to school in a tin-roof shack. His father, my grandfather, was a cook, a domestic servant."[19] He says about his mother: "She was born in a town on the other side of the world, in Kansas. Her father worked on oil rigs and farms through most of the Depression. The day after Pearl Harbor he signed up for duty, joined Patton's army and marched across Europe. Back home, my grandmother raised their baby and went to work on a bomber assembly line. After the war, they studied on the G.I. Bill, bought a house through FHA, and moved west in search of opportunity."[20]

As he reminds us throughout the speech, his focus is on the promise of a tolerant, generous, and connected (and implicitly diverse) America. There are only a few parts of the speech where Obama engages in what might be termed racialized discourse, and often those moments are somewhat coded. For example, about a third of the way into the speech, when discussing the needs of average Americans, Obama describes a "young woman in East St. Louis, and thousands more like her, who has the grades, has the drive, has the will, but doesn't have the money to go to college."[21] While there is no explicit mention that the young woman in question might be black, if you know the demographics of East St. Louis, where approximately 98 percent of all residents are black, you can infer that this young woman unable to afford college is probably black. He also alludes to black communities when he declares: "If there's a child on the South Side of Chicago who can't read, that matters to me, even if it's not my child."[22] Again, most people familiar with Chicago know that its South Side has long been the home of an overwhelming proportion of its black residents.

In another part of the speech, in which Obama explains that average Americans do not want government handouts and are willing to do their part in the fight to make the country better, he moves on from a reference to inner-city neighborhoods to an explicit mention of black communities: "Go into any inner-city neighborhood, and folks will tell you that government alone can't teach kids to learn. They know that parents have to parent, that children can't achieve unless we raise their expectations and turn off the television sets and eradicate the slander that says a black youth with a book is acting white."[23] A similar explicit mention of a racialized community is made: "If there is an Arab American family being rounded up without benefit of an attorney or due process that threatens my civil liberties."[24]

The most forceful mention of race in the speech is his rebuttal to those who, he suggests, seek to divide us by highlighting racial differences. Obama argues toward the latter part of his speech that "Even as we speak, there are those who are preparing to divide us, the spin masters and negative ad peddlers who embrace the politics of anything goes." In his repudiation of such politics, Obama challenges the divisions that the "spin masters" have set forth. "Well I say to them tonight, there's not a liberal America and a conservative America—there is the United States of America. There's not a black America and white America and Latino America and Asian America; there's the United States of America."[25] This theme of challenging existing notions of a divided nation became a mantra of presidential candidate Obama as he repeatedly declared in the face of different divisions that there is one United States of America that connects us all.

After watching or reading Obama's 2004 Democratic National Convention speech, you come away knowing that it is historic in its structure, message, response, and messenger. And, in particular, it is the messenger who must be interrogated when trying to understand the racial messages of this speech. We have to factor into our analysis that at the podium was a well-polished individual who was undoubtedly read as black by most television viewers, regardless of his ambiguous racial positioning early in the speech. The speech, in and of itself, however, largely stayed away from any significant and sustained mention of race. Indeed, it is the diminished importance given to race and racial division in the United States that is most glaring when analyzing the speech through a racial lens. Both directly and indirectly, this is a speech largely about class inequality that shies away from explicit racial references. Of course, this is not surprising given that candidates Obama and Kerry would both need the votes of a significant number of whites in order to win their elections in November 2004.

When the topics of race or, specifically, black communities are directly engaged in this speech, it is usually through the frame of a deficit model. We hear about a young black woman without the money to attend college, black children on the South Side of Chicago who cannot read, black children who are underachieving because of low expectations, black parents who need to parent by turning off the television sets, and the belief by young blacks that studying is acting white. I do not believe this imagery is intentionally meant to demean black people, but it is not surprising that a political candidate, even a black one, in crafting a speech for a wide audience would refer to deficit-based stereotypes that are most widely recognized, resonate, and embraced by white audiences and journalists.

In the commentaries that followed the speech, reporters were clearly taken with its brilliance, but they also highlighted Obama's willingness to take on the "bad behavior" of black people. For example, on PBS Mark Shields, when discussing Obama's comments about parents turning off the television sets and eradicating the idea that black youth having a book is acting white, said, "Obama is the only person who could have said it and he said it so well."[26] Another commentator on the program said, "Forget uniters and dividers, tonight we heard from a transcender." While this speech would establish Obama as a transcender and a player on the national stage, the racial discourse contained in this historic speech did little to transcend or even alter the racial dialogue of the country. Instead, it was Obama's personification of a new blackness and a new black politics—the third wave—that reinscribed the racial discourse, at least among those whites who believe that blacks should stop complaining and do the hard work that is demanded of every individual in the postracial social order. In Obama, and more specifically in the words of his speech, many whites saw the promise of transcending the established racial order and truly moving toward a postracial society.

While this 2004 speech was never intended to be a discussion of race, his 2006 "More Perfect Union" speech in Philadelphia had to be one. The immediate factor dictating the speech was the controversy surrounding Obama's former minister, the Reverend Jeremiah Wright Jr. Reverend Wright had served as pastor of Trinity United Church of Christ for over thirty years. It was Wright's teaching and preaching that had brought Obama to the Christian faith. Theirs was an intimate relationship, with Reverend Wright officiating at the wedding of Robinson and Obama and later baptizing their two daughters. So it created great difficulty for the Obama campaign when the press swarmed to cover to Reverend Wright and his seemingly extreme views on race, racism, and white supremacy in the United States.

Increasingly, stories in major newspapers and magazines and—probably most explosively—videos on YouTube emerged, highlighting some of Reverend Wright's most exaggerated and decontextualized statements, showing a few provocative minutes of much longer sermons. In these videos, Reverend Wright is seen making extreme and, to many, offensive statements. In one video, Wright says, "See the government gives them the drugs, builds bigger prisons, passes a three-strike law, and then wants us to sing 'God bless America.' No, no, no.... Not God bless America, God damn America... for treating her citizens as less than human."[27] He also refers to the United States as the "US of KKK-A."[28] In another video, he contrasts Obama's experience as a black man in a racist country with Hillary Clinton's positioning as a white women, stating, "Hillary ain't never been called a nigger."[29] In yet another video, Wright tries to dissuade black Americans from the belief that former president Bill Clinton "was good to" black people, saying that "he did the same thing to us that he did to Monica Lewinsky."

As we might expect, support for Obama became less secure among white voters in response to the media frenzy surrounding him and Wright. And although Obama tried to assure the public that he did not share many of the views expressed by Wright, it was a tough sale with few believers. It was in this context of increased and negative media coverage of his ties to Wright that Obama announced he would give a speech on race. So on March 18, 2008, presidential candidate Barack Obama took the stage at the National Constitution Center in Philadelphia, standing between two flags, and began his speech by quoting the words "We the people, in order to form a more perfect union."[30]

For the next forty minutes, he outlined the history and future of race relations and structural racism in the United States.

He starts by locating slavery and racism squarely at the founding of the democracy and in the country's most cherished political document, the Constitution. He then proceeds to outline both the ways the struggles and actions of ordinary Americans have worked to narrow the inequalities experienced and the gap between our ideals and the inequalities experienced by many groups. He notes that it is this tradition of struggle that his campaign seeks to continue.

After these largely introductory remarks, Obama returns to familiar themes of the connectedness of the nation, even though "we may have different stories."[31] He also invokes his biography again, but this time it is completely racialized, marking his relationship to the racial history of this country. He no longer talks of a father from Kenya and a mother from Kansas, leaving it to his audience to assign races to his family, and instead, in this speech on race, provides the racial labeling himself.

> I am the son of a black man from Kenya and a white woman from Kansas. I was raised with the help of a white grandfather who survived a depression to serve in Patton's army during World War II and a white grandmother who worked on a bomber assembly line at Fort Leavenworth while he was overseas. I've gone to some of the best schools in America and lived in one of the world's poorest nations. I am married to a black American who carries within her the blood of slaves and slave owners—an inheritance we pass on to our two precious daughters. I have brothers, sisters, nieces, nephews, uncles, and cousins, of every race and every hue, scattered across three continents, and for as long as I live, I will never forget that in no other country on Earth is my story even possible.[32]

It is only after this autobiographical delineation that Obama directly confronts the controversy surrounding Wright, condemning his former pastor for using "incendiary language to express views that have the potential not only to widen the racial divide, but views that denigrate both the greatness and the goodness of our nation, that rightly offend white and black alike."[33] He goes on to say that Wright's remarks provide a "profoundly distorted view of this country—a view that sees white racism as endemic, and that elevates what is wrong with America above all that we know is right with America."[34] He then makes the differences of opinion on race and racism that exist between himself and Wright a generational divide, not too unlike Matt Bai's article on the end of black politics. Obama details what we might call a pre-civil-rights-movement racial understanding in the behavior of both Reverend Wright and his white grandmother and posits that understanding in opposition to a more enlightened understanding of race evident in a young generation of Americans today.

In both Wright and his grandmother, who, Obama confesses, had expressed her fear of black men who passed her on the street and "who on more than one occasion has uttered racial or ethnic stereotypes that made me cringe,"[35] we are invited to see individuals who were raised during the height of racial divisions, institutionalized through systems such as Jim Crow, and who in many ways are unable to fully embrace the changing vision and reality of race in America. Obama explains, "For the men and women of Reverend Wright's generation, the memories of humiliation and doubt and fear have not gone away; nor has the anger and bitterness of those years."[36]

He similarly details what he believes to be the bitterness and anger that exists among some whites, especially working- and middle-class whites. Obama argues that whites have been told by politicians, talk show hosts, and others to blame blacks or immigrants for the difficulties they have experienced, instead of "the real culprits of the middle-class squeeze—a corporate culture rife with inside dealing, questionable accounting practices, and short-term greed; a Washington dominated by lobbyists and special interests; economic policies that favor the few over the many."[37]

As he begins to wind down, Obama argues that blacks must be willing to accept and embrace the fact that we are not "still irrevocably bound to a tragic past" and that "America can change."[38] Whites, he suggests, must be willing to acknowledge "that what ails the African-American community does not just exist in the minds of black people; that the legacy of discrimination and current incidents of discrimination, while less overt than in the past, are real and must be addressed. Not just with words, but with deeds."[39] He then returns to his familiar theme of a connected America, in which we all rise or fall together.

> At this moment, in this election, we can come together and say, "Not this time." This time we want to talk about the crumbling schools that are stealing the future of black children and white children and Asian children and Hispanic children and Native American children. This time we want to reject the cynicism that tells us that these kids can't learn, that those kids who don't look like us are somebody else's problem. The children of America are not those kids, they are our kids, and we will not let them fall behind in a twenty-first-century economy. Not this time.[40]

In one of the final sections of this speech, Obama returns to the idea of a generational divide. This time, the reference is used to mark not the intractability of outdated racial views but the possibility of change. He states, "This union may never be perfect, but generation after generation has shown that it can always be perfected. And today, whenever I find myself feeling doubtful or cynical about this possibility, what gives me the most hope is the next generation—the young people whose attitudes and beliefs and openness to change have already made history in this election."[41]

President Obama was correct in noting that the participation of young people had and would make the 2008 presidential election historic. As discussed in chapter 5, young Americans, in particular young black Americans, turned out to vote for Obama in record numbers. Clearly, in Obama they saw a candidate they could believe in. What is less clear is whether voting for Obama also signaled the changed attitude toward the country and specifically the topic of race that Obama suggests in his "More Perfect Union" speech.

While this speech was also widely praised, any number of critiques have been offered and concerns raised regarding it. For example, some push back at the idea that we can equate the racial reasoning of Reverend Wright's and Obama's grandmother as Obama does in his speech. Critics argue that Wright was describing and reacting truthfully to the systematic racism that has been present in this country since its founding. Obama's grandmother is instead reacting to a set of stereotypes of black people that have been used to preserve a racial order in which blacks are portrayed as dangerous, providing just one of many explanations for their persistence at the bottom of the racial hierarchy. Reverend Wright's words come from a position of marginalization and Obama's grandmother's words from a position of relative privilege in the racial landscape of the country. To equate them seems, if not misleading, less nuanced than one would like.

Similarly, I am concerned that Obama uses the "More Perfect Union" speech to once again tell black parents and black people that they have to own up to their personal responsibility, something he rarely if ever communicates to whites. Specifically, in the speech he states, "And it means taking full responsibility for our [African-American] lives—by demanding more from our fathers, and spending more time with our children, and reading to them, and teaching them that while they may face challenges and discrimination in their own lives, they must never succumb to despair or cynicism; they must always believe that they can write their own destiny."[42]

These critiques of the speech and others have now been logged and recorded in the continuing public dialogue on Obama's racial politics. I am, however, interested in whether the racial discourse found in the two speeches I have discussed corresponds to the racial attitudes of black youth today. As we enter the age of Obama with the number of third-wave candidates who are thought to transcend race increasing, does their positioning of themselves as both in and outside traditional racial categories and politics correlate to the way a new generation of young adults also understand race in this country, in particular black youth? In their lives and articulated concerns are we witnessing the end of black politics? As I argued in chapter 4, in 2005 significant differences still existed between the racial attitudes of, in particular, white and black youth. Now the question is whether those differences in the racial politics of young people still exist and whether a similar divide exists between the racial discourse of President Obama and the racial attitudes of black youth.

Underlying the idea that we are now at a point where we can abandon black politics is the belief that racism, while a major problem in the past, no longer significantly alters the life chances of individuals in the United States. To assess whether young people from different racial and ethnic groups believe that the election of President Obama signals the end of racism as a major problem in the United States, we asked 18- to 30-year-old respondents to give us their reaction to the following: "Some people say that the election of Barack Obama as president of the United States suggests that racism no longer exists in American society and politics. Would you say—(1) racism remains a major problem in our society; (2) racism exists today but is not a major problem; (3) racism once existed but no longer exists in our society; or (4) racism has never been a major problem in our society. Table 6.1 details how perspectives on this question differ by racial and ethnic group.

As is evident from the data, black youth and young adults, six months into Obama's first term as president, still overwhelmingly believe that racism remains a major problem in the United States. Clearly, far from embracing the belief that we have reached a point where race and something called black politics no longer matters, these young people believe that racism is still a major problem for our society and politics. Possibly it is the stories of the killing of black youth in cities like Chicago that travel around the world, or these respondents' more

TABLE 6.1   Perspectives on Racism since the Election of President Obama

Respondents by race/ ethnicity (%)	Racism remains a major problem (%)	Racism exists but not a major problem (%)	Racism no longer exists in our society (%)	Racism never a major problem in society (%)
Black youth	69	29	1	1
White youth	32	63	3	2
Latino youth	51	41	5	3

Source: 2008 Mobilization, Change, and Political and Civic Engagement

localized experience with the disproportionate impact of incarceration and unemployment on black youth that solidifies their belief that, yes, racism is still a major problem. Whatever the genesis of their perspective, it flies in the face of those who have pronounced this the postracial era. It also challenges those third-wave black politicians who seek to minimize the significance of race today.

To further explore this line of inquiry, we asked a similar question, probing whether young people believe that blacks have achieved racial equality. Specifically, we asked whether blacks (1) have achieved racial equality; (2) will soon achieve racial equality; (3) will not achieve racial equality in the respondent's lifetime; (4) will never achieve racial equality. Table 6.2 shows the responses.

Not surprisingly, black youth are less likely than other young people to believe that blacks have achieved racial equality. Only 13 percent of young black Americans believe that blacks have already achieved racial equality, compared to 51 percent of young whites. As has been found previously, Latino youth represent the midway point between blacks and

TABLE 6.2   Blacks Achieve Racial Equality

Race/ethnicity of respondent	Have achieved racial equality (%)	Will soon achieve racial equality (%)	Will not achieve racial equality in your lifetime (%)	Will never achieve racial equality (%)
Black	13	46	28	13
White	51	28	14	7
Latino	32	36	26	6

Source: 2008 Mobilization, Change, and Political and Civic Engagement

whites in the assessment of the racial equality of blacks, with 32 percent of Latinos believing that blacks have achieved racial equality. If there is more encouraging news to be taken from this analysis, it's that a majority—59 percent—of black youth aged 18–30 believe that racial equality has been or will soon be achieved. This statistic, highlighting what might be the racial optimism of young black Americans, is generally aligned with the racial analysis put forth by many third-wave politicians.

Of course, when trying to assess racial progress in the country, one must ask about the prospects of other groups of color. Tables 6.3 and 6.4 contain data on how young people across racial and ethnic groups evaluate the racial equality of Latinos and Asians. Black respondents assessed the racial equality of Latinos almost exactly as they evaluated their own. Only 14 percent of black youth opined that Latinos have achieved racial equality. This number is nearly identical to the 13 percent of black youth who believed that blacks had achieved racial equality. Literally across all the categories, there was very little difference in how black youth appraised the racial equality of Latinos compared to their own.

While black youth reported that they and their Latino brothers and sisters shared a similar racial position, Latino youth were more likely to say that blacks had achieved racial equality compared to themselves. Specifically, 32 percent of Latino youth believed that blacks have achieved racial equality, compared to 19 percent of Latinos who believed that Latinos have achieved racial equality. Greater racial optimism was evident in the number of respondents who choose the category "Latinos will soon achieve racial equality." Nearly a majority of Latino youth—48 percent—placed themselves in this category. As with their assessment of the racial progress of blacks, about one-third of Latinos believed that racial equality will never be achieved or at least not in their lifetimes.

TABLE 6.3   Latinos Achieve Racial Equality

Race/ethnicity of respondent	Have achieved racial equality (%)	Will soon achieve racial equality (%)	Will not achieve racial equality in your lifetime (%)	Will never achieve racial equality (%)
Black	14	49	28	9
White	33	41	19	7
Latino	19	48	25	8

Source: 2008 Mobilization, Change, and Political and Civic Engagement

Interestingly, when asked about the racial achievement of Latinos, white youth and young adults were more likely to believe that blacks and Asians have achieved racial equality compared to Latinos. While consistently optimistic about the prospects of racial equality for all groups, white youth were more likely to say that Latinos will soon achieve racial equality than to believe that they have already achieved racial equality. This is different than the findings in table 6.2 that 51 percent of white youth believed that blacks have achieved racial equality and in table 6.4 that 52 percent of white youth indicated that they believed Asians have achieved racial equality.

Black youth were much more likely to believe that Asians have achieved racial equality in the United States, compared to themselves or Latinos. Only 13 percent of black youth believed that blacks have achieved racial equality. Similarly, only 14 percent reported that Latinos have achieved racial equality. In contrast, 36 percent believed that Asians have achieved racial equality, followed up with another 39 percent who stated that Asians will soon achieve racial equality. Latino and white youth were much more likely to assess the racial trajectory of Asians as being analogous to that of blacks, with a majority of white youth believing that both blacks and Asians have already achieved racial equality and about one-third of Latino youth stating that both blacks and Asians have achieved racial equality.

It is clear that while all the groups represented in these tables are generally more optimistic than pessimistic about the racial trajectory of specific racial groups, a majority of black and Latino youth still believe that racism is a major problem in American society and are not prepared to declare the end of racism, the end of black politics, or the emergence of the postracial era. Instead, black and Latino youth seem cautiously optimistic about what is possible in terms of changing the

TABLE 6.4   Asians Achieve Racial Equality

Race/ethnicity of respondent	Have achieved racial equality (%)	Will soon achieve racial equality (%)	Will not achieve racial equality in your lifetime (%)	Will never achieve racial equality (%)
Black	36	39	19	6
White	52	30	12	6
Latino	31	42	21	6

Source: 2008 Mobilization, Change, and Political and Civic Engagement

racial terrain of the nation. Their optimism is a bit more constrained than that of third-wave black candidates who seem to suggest through their behavior that race is a topic that does not deserve sustained and serious consideration. Generally, third-wavers only raise the topic of race when they are pushed. However, while black youth are less likely to embrace the rhetoric of racial transcendence that is often associated with third-wavers, these young people are still committed to a politics of change as articulated by President Obama. In fact, when we asked how much change has occurred in the country since President Obama took office, the majority of white, black, and Latino youth stated that big or at least some change had taken place in the first six months of Obama's presidency. The specific numbers are displayed in table 6.5. Again, belief in Obama's ability to effect at least some change is greater among black youth than among Latino and white youth.

DETAILING RACISM IN THE LIVES OF YOUNG BLACK AMERICANS

As noted in earlier chapters, statistical data can only take us so far in understanding the attitudes and ideas of black youth on a topic such as the existence of race and racism in the United States. In an attempt to dive deeper into the perspectives of black youth, I want to briefly revisit the focus group discussed in chapter 5 to hear what young blacks had to say about the role of race and racism in their lives. This focus group was conducted three months after President Obama's election and weeks after his inauguration. The group consisted of young black people from Chicago aged 18–24. Again, they are not a representative sample but instead a group of young black people who were willing to share their senses of the challenges they face and prospects for their future.

TABLE 6.5 Change since President Obama Took Office

Race/ethnicity of respondent	Big change (%)	Some change (%)	Very little change (%)	No change (%)
Black	17	63	15	2
White	11	40	35	10
Latino	14	50	26	6

Source: 2008 Mobilization, Change, and Political and Civic Engagement

Although the young people in our focus group were very excited about Obama's election, they were also clear that racism and the need for black politics still existed. In their lives they saw a disparity between the opportunities afforded them and those provided to other groups, in particular white Americans. In their words one does not hear a desire for an outlandish political agenda but the desire for one quite similar to what other Americans want. These young people want affordable housing in their neighborhoods, safe neighborhoods free from violence, jobs with which they can support their families, and a better education for themselves and their children. They worry, however, that these basic provisions for a good and decent life will not be available to them even in the limited quantity that their parents were able to access. One young man explained, "My father did work in the same job since I was born. But now you can maybe work a year, if that." Another young man stated, "Companies that were around for many years are going away. There are a lot more smaller stores that were around neighborhoods that have gone away because of what they call big-box stores like your Wal-Marts and Kmarts and all of those stores. And people are getting laid off and even big companies, car companies, and places that provided jobs for families for decades are leaving and jobs are leaving."

In the words of these young people, one hears a strained search for a good and productive life. Nearly all of the participants, when asked what they hoped for, included in their answer "being financially secure." Beyond financial security, however, many of them wanted a better life not only for themselves but their children. A young woman explained, "I just don't want my baby to be raised in the environment and situation that I have been in. I want a better life for her." These are familiar words and hopes that have often been cast as part of the American dream. Everyone wants a better life for his or her children. But in the case of these young blacks, many believe that their ability to attain the American dream of generational progress is still blocked by race and racism, for it impacts the resources they are afforded and the basic conditions they experience. The same young woman, when asked what a different environment for her daughter would look like, said, "just not a lot of drugs mess all around the house or people fighting, people shooting, because we see it all in our neighborhood."

Many of the young people in our focus group described living conditions that they believed would be unacceptable if they existed in many white communities. One young woman raised the issue of housing and how gentrification was driving black people from their neighborhoods.

There is housing in our area too and it's being sold but its gentrification, it's not meant for me. It's never meant for me because what gentrification is, is they put up these condos and these little box houses and they skyrocket the prices of them and the people in the community can't afford it. So the property taxes go up and you can no longer afford your home. They give vouchers out to the suburbs and the problem I have with that is like we have culture within these communities so you're placed outside your element where you do not belong. It's like you're isolated and it's like why do I have to go.

Similar concerns about the poor condition of black communities were expressed on numerous topics, ranging from oft-heard issues of violence and educational quality to newly discussed disparities such as those surrounding healthy food choices. One respondent explained that differences in food quality and availability are reflected in the grocery stores in black neighborhoods compared to wealthier neighborhoods. He said, "I work in Englewood [a black poor and working-class community], at an elementary school and there are corner stores around and these kids eat so much junk, and I remember I use to eat it when I was younger too, but as far as health-wise, like we only have corner stores. Then you go to a wealthier neighborhood and you have like Whole Foods, Trader Joe's, so you see all these wonderful stores in these communities." Just like black voters over forty years ago, who looked to first-wave black officials to address the racial inequality that blocked the progress of black people in the realms of housing, jobs, and health care, this generation of young black Americans still believes that racial inequality is a major problem that continues to block their progress. Numerous members of the group told stories of harassment by the police that easily could have been told forty years ago. And while daily harassment by the police seems almost natural to these young people, it did not appear to be what they were most concerned about. Instead, they repeatedly returned to the subject of how race constrains the opportunities they need to move up and move out. They talk about how racism leads to living in resource-poor neighborhoods and attending resource-poor schools. A number of respondents commented on how the geographic segregation of black people limits their access to opportunity and long-term mobility.

If me and her [another focus group participant] have a kid together and we raise our kid in Lincoln Park [an affluent white Chicago neighborhood] somewhere where the lights shine bright and stuff like that.

Yeah, she's a black kid but she's been raised in an environment where, good schooling, good [food], got the Whole Foods down the corner so she's eating well now. And our baby here is going to grow up to live a good life and she's going to raise her kids in that same environment. You know, our kids and our offspring, just our family, they're going to be good. But for the rest of us [black people] at large, we're still in that downward spiral.

Another young man explained it this way:

You take all of us who, this is just a make-believe situation here, you take all of us who don't have anything, never had anything, put us all in one area and pretty much don't give us anything to survive off of, and say okay, you guys go in this area and see you guys later and hopefully everything goes good. We're animals. We don't have anything, we're hungry, it's every man for ourselves. I'm going to kill you to get that. And that's pretty much how we've all been...the area, the environment that we've been raised in for years. Nobody cares, like I said earlier, and that's just where the problem is.

Despite their position that in many ways the government and larger society have walled them off without adequate resources, this generation, like those before them, also understands that black Americans must continue to do their own work to improve their lives. For example, when asked what blacks need to do to get ahead, the young people in our focus group gave answers such as "work hard," "be educated," "stop being lazy and opening your mouth, ain't nobody going to give you nothing," and "stop complaining." Further, as I discussed in chapter 3, these young people are well-versed in a neoliberal discourse built around privatizing failure, so they are quick to point out the personal failings of other black people. One young woman noted that black "men [are] not being men, not taking care of kids, I mean not raising their children right. And these kids are coming out on the street being raised by TV but also people who never had fathers."

However, despite their recognition that individuals need to personally use the limited agency they have to make their lives better, nearly all the respondents agreed that there were different rules for blacks than for other groups. For example, when considering the difficulty black men have in getting a job a young man explained, "You can't really get a job. You sign all the applications but you don't get hired. [Moderator: "Why do you think this is the case?"] I just think it's the color. What white people see on TV, on the news. . . . They'll see it on the news and see us coming to stores with our applications. Maybe they see a tattoo or something and they judge us by that." Another young man later explained that black youth have to engage in different strategies that others, specifically whites, don't expect from young blacks to try and get ahead.

> Can't bow down. Me personally, I defeat it with my intelligence. I mean I know…it's like doing a left hand lay-up when they're used to you playing with your right. It's like it catches them off guard. I mean, you know, generally when I meet somebody or go for an interview somewhere it's someone of the Caucasian race. They're expecting one thing, a certain thing that they've been taught to expect of people of African descent, you know. And it almost kind of sounds bad, but they say oh, this guy's actually not a drug dealer or whatever. He's in school or he's working, and talks with intelligence. And that almost like, it's that left hook when they're expecting the right.

This group of young people, although exuberant over the first African-American president, realize that they cannot count on him or any other politician to singly change their condition. They understand that for their lives to improve, a number of entities must change—the government, employers, teachers, parents, and young people themselves. In their discussions one gets the sense that they believe that change is possible, but not directed by one person, even if that person is President Obama. One young woman explained that "Obama is not the only one, it's been many, he's one of many."

A vision of black politics that is focused on community action, not following ordained leaders, is heard repeatedly in the words of these young people. One young woman stated that the election of President Obama "told us American people that the power is in our hands and however you want this country ran we pretty much can decide that. I think everyone realized that and saw it for themselves this time around." Another young person explained, "It's not good enough if one guy makes it. That's not good for everybody in general, so everyone, if all of us can come out of it, then we can say we've done something to make change happen. But for one man to come out of it, that's not good enough. In fact, that's not doing anything at all."

Throughout the pages of this book, black youth have indicated through their answers to surveys, comments in focus groups, and in-depth interviews that they are looking forward to the day when race is no longer a factor in determining the quality of their schooling, their access to health care and quality food, how they are treated by the police, and whether they are able to land good jobs and have promising careers. If there is any group interested in the postracial moment where there actually could be an end to black politics, it is probably young black Americans. Unfortunately, for this generation of young blacks and the nation, we have not reached that moment.

Far from the election of Barack Obama signaling the end of black politics, in some sectors of the country his election has unleashed an unbridled racism that has not been witnessed in such regularity for some time. Whites who have been affected by layoffs and the failing economy, the escalating cost of health care, the bottoming out of the housing market, and the decline in our public schools have been motivated by radio and talk show hosts to rebel and to once again blame black people, immigrants, and, of course, our first black president for their predicament. They have in response held "tea parties" and "9/12 rallies" in which President Obama has been demeaned and depicted as Other, an unspeakable evil on a par with Adolph Hitler. As many traditional journalists and pundits have claimed, vilification of a sitting president is part of the vitriolic politics we call American politics. But others, including former president Jimmy Carter, have suggested that what we are witnessing in the backlash against President Obama is the continuing racist attitudes and behaviors of some whites, individuals who instinctively focus on racial explanations for their difficulties instead of pointing to the capitalist greed and neoliberal policies that have dismantled many of the protections middle- and working-class people depend on. Such a backlash, therefore, demands the continuation of black politics, if only to provide a counter to the outlandish and racist politics of some on the extreme right wing.

It is important to remember that the election of President Obama also serves to highlight, again, the bifurcation in black communities that continues, including among young black Americans. There are those young people in black communities who are positioned to benefit from the election of President Obama. They have been educated in private schools, either because their parents could pay the tuition outright or because someone somewhere believed them worthy of a scholarship. There are others who were educated in good public schools or charter schools where good instruction is valued above testing. Many of these young blacks not only voted for Obama, they worked on his campaign, and started Yes We Can! groups on Facebook. These young people seem to make healthier life decisions about, for example, when to have children, probably because they are presented with more activities during school, after school, and on the weekends so that self-destructive options do not take up as much space in their lives. The truth, of course, is that these young blacks are also better able to bounce back from bad decisions, given their access to supplemental resources. These are the young black people who are more likely to directly benefit from the election of President Obama. They are the black people whom corporations, universities, and governments are also more likely to hire as they look for talented individuals who will further their goals.

There are other young black people who, while they voted for President Obama, may not see the direct impact of his victory in their lives for some time. These young people were no less enthusiastic about Obama's candidacy. They wore T-shirts and buttons supporting Obama, wrote about and discussed his campaign and potential presidency in their classrooms, and returned to homes and apartments where Obama campaign signs were pasted in the windows. These young black people, however, go to subpar schools, underfunded by the city, state, and federal government, few of whose graduates attend college. They live in neighborhoods where gang activity and the wrong policing strategies threaten the safety of neighborhood residents and significantly reduce their life options and choices. Faulty decision-making among this group tends to have an exponential negative impact in their lives, since there are few outside and internal resources to help attenuate the impact of an unplanned pregnancy, dropping out of school, or being arrested. And while some from this group of young blacks will find a way to better their station in life, many will spend their lives trying to get ahead and recover from policies, institutions, and choices that are unforgiving in their closing of possibilities.

The politics of third-wave black politicians seem especially relevant and useful to the first group of young blacks, who probably will be able to continue to make significant strides in America by framing their struggles as part of the promise of American democracy without any sustained discussion of and attention to race. These young people, like Obama, embody what is thought to work in our democracy and government. They are the poster children for programs like affirmative action and Headstart and for the dialogue that has now been going on for decades on "the importance of diversity." They represent the potential of the country to produce a new group of leaders who—as participants in the narrow political party structure or as outside agitators in support of those most marginalized—will push the country forward toward a more diverse and inclusive democratic process.

I am concerned, however, with what type of politics not only will save the physical lives of young blacks in the second category described above but also will transform the totality of their lived experience, empowering them with equal opportunities to live a fulfilling and joyful life. As was clear in the words of many of these young people, they believe that race is still a major factor in determining their life opportunities, so a politics led by third-wave politicians unwilling to take on the question of race forcefully and continuously may not serve this group of young blacks very well. As in the past, it will probably be the organizers, advocates, and communities outside the traditional political power structure who will do the hard work of changing the life trajectory of marginalized black youth and holding third-wave black politicians accountable.

While I can say for sure that as a nation we have not reached or seen the end of black politics, the answers to other crucial questions are less clear. How will American politics and the American people respond to the desperate lived condition of some black youth? How will we address the continued alienation of black youth toward the state, even in the age of Obama? How will we facilitate the continued participation of black youth in the political process after Obama? How will we calm the moral panic in black communities about black youth and produce a moral politics that can be embraced by black youth? How do we fundamentally better the lives of marginalized young black people, demanding their full equality?

The first step in addressing all of these questions has to be acknowledging and treating young blacks as equal and full members of the larger political community whose perspectives are central to how we understand the successes and failures of our politics. When we include black youth as full and equal members, it means that we acknowledge their worth and will pursue a politics that reflect that understanding. As a first step, it means that we will provide them with the necessities to be active participants in the democratic process, and that means addressing some basic inequalities. For example, it means dedicating more money, effort, and will to specific policies and programs, such as quality education for marginalized youth, especially young black people who suffer from dropout rates of nearly 50 percent in some urban cities. It means designating more money to health programs accountable for erasing the disproportionate impact of HIV/AIDS, sexually transmitted infections, and mental health problems among black youth. It means that it can never be acceptable to have members of our community killed on the way to or from school—a way of life that black children in Chicago and other major cities have endured for far too long. As equal members of our political community, their future is literally our future, their suffering our suffering. And while President Obama has supported legislation in these areas, for example, bolstering community colleges and historically black colleges and universities as well as expanding health care and funding for public education, more, much more, must be accomplished.

In addition to addressing the material needs of black youth, equal membership in the political community must also mean, as scholar john a. powell puts it, "expanding the choices that people have to lead lives they value."[43] He continues, "Fundamental to enlarging choices is building human capabilities—the range of things that people can do or be in their lives. The most basic capabilities for human development are to lead long and healthy lives, to be knowledgeable, to have access to resources needed for a decent standard of living, and to be able to participate in the life of the community." We must therefore expand the civic capacity of young black Americans to fully engage in the politics of the country through which decisions about the distribution of resources and the country's priorities are debated and decided. If we start by ensuring the political equality of young blacks and demanding the resources and institutional arrangements necessary for "an environment in which people can develop their potential and lead productive, creative lives in accord with their needs and interests," then we have begun the process of transforming their lives and the country.[44]

Of course, once young blacks have been accepted as full and equal members of the political community and been provided with the equal opportunities dictated by full membership, then we as a community and a nation can legitimately ask things of young black Americans. We can demand that they respect every other member of the community and demonstrate not only tolerance but acceptance of the rights of others. For instance, the attitudes among young blacks that would deny gay members of our community the right to marry would not be accepted. Similarly, we would expect them, if provided real opportunity, to select those choices that further their lives and improve the public good of all the members of our society.

It is ultimately the question of how to promote the membership and participation of black youth in the life of the community, the heart of our democracy, that has been the focus of this book. As nation and community, we must renew our commitment to black youth, following their lead as they help us to reconceptualize what constitutes meaningful politics, whose lives are valued, protected, and enriched, and how to produce a moral politics through which all are allowed, encouraged, and provided with the means to be full and equal members of our political community. Black youth can help us to remix our democratic principles and practices, recognizing that full membership and the participation of all must be the basis for American politics in the twenty-first century.

"A Change Is Gonna Come"

Policy and Politics

W HILE MANY OF us in the academy may be comfortable making broad statements about what we must do as a nation to move the argument forward (and end a book), others will no doubt be left wanting without a more practical and concrete discussion about how to advance this struggle. In an attempt to start the conversation about what specific policies might constitute part of a political agenda to empower black youth in the United States, I offer what I believe are some of the best policy suggestions that have come to my attention. This is not a comprehensive list of all policy interventions, but a short list of suggested initiatives that others have developed.

Before briefly outlining these possible interventions, I want to be clear that none of them will come to fruition without the mobilization of significant numbers of individuals and groups demanding a change to the second-class status of too many young black people. Furthermore, the true empowerment of young people cannot be imposed on them. It is a process that must develop from *their* leadership, insight, and experience. Older folks like me must be prepared to follow, challenge, debate, and yes, defer to young activists, advocates, organizers, and young black people who live the contradictory and complicated reality that the book details. With all this in mind, below are suggested interventions/initiatives in six policy areas I think the country should pursue to *begin* the process of radically altering the lives and status of young black Americans.

MAKING POSTSECONDARY
EDUCATION ACCESSIBLE

Whereas Americans once needed only a high school degree to compete for living-wage jobs, we now recognize that the certificate of entry into such a competition is a college diploma. The goal, therefore, must be to make college affordable and to prepare young black students for its rigors—financial, social, and intellectual. Toward the goal of making college more affordable a number of reports have suggested that the national government consolidate at least three federal financial aid sources—Pell grants, loans, and work-study. The idea would be to guarantee financial access to college through funding from these three sources by a need-based assessment. Students from families with fewer resources would have more grants as part of their package, while students from families with higher socioeconomic status would receive packages in which loans make up a larger percentage of financial support. Every student would be expected to contribute to their education either through part-time work requirements while in school (work-study) or by agreeing to take on community service jobs during the summers and for a year or two after graduating. Demos, an influential liberal think tank, recently issued a report that discusses in detail a similar idea called "The Contract for College."[1]

In addition to making college financially affordable we also must provide an educational infrastructure that meets the needs of every student. This means recognizing the role that community colleges, public universities, and historically black and other minority-serving institutions play in making postsecondary education available to black youth. Greater resources must be directed to those institutions willing and able to increase access to such youth, especially those most disadvantaged. The Obama administration and Congressional Democrats have put forward a number of programs such as the Community College and Career Training Program to help two-year postsecondary education institutions with programs that will turn out productive workers. These initiatives are a good start in rethinking the pathway to good jobs and full lives, but they represent only a start—both in terms of funding and providing the quality education that black youth deserve. Yes, we want to use postsecondary education to impart valuable skills needed for black youth to compete in the labor market. That said, it is worth noting that at more elite institutions, access to education is not only about securing higher-paying jobs but also enriching one's life through the introduction to and engagement with intellectual ideas. This also should be part of the postsecondary education that we provide black youth across the class divide.

GRADUATING FROM HIGH SCHOOL

While finishing college will be the goal for many young people, we must also recommit ourselves to ensuring that the high school graduation rates of youth in inner-city schools rise dramatically. As noted earlier, in some urban areas the dropout rate for black males is 50 percent or more. This is unacceptable. A report, *Left Behind in America: The Nation's Dropout Crisis*, by the Center for Labor Market Studies and the Alternative Schools Network, details the devastating economic impact of dropping out on the 6.2 million young people aged 16–24 who left high school without diplomas by 2007.[2] In the report, the authors urge the immediate adoption of the Hope & Opportunity Pathways through Education (Hope USA) initiative that would use federal funds to match those from state and local school districts in programs to re-enroll young dropouts. A number of such programs have been developed, and generally these initiatives aim to provide such students with both a high school degree and marketable vocational skills. The most successful of these programs include small alternative school settings, year-round afterschool and summer activities, support from mentors, experienced staffs, and yearlong access to job opportunities.

SECURING MEANINGFUL EMPLOYMENT

Suggesting that we create jobs through the green economy has become almost passé now, but I want to return to the idea once again. When reviewing proposals to put young people back to work, especially non-college bound young people who are disproportionately black, one is confronted with two realities: first, there aren't a lot of new ideas out there for getting young black people either to work or back to work; and second, more and more economists and policy-makers are arguing that there is a real opportunity to create new jobs through the green economy. San Francisco State professor Rachel Pinderhughes notes that many of the jobs will be "manual labor jobs in businesses whose goods and services directly improve environmental quality."[3]

While I do not hold out great hope for the green economy rescuing the economic plight of many young black people, I also realistically understand that the manufacturing and service sector do not offer much hope on that front either. So given the limited choices for job expansion, I think devoting resources to the greening of our economy makes sense, at least for now. Such a project will only have an impact on the employment opportunities of black youth if the additional resources allocated by governments and industries are tied to requirements for job training programs and reinvestment in black and poor communities. The focus has to be on producing entry-level jobs, training, and employment mobility or growth for those who are currently unemployed, underemployed, or otherwise hard to employ.

In addition to investing in the green economy, others have advocated that the government reinvest in traditional job training programs. The Center for Law and Social Policy has advocated for the Obama administration to "provide $500 million to re-activate and expand the Youth Opportunity Grant program in WIA [the Workforce Investment Act of 1998], targeted to communities of high youth distress, to reconnect dropouts and other high risk youth to education, training and employment."[4] Still others suggest that we focus on fostering entrepreneurship among young people of color and creating jobs for them in small and neighborhood businesses.

ENDING VIOLENCE

In the area of violence, there seems to be increasing support for the use of more traditional means of intervention such as adult and peer-to-peer mentoring programs, an extension of the school day, and more recreational programs on weekends and evenings as well as during summers. The use of peers as educators, mentors, advocates, and organizers is critical in the development of such programs. Advocates suggest that programmatic interventions should start early in a child's life and that an intensified effort to foster participation in such programs should happen during the teenage years when the danger of engaging in violent, high-risk behavior is at its peak. While many of these programs operate at the individual, community, or school level, national and statewide efforts to pass legislation that will regulate and disrupt the sale and resale of firearms must also be continued.

CHALLENGING INCARCERATION

Efforts to reform our ineffective incarceration policies have been ongoing for some time. Activists have fought to change our funding priorities from arrest and incarceration to prevention and treatment. We must revise our current laws that continue to send disproportionate numbers of black youth to jail for nonviolent and drug-related offenses. Community-based justice programs and the provision of drug treatment instead of traditional incarceration is one approach to lessen the number of young people sentenced to jail or prison for nonviolent drug offenses. For those young people already incarcerated, we must provide more coordinated and extensive support as they re-enter their communities. If we intervene by helping them enter a job training program or a community college, we lessen the probability that they will be incarcerated in the future. Denying those who were formally incarcerated basic rights such as the right to vote or to receive government aid for their education only prolongs their punishment, increases their alienation, and impedes integration back into their communities and families as contributing members.

PROMOTING CIVIC AND POLITICAL ENGAGEMENT

None of the issues detailed in the book will be addressed without the mobilization of young people to demand the resources they need to excel. As was witnessed in the 2008 presidential election, if given candidates and causes that they believe in young people across racial groups will become active in the political process. What the last election also demonstrated was that resources make a difference in participation. While 62 percent of college-bound youth went to the polls in 2008, only 32 percent of non-college bound youth participated.[5] We can help to facilitate increased participation across class, race, gender, and education by providing meaningful opportunities for political and civic engagement to all young people through our schools and other community-based organizations. Through sustained and regular participation throughout adolescence young people, especially those with fewer resources, develop patterns of civic and political engagement. The authors of the report *An Inequitable Invitation to Citizenship:*

Non-College Bound Youth and Civic Engagement suggest that the use of technology, social media tools, and social networking sites be used more extensively to engage young people in civic and political activism.[6] Another proven route to facilitating activism and participation is to offer more meaningful service learning opportunities to youth in schools, making sure that young people in public, urban, and struggling schools are provided the same quality of service learning experiences as other young people.

Again, this very brief mention of possible interventions that could improve the life of young black people is not meant to be comprehensive. It is just the beginning of our conversation about the battles that must be waged if we are to offer young black people the opportunity to have meaningful and satisfying lives. None of the programs mentioned would benefit only black youth. All of these ideas would help to change the life trajectory of poor and marginal youth who are disproportionately young people of color. Most important, the adoption of these policies and others would signal to black youth that they are full members of our political community in whose future we will invest and protect.

Appendix A

TABLE A.1 Description of Variables from the Black Youth Project Survey Used in Analysis

Variable	Variable Label/Number	Direction of Variable Coding
Respondent education	A5	Increasing = more education [1 = GED … 7 = PhD]
Respondent age	main_age	Increasing = higher age [15–25]
Respondent sex	main_sex	Increasing = female [1= male, 2= female]
Family SES index	k1, k2_recode, l26_recode, l27, 115_recode, 120_recode	Increasing = higher SES
Respondent race	race_grp_big3	1 = White 2 = Black 3 = Latino
Youth 2004 vote	D3	(0 = No) (1 = Yes)
Linked fate recode	j9_recode	Increasing = stronger linked fate
Political efficacy recode	c12_recode	Increasing = more efficacy
Parental political interest	d1_recode	Increasing = more parental interest
Perceptions of systematic racism scale	f11_recode, j4_recode	Increasing = increasing perceptions of systematic racism [scale ranges from 2 to 10, mean = 6.8]
Personal discrimination	j11_recode, j13_recode, j14_recode	Increasing = more discrimination [index ranges from 3 to 15, mean = 6.1]

(continued)

Variable	Variable Label/Number	Direction of Variable Coding
Personal racism	j10_recode	Increasing = more discrimination
Perceptions of state racism	j5_recode, d25_recode, f10_recode	Increasing = increasing perceptions of state racism
Rap music exposure index	b1_recode, b5_recode	Increasing = increasing exposure [index ranges from 2 to 12, mean = 7.6]
Personal efficacy	c2_recode, c6_recode, c7_recode	Increasing = increasing efficacy [scale ranges from 5 to 12, mean = 9.8]
Religious activity index	e4, e5, e6	Increasing = increasing religious activity [index ranges from 3 to 18, mean = 10.3]
Belief in God	e1_recode	
Immigrant status	l1, l2, l3	Increasing foreignness [scale range from 0 to 7, mean = 1.2]
Government orientation scale	c14, c15	Increasing = better feelings about government officials [scale ranges from 2 to 8, mean = 4.8]
Inclusion/Equality	d24_recode	Increasing = increasing perceptions of inclusion/ equality
Opportunity	d26_recode	Increasing = increasing perceptions of opportunity
Alienation	Government orientation, d24_recode, d26_recode	Increasing = feel less politically alienated
Religiosity	E1	Increasing = so that religion is more important in one's life
Positive view	J8_recode	Increasing = increasingly believe other racial groups view their own racial group positively
Morals	New_h30, new_h31, new_h32	Increasing = increasing moral values
Rap attitudes	New_b8, new_b11, new_b12	Increasing = increasing negative views about rap music videos
Social support	New_c4, new_c5	Increasing = feel stronger sense of social support
Pregnancy consequences	New_h33, new_h34	Increasing = agree that there are negative consequences to pregnancy

Variable	Variable Label/Number	Direction of Variable Coding
Teenagers and sex	New_h23, new_h24	Increasing = agree it's okay for teenagers to have sex, if in a serious relationship and/or emotionally ready
Self-esteem	New_c1, new_c2, newc3	Increasing = have high self-esteem
Organization/group	D18_recode	(0 = No) (1 = Yes)
In school	A2	(0 = No) (1 = Yes)
Sex education	A11	(0 = No) (1 = Yes)
Racial diversity		Increasing = increasing diversity
Neighborhood SES	%Unmarried female hshlds, %unmarried female hshlds with children, %college grad_recode, %hshlds with 5 or more persons, %renter occupied hshlds, %income below pov, %unemployed, %non-citizen	Increasing = higher neighborhood SES
Listen to rap music	B1	Increasing = listen to little or no rap music
View rap music programming	B5	Increasing = view little or no rap music programming
Politicizing rap music	B9	Increasing = disagree rap music should be more political
Oral sex	H1	(1 = Yes) (2 = No)
Sexual intercourse	H5	(1 = Yes) (2 = No)
Been or gotten someone pregnant	H11	(1 = Yes) (2 = No)
Had an abortion (personally or partner)	H12	(1 = Yes) (2 = No)
Willingly tested for STIs	H14	(1 = Yes) (2 = No)
Willingly tested for HIV/AIDS	H15	(1 = Yes) (2 = No)
Feel in control when having sex	H21	Increasing = do not feel in control

(continued)

Variable	Variable Label/Number	Direction of Variable Coding
Feel good about themselves when having sex	H22	Increasing = do not feel good about themselves
Okay to have sex if in a serious relationship	H23	Increasing = do not believe it is okay to have sex
Okay to have sex if emotionally ready	H24	Increasing = do not believe it is okay to have sex
Okay to have sex if using protection	H25	Increasing = do not believe it is okay to have sex
Premarital sex	H30	Increasing = believe it is not always wrong to have premarital sex
Homosexuality	H31	Increasing = disagree homosexuality is always wrong
Abortion	H32	Increasing = disagree abortions are always wrong
Pregnancy will embarrass family	H33	Increasing = disagree pregnancy will be embarrassing for family
Personally feel embarrassed about pregnancy	H34	Increasing = disagree they will be embarrassed by pregnancy
Stay with partner if pregnant	H35	Increasing = do not believe they have to stay with baby's father/mother
Pregnancy will make achieving goals difficult	H36	Increasing = pregnancy will not make their goals harder to achieve
Government should offer benefits to married couples	H26	Increasing = government should not have to offer benefits to married couples
Legalize same-sex marriage	D21	Increasing = disagree government should make same-sex marriages legal
Ability to have abortion without parental consent	H28	Increasing = abortions should not be allowed without parental consent
Make abortions illegal	D22	Increasing = disagree government should make abortions illegal
Make sex education mandatory	H27	Increasing = sex education should not be mandatory

Variable	Variable Label/Number	Direction of Variable Coding
Make condoms available at high schools	H29	Increasing = condoms should not be available in high school
Abstinence-only programs	D23	Increasing = disagree government should only fund abstinence-only programs
Rap music videos contain too many references to sex	B8	Increasing = disagree that rap music videos contain too many references to sex
Rap music videos contain too many references to violence	B10	Increasing = disagree that rap music videos contain too many references to violence
Rap music videos portray black women in bad and offensive ways	B11	Increasing = disagree that rap music videos portray black women in bad/offensive ways
Rap music videos portray black men in bad and offensive ways	B12	Increasing = disagree that rap music videos portray black men in bad/offensive ways
Government is run by a few big interests	C15	Increasing = disagree government is run by a few big interests
Leaders in government care very little about people like me	C14	Increasing = disagree leaders care very little about people like them
Government treats immigrants better than black people	D25	Increasing = disagree that government treats immigrants better than black people
If more white people had AIDS, government would do more to find cure	F10	Increasing = government would not do more to find cure
It is hard for young black people to get ahead because of discrimination	J2	Increasing = disagree that it is hard for young black people to get ahead
Black youth receive a poorer education than whites	J4	Increasing = disagree black youth receive a poorer education

(continued)

Variable	Variable Label/Number	Direction of Variable Coding
Police discriminate more on black youth than whites	J5	Increasing = disagree that police discriminate more on black youth
Respondent feels like a full and equal citizen	D24	Increasing = respondent does not feel like a full and equal citizen
In the U.S., everyone has an equal chance to succeed	D26	Increasing = disagree that everyone has an equal chance to succeed
Contacted a public official	D3	(0 = No) (1 = Yes)
Given money to a candidate	D11	(0 = No) (1 = Yes)
Worked or volunteered on a political campaign, for a candidate, or for a party	D12	(0 = No) (1 = Yes)
Been active in or joined a political group	D9	(0 = No) (1 = Yes)
Written an article or letter to the editor about a political issue or problem	D15	(0 = No) (1 = Yes)
Worked with people in the neighborhood on a political issue or problem	D14	(0 = No) (1 = Yes)
Talked with family or friends about a political issue, party, or candidate	D13	(0 = No) (1 = Yes)
Wrote a blog or sent an e-mail	D10	(0 = No) (1 = Yes)
Signed a paper or e-mail petition	D5	(0 = No) (1 = Yes)
Engaged in buycotting	D8	(0 = No) (1 = Yes)
Attended protest meeting, demonstration, or sit-in	D6	(0 = No) (1 = Yes)
Boycotted	D7	(0 = No) (1 = Yes)

Variable	Variable Label/Number	Direction of Variable Coding
Member of an organized group	D18	(0 = No) (1 = Yes)
Engaged in organized volunteer or community-service work	D19	(0 = No) (1 = Yes)
Attended religious service at least once a week	E4	Increasing = rarely or never attends religious services
Served on a committee, organized a meeting, helped with special project at place of worship at least once or twice a month	E5	Increasing = rarely or never engages in activities at place of worship
Engaging in number of political acts		Number of political acts mentioned

TABLE A.2   Description of Variables from the Cosby Survey used in Analysis

Variable	Variable Label/Number	Direction of Variable Coding
Income	PPIMCIMP	Increasing = higher income
Encourages having sex too early	Q8_1	(0 = No) (1 = Yes)
Encourages multiple sexual partners	Q8_2	(0 = No) (1 = Yes)
Encourages taking drugs such as marijuana	Q8_3	(0 = No) (1 = Yes)
Encourages illegal activity such as selling drugs	Q8_4	(0 = No) (1 = Yes)
Encourages taking school less seriously	Q8_5	(0 = No) (1 = Yes)
Encourages disrespect of elders	Q8_6	(0 = No) (1 = Yes)
Encourages having babies before married	Q8_7	(0 = No) (1 = Yes)
Encourages disrespect of police	Q8_8	(0 = No) (1 = Yes)
Encourages violent behavior	Q8_9	(0 = No) (1 = Yes)
Encourages poor treatment of women	Q8_10	(0 = No) (1 = Yes)
Most of their problems arise because of their own bad decisions and behaviors	Q1	Respondents answered (1) to Q1
Black youth are making some bad personal decisions, but they also face substantial discrimination	Q1	Respondents answered (2) to Q1
Things like discrimination and a lack of jobs are the real reasons black youth find it hard to get ahead	Q1	Respondents answered (3) to Q1

TABLE A.3 Description of Variables from the MCPCE Survey used in Analysis

Variable	Variable Label/Number	Direction of Variable Coding
Respondent education	PPEDUC	Increasing = more education [1 = GED … 7 = PhD]
Respondent age	PPGENDER	Increasing = higher age [18–30]
Respondent sex	PPAGE	Increasing = female [1 = male, 2 = female]
Family income	PPINCIMP	Increasing = higher income
Respondent race	race	1 = White
		2 = Black
		4 = Asian
		8 = Latino
Youth 2008 vote	Q2_1, q2	(0 = No) (1 = Yes)
Linked fate recode	Q79, Q79_1 (wave 1)	Increasing = stronger linked fate
	Q78, Q78_1 (wave 2)	
Political efficacy recode	Q42 (wave 1)	Increasing = more efficacy
	Q40 (wave 2)	
Party identification	Partyid7	Increasing from strong Republican to strong Democrat
Inclusion/equality	Q52	Increasing = increasing perceptions of inclusion/equality
Opportunity	Q48	Increasing = increasing perceptions of opportunity
Government is run by a few big interests	Q45	Increasing = disagree government is run by a few big interests
Leaders in government care very little about people like me	Q44	Increasing = disagree leaders care very little about people like them

TABLE A.3 (Continued)

Variable	Variable Label/Number	Direction of Variable Coding
Contacted a public official	Q8	(0 = No) (1 = Yes)
Given money to a candidate	Q6 (wave 1)	(0 = No) (1 = Yes)
	Q5 (wave 2)	
Worked or volunteered on a political campaign, for a candidate, or for a party	Q7 (wave 1)	(0 = No) (1 = Yes)
	Q6 (wave 2)	
Been active in or joined a political group	Q17	(0 = No) (1 = Yes)
Written an article or letter to the editor about a political issue or problem	Q11	(0 = No) (1 = Yes)
Worked with people in the neighborhood on a political issue or problem	Q22	(0 = No) (1 = Yes)
Talked with family or friends about a political issue, party, or candidate	Q21	(0 = No) (1 = Yes)
Called a radio show	Q12	(0 = No) (1 = Yes)
Attended meetings, rallies, speeches, or dinners in support of a candidate	Q4	(0 = No) (1 = Yes)
Had a campaign button, political sticker, or sign in your window	Q5	(0 = No) (1 = Yes)
Attended a meeting of a local government board or council	Q9	(0 = No) (1 = Yes)
Tried to involve others in election, including going door to door, making phone calls, collecting signatures, and passing out literature	Q14	(0 = No) (1 = Yes)

Variable	Variable Label/Number	Direction of Variable Coding
Signed a paper or e-mail petition	Q10	(0 = No) (1 = Yes)
Engaged in buycotting	Q16 (wave 1) Q14 (wave 2)	(0 = No) (1 = Yes)
E-mailed the editor or manager of a newspaper, television station, or Web site about a political issue or candidate	Q20	(0 = No) (1 = Yes)
Got campaign/candidate information from Facebook/MySpace (30)	Q30 (wave 1) Q31 (wave 2)	(0 = No) (1 = Yes)
Written a blog about a political issue, candidate, or political party	Q19	(0 = No) (1 = Yes)
Written or forwarded an e-mail, signed an e-mail petition, or posted a comment to a blog about a political issue, candidate, or party	Q18	(0 = No) (1 = Yes)
Member of an organized group	Q25 (wave 1 only)	(0 = No) (1 = Yes)
Engaged in organized volunteer or community-service work	Q24	(0 = No) (1 = Yes)
Engaging in number of political acts		Number of political acts mentioned
Black equality	Q71_1	Increasing = less racial equality
Latino equality	Q71_2	Increasing = less racial equality
Asian equality	Q71_3	Increasing = less racial equality
Perspective on racism since the election of Barack Obama	Q69 (Wave 2 only)	Increase = racism continues to be a major problem

Notes

Chapter 1

1. Elijah Anderson, *Streetwise: Race, Class, and Change in an Urban Community* (Chicago: University of Chicago Press, 1992); Elijah Anderson, *Code of the Street: Decency, Violence, and the Moral Life of the Inner City* (New York: Norton, 1998); Carl Husemoller Nightingale, *On the Edge: A History of Poor Black Children and Their American Dreams* (New York: Basic Books, 1993); Mary Pattillo-McCoy, *Black Picket Fences: Privilege and Peril among the Black Middle Class* (Chicago: University of Chicago Press, 1999); Anne Arnette Ferguson, *Bad Boys: Public Schools in the Making of Black Masculinity* (Ann Arbor: University of Michigan Press, 2001).

2. Throughout this book I will use the categories white, Latino, Asian, and black to separate and divide by race the young people discussed. I recognize that some Latinos also identify as white racially. In the analysis provided we make the arbitrary decision to separate and group together all those who identify as Latino as distinct from those young people who identify as only white.

3. These data were collected from July to November 2005. There were 1,590 total respondents to the survey. The Black Youth Project research team developed and tested the questionnaire. The actual administration of the survey was done by the National Opinion Research Center at the University of Chicago under the title "Youth Culture Survey." For more information on the survey and methodology and to download the data, go to www.blackyouthproject.com.

4. The MCPCE Study is funded by the Ford Foundation with support from the University of Chicago. Cathy J. Cohen is principal investigator and research director; Michael C. Dawson is co–principal investigator. The Knowledge Networks panel is drawn from a random sample of the population of households in the United States. The survey sample for the MCPCE survey is a nationally representative panel that includes oversamples of blacks, Latinos, Asians, and young people aged 18–35. One-third of the Latino respondents came from Spanish-language-dominant homes and

received the questionnaire in Spanish. For more information on the survey and methodology and to download the data go to the Web site of the study, www.2008andbeyond.com.

5. Charles M. Blow, "No More Excuses?" *New York Times*, January 23, 2009, www.nytimes.com/2009/01/24/opinion/24blow.html.

6. V. Dion Hayes, "Blacks Hit Hard by Economy's Punch," *Washington Post*, November 24, 2009, www.washingtonpost.com/wp-dyn/content/article/2009/11/23/AR2009112304092.html?referrer=emailarticle.

7. Sentencing Project, "Racial Disparity" section, www.sentencingproject.org/template/page.cfm?id=122.

8. Sentencing Project, "Women in the Criminal Justice System: Briefing Sheets" (May 2007), www.sentencingproject.org/doc/publications/womenincj_total.pdf.

9. Adam Liptak, "U.S. Prison Population Dwarfs That of Other Nations," *New York Times*, April 23, 2008, www.nytimes.com/2008/04/23/world/americas/23iht-23prison.12253738.html?_r=1.

10. "The Racial Gap in High School Graduations Leaves Blacks Far behind Whites in College Eligibility," *Journal of Blacks in Higher Education Weekly Bulletin*, August 6, 2009, www.jbhe.com/latest/news/8–6–09/racialgap.html.

11. Bernadette D. Proctor and Joseph Dalaker, *Poverty in the United States: 2001*, U.S. Census Bureau, Current Population Reports, 60–219 (Washington, D.C.: U.S. Government Printing Office, 2002).

12. National Center for Children in Poverty, "Basic Facts about Low-income Children: Children under Age 18," 2008, www.nccp.org/publications/images/BF018-fig7.jpg.

13. U.S. Department of Labor, Bureau of Labor Statistics, "The Employment Situation: December 2003," news release, January 2004, USDL 04-07.

14. U.S. Department of Labor, Bureau of Labor Statistics, "Labor Force Statistics from the Current Population Survey," October 2009, http://data.bls.gov/PDQ/servlet/.

15. Tamara Draut, "Economic State of Young America," *Demos: A Network for Ideas & Action* (Spring 2008): 8.

16. Kathy Bergen, "African Americans Hit Inordinately Hard by Recession: Staggering High Unemployment among Black Middle Class Wipes Out a Generation of Wealth," *Chicago Tribune*, November 6, 2009, http://archives.chicagotribune.com/2009/nov/06/business/chi-fri-black-jobs-nov06.

17. McKinsey & Company, "The Economic Impact of the Achievement Gap in America's Schools: Summary of Findings," Social Sector Office (April 2009): 5.

18. David Harvey, *A Brief History of Neoliberalism* (New York: Oxford University Press, 2007).

19. Amartya Sen, *Development as Freedom* (New York: Anchor Books, 1999), xi–xii.

20. Derrion Albert, "Beating Death: 4 Teens Charged with Murder," *Huffington Post*, September 28, 2009, www.huffingtonpost.com/2009/09/28/derrion-albert-beating-de_n_302321.html.

21. "Youth Violence in America: How Can We Stop It?" *Huffington Post*, October 7, 2009, www.huffingtonpost.com/2009/10/07/youth-violence-in-america_n_313141.html.

22. Ed Pilkington, "Chicago's Murdered Children," *Guardian*, August 11, 2009, www.guardian.co.uk/world/2009/aug/11/chicago-children-murders/print.

23. Barack Obama, "Remarks of Senator Barack Obama on Chicago Violence," July 15, 2007, www.obama.senate.gov.

24. Pilkington, "Chicago's Murdered Children."

25. Tera Williams, "Mom of Teen Who Was Beaten to Death Speaks Out," MyFoxChicago, September 26, 2009, www.myfoxchicago.com/dpp/news/metro/derrion_albert_mom.

Chapter 2

1. Dahleen Glanton and Kayce T. Ataiyero, "'N-word' Gets Symbolic End," *Chicago Tribune*, July 10, 2007, http://archives.chicagotribune.com/2007/jul/10/news/chi-naacp10jul10.

2. The ironic and sad fate of former mayor Kwame Kilpatrick is discussed in chapter 3.

3. Similar to Clarence Thomas labeling the sexual harassment accusations against him a "high-tech lynching," Kilpatrick would also state that the "lynch-mob mentality" he faced threatened the lives of his wife and children and was motivated by the media's endless pursuit of high Nielsen ratings.

4. "NAACP Delegates 'Bury' N-word in Ceremony," MSNBC, July 7, 2009, www.msnbc.msn.com/id/19680493/.

5. Many readers may remember the controversy that surrounded Don Imus when on April 4, 2007, he referred to the Rutgers University women's basketball team as a bunch of "nappy-headed hos." After significant protests, primarily by civil rights organizations, and eventual abandonment by many of his top sponsors, Imus was fired from his very popular radio show, *Imus in the Morning*, later that month. In November 2007, Imus returned to the air on Citadel Media's WABC in New York.

6. Suzette Hackney, "Detroit Funeral Aims to Bury Racial Slur," *USA Today*, July 9, 2007, www.usatoday.com/news/nation/2007-07-09-naacp_N.htm.

7. Glanton and Ataiyero, "'N-word' Gets Symbolic End."

8. Quotation from in-depth interview, Black Youth Project Survey, 2006. The Black Youth Project, a research initiative headed by Cathy J. Cohen at the University of Chicago, examines the attitudes, resources, and culture of African-American youth aged 15–25, exploring how these factors and others influence their decision-making, norms, and behavior in critical domains such as sex, health, and politics. The first phase of the research focused on mounting a new national survey of young people aged 15–25 with an oversample of African-Americans. There were 1,590 respondents to the 45-minute telephone survey conducted between July and November 2005. The primary sampling mode was a national random digit dial conducted by the National Opinion Research Center. A secondary oversample of blacks and Hispanics was used to supplement low N from those groups in the primary sample. Participants in the oversample came from areas of the United States with at least 15 percent black or Hispanic populations. There was also an oversample of respondents in the Chicago area. The response rate for the telephone surveys was 62 percent. During the second

phase of the project, researchers conducted in-depth interviews with African-American respondents of the new national survey. Thirty-seven young people between the ages of 15 and 25 were interviewed in 2006, prior to the historic campaign and election of Barack Obama. Respondents to the Black Youth Project national survey in 2005 were asked if they would be willing to be interviewed at a later date. Thirty of the previous respondents and an additional five men who did not take part in the original survey were interviewed over the summer and fall of 2006. Interviewees lived in four midwestern cities: Chicago, St. Louis, Milwaukee, and Detroit. We matched the race and gender of the interviewer with the interviewee. All those who were interviewed received $50. Generally, interviews lasted approximately one hour. The third phase of the project will explore the themes and narratives found in the most popular rap songs through the methodology of content analysis.

9. Quotations from in-depth interviews, Black Youth Project Survey.
10. The term "black crusader" was used in the episode "Cleveland" of the comedy series *30 Rock* on NBC. In the segment, a black comedian believes that the black crusaders, led by Bill Cosby and Oprah Winfrey, are out to get him for making black people look bad.
11. Martin Gilens, "Race and Poverty in America: Public Misperceptions and the American News Media," *Public Opinion Quarterly* 60 (1996): 515–41.
12. Cathy J. Cohen, *African-American Cosby Study* (2007). This study was a national representative survey of 500 black Americans aged 30 and older administered by Knowledge Networks during April 2007. Respondents are part of the Knowledge Networks online research panel, which is representative of the entire U.S. population. The completion rate was 61.4 percent. Unlike other Internet research that covers only individuals with Internet access who volunteer for research, Knowledge Networks surveys are based on a sampling frame that includes both listed and unlisted numbers and is not limited to current Web users or computer owners. Panel members are randomly recruited by telephone, and households are provided with Internet access and hardware if needed. Knowledge Networks selects households using random digit dialing.
13. Stanley Cohen, *Folk Devils and Moral Panics: The Creation of the Mods and Rockers*, 3rd ed. (New York: Routledge, 2002).
14. Michael C. Dawson, *Behind the Mule: Race and Class in African-American Politics* (Princeton, NJ: Princeton University Press, 1994).
15. "Bill Cosby's Confused Notion of 'Responsibility'" *The Black Commentator*, June 3, 2004, www.blackcommentator.com/93/93_cover_cosby.html.
16. Oscar Lewis, "The Culture of Poverty," in *On Understanding Poverty: Perspectives from the Social Sciences*, ed. D. Moynihan (New York: Basic Books, 1968), 187–200; Charles Murray, *Losing Ground: American Social Policy, 1950–1980* (New York: Basic Books, 1984).
17. See for example Cornel West's comments on NPR, www.npr.org/templates/dmg/dmg_wmref.php?prgCode=TAVIS&showDate=26-May-2004&segNum=3&mediaPref=WM&sauid=U561620481156445359625&getUnderwriting=1,

The *Tavis Smiley Show*, May 25, 2004; Hamil R. Harris, "Some Blacks Find Nuggets of Truth in Cosby's Speech, Others Say D.C. Remarks about Poor Blacks Went Too Far," *Washington Post*, May 25, 2004, www.washingtonpost .com/wp-dyn/articles/A55656-2004May25.html; and interview with Reverend Jesse Jackson, Fox News, July 2, 2004, www.foxnews.com/printer_friendly_ story/0,3566,124818,00.html.

18. Henry Louis Gates, "Breaking the Silence," *New York Times*, August 1, 2004.

19. William Bennett, *Bill Bennet's Morning in America*, http://mediamatters.org/ items/200509280006; Don Imus, *Imus in the Morning*, video, www.youtube .com/watch?v=RF9BjB7Bzr0.

20. Martin Gilens, *Why Americans Hate Welfare: Race, Media, and the Politics of Antipoverty Policy* (Chicago: University of Chicago Press, 2000).

21. Eric Michael Dyson, *Is Bill Cosby Right?: Or Has the Black Middle Class Lost Its Mind* (New York: Basic Civitas Books, 2006), xvi.

22. Don Imus and his staff, *Imus in the Morning*, MSNBC, April 4, 2007, transcript available at http://mediamatters.org/items/200704040011.

23. Don Imus, *Imus in the Morning*, April 10, 2007, and *The Today Show*, ABC, April 10, 2007; transcripts available at http://mediamatters.org/ items/200704100020?f=i_related.

24. Cathy J. Cohen, *Black Youth Project: Research Summary* (2007), www .blackyouthproject.com/writings/research_summary.pdf, 19. See also Jeff Chang and Dave Zirin, "No Scapegoats: The Other Side of Hip-Hop," *Los Angeles Times*, April 23, 2007, www.latimes.com/news/opinion/ la-oe-zirin23apr23,0,3088270.story?coll=la-opinion-rightrail.

25. Angela Davis, *Women, Culture, and Politics* (New York: Random House, 1989); Paula Giddings, *When and Where I Enter: The Impact of Black Women on Race and Sex in America* (New York: Bantam, 1988).

26. Tracey Denean Sharpley-Whiting, *Pimps Up, Hos Down: Hip Hop's Hold on Young Black Women* (New York: New York University Press, 2007).

27. Tricia Rose, "Never Trust a Big Butt and a Smile." *Camera Obscura* 23 (1991): 108–31; Robin Roberts, "Music Videos, Performance and Resistance: Feminist Rappers," *Journal of Popular Culture* 25 (1991): 141–52.

28. Quotation from in-depth interview, Black Youth Project.

29. Stanley Cohen, "Mods, Rockers, and the Rest: Community Reaction to Juvenile Delinquency," *Howard Journal* 12, 2 (1967): 121–30.

30. Phillip Jenkins, *Moral Panic: Changing Concepts of the Child Molester in Modern America* (New Haven, CT: Yale University Press, 1998).

31. Erich Goode and Nachman Ben-Yehuda, *Moral Panics: The Social Construction of Deviance* (Oxford: Blackwell, 1994), 15.

32. Howard S. Becker, *Outsiders: Studies in the Sociology of Deviance* (New York: Free Press, 1973).

33. Cohen, "Mods, Rockers, and the Rest."

34. Goode and Ben-Yehuda, *Moral Panics*, 24.

35. Jenkins, *Moral Panic*, notes the different degrees of power held by competing interest groups and stakeholders in shaping the framing of moral panics, the perceived implications, and the response to that particular framing.

36. Evelyn Brooks Higginbotham, *Righteous Discontent: The Women's Movement in the Black Baptist Church, 1880–1920* (Cambridge, MA: Harvard University Press, 1993).

37. Ibid., 188.

38. Ibid., 193.

39. W. E. B. Du Bois, *The Philadelphia Negro: A Social Study*, 2nd ed. (Philadelphia: University of Pennsylvania Press, 1996); William Julius Wilson, *The Truly Disadvantaged: The Inner City, the Underclass, and Public Policy* (Chicago: University of Chicago Press, 1987).

40. Cohen, *Black Youth Project: Research Summary*.

41. Cohen, *Black Youth Project: Research Summary*.

42. Tony Roshan Samara, "Youth, Crime and Urban Renewal in the Western Cape," *Journal of Southern African Studies* 31, 1 (March 2005): 209–27; Stuart Hall, Chas Critcher, Tony Jefferson, John N. Clarke, and Brian Roberts. *Policing the Crisis: Mugging, the State and Law and Order* (New York: Palgrave Macmillan, 1978).

43. Celeste Watkins-Hayes, *The New Welfare Bureaucrats: Entanglements of Race, Class, and Policy Reform* (Chicago: University of Chicago Press, 2009).

44. Mary Pattillo, *Black on the Block: The Politics of Race and Class in the City* (Chicago: University of Chicago Press, 2007).

45. Cathy J. Cohen, *The Boundaries of Blackness: AIDS and the Breakdown of Black Politics* (Chicago: University of Chicago Press, 1999).

46. John McWhorter, *Losing the Race: Self-sabotage in Black America* (New York: Perennial, 2001), 37.

47. Ibid., 2.

48. Ibid., 39.

49. Juan Williams, *Enough: The Phony Leaders, Dead-end Movements, and Culture of Failure That Are Undermining Black America—and What We Can Do about It* (New York: Crown, 2006), 126–27.

50. Stanley Crouch, *The Artificial White Man: Essays on Authenticity* (New York: Basic Books, 2004), 10.

51. Spike Lee, "Spike Lee Denounces Rap Music," *Urban Grounds*, November 4, 2005, http://urbangrounds.com/2005/11/04/spike-lee/; Wynton Marsalis, http://blogcritics.org/archives/2003/10/02/110040.ph.

52. Schott Foundation for Public Education, "Given Half a Chance: The Schott 50 Report on Public Education and Black Males" (2008), www.blackboysreport.org/files/schott50statereport-execsummary.pdf.

53. Cohen, *African-American Cosby Study* (2007). It is important to note that an additional 30 percent of older African Americans believe that "while black youth face some discrimination, most of their problems arise because of *their own bad decisions and behaviors*." Only 18 percent of older blacks attribute the difficulties that black youth face to primarily "things like discrimination and a lack of jobs."

54. The "perp walk" is slang for the police practice of walking a suspect in front of members of the media, especially television camerapersons, so they can record an image for a later broadcast.

55. Cohen. *The Boundaries of Blackness*, 75.

Chapter 3

1. See "Kwame Kilpatrick: A Mayor in Crisis" at http://detroit.about
   .com/gi/o.htm?zi=1/XJ&zTi=1&sdn=detroit&cdn=citiestowns&tm=1
   5&gps=106_1666_1259_875&f=00&su=p284.9.336.ip_p554.12.336
   .ip_&tt=2&bt=1&bts=0&zu=http%3A//www.freep.com/apps/pbcs.dll/
   article%3FAID%3D/99999999/NEWS01/80124052%26template%3Dthem
   e%26theme%3DKILPATRICK012008.

2. Jill Smolowe, "Autumn of His Life?" *Time*, July 21, 1997, www.time.com/
   time/magazine/article/0,9171,138024,00.html?iid=digg_share.

3. Elijah Anderson, *Streetwise: Race, Class, and Change in an Urban Community*
   (Chicago: University of Chicago Press, 1992); Frank F. Furstenberg, Jr.,
   S. Morgan, K. A. Moore, and J. C. Peterson, "Race Differences in the
   Timing of Adolescent Intercourse," *American Sociological Review* 52 (1987):
   511–18; Dennis P. Hogan and Evelyn M. Kitagawa, "The Impact of Social
   Status, Family Structure, and Neighborhood on the Fertility of Black
   Adolescents," *American Journal of Sociology* 90, 4 (1985): 825–55.

4. Bill Cosby and Alvin F. Poussaint, *Come On People: On the Path from Victims to
   Victors* (Nashville: Thomas Nelson, 2007); John McWorter, *Winning the Race:
   Beyond the Crisis in Black America* (New York: Gotham, 2006).

5. Tommie Shelby, "Justice, Deviance, and the Dark Ghetto," *Philosophy and
   Public Affairs* 35 (2007): 144.

6. Sam Roberts, "Two-parent Black Families Showing Gains," *New York Times*,
   December 17, 2008, www.nytimes.com/2008/12/17/us/17census
   .html?_r=1.

7. Kaiser Family Foundation, "Sex on TV: A Biennial Report to the Kaiser
   Family Foundation" (February 2003); K. L. Brewster, "Race Differences
   in Sexual Activity Among Adolescent Women: The Role of Neighborhood
   Characteristics," *American Sociological Review* 59 (1994): 408–24; Furstenburg
   et al., "Paternal Participation and Children's Well-being after Marital
   Dissolution," *Americal Sociological Review* 52 (1987): 643–52; Hogan
   and Kitagawa, "The Impact of Social Status, Family Structure, and
   Neighborhood on the Fertility of Black Adolescents," *American Journal of
   Sociology* 90, 4 (1985): 825.

8. Black AIDS Institute, "Shocking Study on Black Teen STD Rates Raises
   Troubling HIV Questions As Well," March 13, 2008, www.blackaids.org.

9. For example, the Centers for Disease Control and Prevention published
   data from the 2001 Youth Risk Behavior Surveillance Survey indicating
   that African-American high school students were more likely than white
   high school students to report having had sex (61 percent and 43 percent,
   respectively); having initiated sex before age 13 (16 percent and 5 percent,
   respectively); having had sex with more than four partners (26 percent and
   12 percent, respectively); and having been pregnant or gotten someone
   pregnant (11 percent and 3 percent, respectively).

10. See, for example, William Julius Wilson, *The Truly Disadvantaged: The Inner
    City, the Underclass, and Public Policy* (Chicago: University of Chicago Press,
    1987).

11. Sandra Sobieraj Westfall, "Bristol Palin, 'My Life Comes Second Now,'" *People*, June 1, 2009, www.people.com/people/archive/article/0OK?20282000,00.html.

12. Fantasia Barrino, "Baby Mama," composed by Barbara Acklin, Eugene Record, Harold Lilly, Vito Colapietro, and Neely Dinkins, Jr., 19 Recordings Limited, 2005.

13. Elizabeth Blair, "Profile: Criticism over *American Idol* Winner Fantasia Barrino's New Single 'Baby Mama,'" *Morning Edition*, NPR, May 24, 2005.

14. Claudia Sandoval, a graduate student at the University of Chicago, helped with much of the statistical analysis thus references to the statistical analysis will include the use of first-person plural pronouns. Ordered probit is used in our analyses because the dependent variables under examination are ordinally scored as a Likert scale.

15. In an attempt to explore what factors might be associated with a feeling of sexual empowerment, we combined two questions into a scale that asked respondents whether they strongly agreed, agreed, neither agreed nor disagreed, disagreed, or strongly disagreed with the each of the following statements: (1) "When I have sex I feel in control," and (2) "When I have sex I feel good about myself." The Cronbach alpha for the sexual control scale is .5650 for blacks, .5749 for whites, .5478 for Latinos, and .5647 for all respondents. We then ran an ordered probit using our sexual feeling scale as the dependent variable. Ordered probit was used because the dependent variables under examination are ordinally scored as a Likert scale. Finally, we used the statistical program Clarify to help identify the relative proportional impact of significant variables. For more information on Clarify see Gary King, Michael Tomz, and Jason Wittenberg, "Making the Most of Statistical Analyses: Improving Interpretation and Presentation," *American Journal of Political Science* 44, 2 (April 2000): 347–61; see also the Clarify Web site, http://gking.harvard.edu/clarify/docs/clarify.html.

16. Family SES is an index of responses to questions about father's and mother's education, reception of government assistance, whether the family rents or owns their home, and family income. For significant parts of our sample, family income was missing. To address this issue, we imputed data using the multiple imputation package from Stata called ICE. Multiple imputation is a statistical technique that allows researchers to derive appropriate estimates for missing data in multivariate analysis. One key element of multiple imputation is that it accounts for variation in the original data and variation in the imputations. The following variables were included in the multiple imputation model for the Black Youth Project data analysis: family income, sex, age, education, sense of linked fate (the degree to which black youth believe that what happens to most black people in this country affects them), public assistance reception, father's education, mother's education, parent's marital status, parent's property ownership, parent's employment history, immigrant status, political efficacy, rap exposure, personal efficacy, urban neighborhood SES, neighborhood

racial diversity, percent white population in neighborhood, percent black population in neighborhood, personal discrimination, systemic racism, belief in God, political alienation, and most of the politial participation variables. For more information on imputation methods see Jeffrey Wayman, "Multiple Imputation for Missing Data: What Is It and How Can I Use It?" paper presented at the annual meeting of the American Educational Research Association, Chicago, April 2003; Patrick Royston, "Multiple Imputation for Missing Values," *Stata Journal* 4 (2004): 227–41; and Gary King, James Honeker, Ann Joseph, and Kenneth Scheve, "Analyzing Incomplete Political Science Data: An Alternative Algorithm for Multiple Imputation" (1999), http://gking.harvard.edu/files/mipres.pdf.

17. Composite score from two questions assessing how often the respondent listens to rap music and watches rap music videos. This variable is a possible alternative or oppositional source of information about the government and the political system.

18. Level of agreement with the statement "I believe that by participating in politics I can make a difference."

19. Our measure of political alienation is comprised of three dimensions and will be discussed extensively in the next chapter. Details of the measure can also be found in the coding sheet entitled "Description of Variables from the Black Youth Project Survey used in Analysis," which details all variables used in analyses throughout the book.

20. For more information on Clarify see the sources cited in note 15.

21. All the findings detailed below assume that all other factors included in our model, except for the one variable or characteristic being discussed, are the same for all respondents being compared; thus, we claim all other factors are constant.

22. In this analysis, we combined three questions that asked whether respondents strongly agreed, agreed, neither agreed nor disagreed, disagreed, or strongly disagreed with the idea that it would be all right if teens had sex under a number of specified conditions. The Cronbach alpha for the teen sexuality scale is .8601 for blacks, .9299 for whites, .8677 for Latinos, and .8889 for all respondents. We also ran an ordered probit and used Clarify for the interpretation of the results.

23. The Cronbach alpha for the morality scale among blacks is .6588, for whites .7895, for Latinos .6861, and for all respondents .7274.

24. We only included the questions (1) "Would having or fathering a baby before you are married be embarrassing to you?" and (2) "Would having or fathering a baby before you were married be embarrassing to your family?" in our scale of pregnancy consequences, since these two questions were the only combination of variables with a Cronbach alpha above .6. The Cronbach alpha for blacks is .7964, for whites .7887, for Latinos .7836, and for all respondents is .7952.

25. Paul Steinhauser, "CNN Poll: Generations Disagree on Same-sex Marriage," CNN.com, May 4, 2009, www.cnn.com/2009/US/05/04/samesex.marriage.poll/index.html?iref=mpstoryview.

26. Chuck Raash, "Generations Reshape Gay Marriage Debate," *USA Today*, May 21, 2009, www.usatoday.com/news/opinion/columnist/raasch/2009-05-21-new-politics_N.htm.

27. Since the Cronbach alpha for the government morality scale among blacks is only .3724, we decided to perform an ordered probit on individual variables in our data set.

28. Tara Parker-Pope, "For Clues on Teenage Sex, Experts Look to Hip-hop," *New York Times*, November 6, 2007, www.nytimes.com/2007/11/06/health/06well.html?ex=1352005200&en=c35f9b1dd8b01b84&ei=5088&partner=rssnyt&emc=rss.

29. Gwendolyn D. Pough, *Check It While I Wreck It: Black Womanhood, Hip-hop Culture, and the Public Sphere* (Boston: Northeastern University Press, 2004), 186–89.

30. Tricia Rose, *The Hip Hop Wars: What We Talk about When We Talk about Hip Hop—And Why It Matters* (New York: Basic Books, 2008), 108–9.

31. The Cronbach alpha for the rap attitudes scale is .8067 for blacks, .8020 for whites, .8016 for Latinos, and .8001 for all respondents.

32. The question of whether rap music videos should be more political did not scale with the other questions about rap music videos used in the rap music video scale.

33. Bakari Kitwana, *Why White Kids Love Hip-Hop: Wankstas, Wiggers, Wannabes, and the New Reality of Race in America* (New York: Basic Books, 2005), 15.

34. Parker-Pope, "For Clues on Teenage Sex."

35. Participants were recruited through advertisements at selected sites, such as universities, community colleges, churches, and youth centers. All respondents received financial compensation for their participation.

36. Wilson, *Truly Disadvantaged*.

37. Intersectional analysis refers to exploring an issue with the understanding that multiple factors and identities contribute to and are important in trying to understand the issue at hand. For example, when talking about the issues black women face, one must take into account issues of race, gender, class, and sexuality. For more discussion of intersectionality see Kimberle Williams Crenshaw, "Mapping the Margins: Intersectionality, Identity Politics and Violence Against Women of Color," *Stanford Law Review* 43, 6 (1991): 1247–49.

38. Cathy J. Cohen, "Deviance as Resistance: A New Research Agenda for the Study of Black Politics," *Du Bois Review* 1 (2004): 27–45.

39. David A. Snow, "Framing Processes, Ideology, and Discursive Fields," in *The Blackwell Companion to Social Movements*, ed. D. A. Snow, S. A. Soule, and H. Kriesi (Oxford: Blackwell Publishers, 2004), 404.

40. "Bill Cosby's Confused Notion of 'Responsibility,'" *The Black Commentator*, June 3, 2004, www.blackcommentator.com/93/93_cover_cosby.html.

41. Christopher Hass, "Barack Obama: Father's Day Speech," *Organizing for America*, June 15, 2008, http://my.barackobama.com/page/community/post/stateupdates/gG5nFK.

42. Gene Seymor, "Black Directors Look beyond Their Niche," *New York Times*, January 9, 2009, www.nytimes.com/2009/01/11/movies/11seym.html.

43. Andre C. Willis, "Tyler Perry's Conservative Tent Revival: Why the Hit Producer's Narrow Evangelism May Not Be Doing Black People Any Good," *Root.com*, March 25, 2008, www.theroot.com/views/tyler-perrys-conservative-tent-revival.

44. A. O. Scott, "Serving a Buffet of Morality and Humor," *New York Times*, March 22, 2008, http://movies.nytimes.com/2008/03/22/movies/22tyle.html.

45. Darryl Fears and Jose Antonio Vargas, "City Says HIV Count Is Likely Too Low," *Washington Post*, March 17, 2009, www.washingtonpost.com/wp-dyn/content/article/2009/03/16/AR2009031600891.html.

46. Barack Obama, "Prepared Remarks of President Barack Obama Back to School Event," September 8, 2009, www.whitehouse.gov/MediaResources/PreparedSchoolRemarks/.

Chapter 4

1. Lisa De Moraes, "Kanye West's Torrent of Criticism, Live on NBC," *Washington Post*, September 3, 2009, www.washingtonpost.com/wp-dyn/content/article/2005/09/03/AR2005090300165.html.

2. On November 14, 2004, Kanye West stormed out of the American Music Awards broadcast after learning he had lost in the category of best new artist to Gretchen Wilson for her song "Redneck Woman." He would later tell reporters, "I felt like I was definitely robbed, and I refused to give any politically correct bullsh—ass comment....I was the best new artist this year"; quoted in James Montgomery, "Heard Him Say! A Timeline of Kanye West's Public Outbursts," MTV.com, www.mtv.com/news/articles/1569536/20070912/west_kanye.jhtml#.

3. Michael C. Dawson, "Katrina, Race and Poverty: Field Report," November 21, 2005, conducted by Knowledge Networks, unpublished.

4. "Jena Six" refers to six African-American youth who were arrested in Jena, Louisiana, on December 4, 2006, and charged with attempted second-degree murder for fighting a white youth, Justin Barker. This fight followed a number of incidents in which black students were harassed and physically attacked by white students at Jena High School. The events surrounding this case, especially the racially exaggerated charges against the six black youth, first attracted attention from black media sources and eventually national media. Successful political mobilization around the case produced a massive march in Jena, Louisiana, on September 2007.

5. Quotation from in-depth interview, Black Youth Project. For more on this project see note 3 of chapter 1.

6. See Daniel Kurtzman, comp., "Stupid Quotes about Hurricane Katrina," http://politicalhumor.about.com/od/currentevents/a/katrinaquotes.htm.

7. In-depth interview, Black Youth Project.

8. De Moraes, "Kanye West's Torrent of Criticism, Live on NBC."

9. See, e.g., Schley R. Lyons, "The Political Socialization of Ghetto Children: Efficacy and Cynicism," *Journal of Politics* 32, 2 (1970): 288–304; Edward S. Greenberg, "Black Children and the Political System," *Public Opinion*

Quarterly 34, 3 (1970): 333–45; and Paul R. Abramson, "Political Efficacy and Political Trust among Black Schoolchildren: Two Explanations," *Journal of Politics* 34, 4 (1972): 1243–75. For more recent work in this area, see Andrea Simpson, *Tie That Binds: Identity and Political Attitudes in the Post–Civil Rights Generation* (New York: New York University Press, 1998).

10. During the 1970s, scholars such as Edward Greenberg, Schley Lyons, Paul Abramson, James W. Clarke, Sarah Liebscutz, and Richard G. Niemi relied on small data sets generated from paper-and-pencil surveys that were conducted in a limited number of schools and community programs to explore the political attitudes of black youth. Working under the rubric of political socialization, most of these studies focused on issues of trust and efficacy and did not explore the political positions of these young people on specific political and public policy issues of the time. Even given the problems associated with these research designs, scholars identified interesting findings, suggesting that African-American youth had lower levels of trust in the government and their political efficacy varied depending on such factors as age and class. Unfortunately, instead of building on the insights learned from such studies and generating data from broader and more reliable research strategies, social science research in this area was severely neglected in the 1980s.

11. See, e.g., Elijah Anderson, *Streetwise: Race, Class, and Change in an Urban Community* (Chicago: University of Chicago Press, 1992), and *Code of the Street: Decency, Violence, and the Moral Life of the Inner City* (New York: Norton, 1998); Carl Husemoller Nightingale, *On the Edge: A History of Poor Black Children and Their American Dreams* (New York: Basic Books, 1993); Mary Pattillo-McCoy, *Black Picket Fences: Privilege and Peril among the Black Middle Class* (Chicago: University of Chicago Press, 1999); Anne Arnette Ferguson, *Bad Boys: Public Schools in the Making of Black Masculinity* (Ann Arbor: University of Michigan Press, 2001).

12. Peter Levine, *The Future of Democracy: Developing the Next Generation of American Citizens* (Hanover, NH: University Press of New England, 2007), 92.

13. Ibid.

14. The mean difference for blacks and whites is significant at the .01 level. The mean difference between blacks and Latinos is not statistically significant. The mean difference between Latinos and whites is significant at the .05 level.

15. The mean difference for blacks and whites is significant at the .001 level. The mean difference between blacks and Latinos is not statistically significant. The mean difference between Latinos and whites is significant at .the 01 level.

16. In-depth interview, Black Youth Project.

17. In-depth interview, Black Youth Project.

18. In-depth interview, Black Youth Project.

19. Latina respondents registered the lowest levels of agreement with this statement, with only 14 percent in accord, marking a 34 percentage difference between their concurrence and that of black women, which registered at 48 percent. The mean difference for blacks and whites is

significant at the .05 level. The mean difference between blacks and Latinos is not statistically significant. The mean difference between blacks and Latinos is statistically significant at the .05 level when testing unweighted data. The mean difference between Latinos and whites is not statistically significant.

20. Difference in means among all three groups is statistically significant at the .001 level.

21. Centers for Disease Control and Prevention, "HIV/AIDS Surveillance in Adolescents and Young Adults (through 2006) Slide Set," www.cdc.gov/hiv/topics/surveillance/resources/slides/adolescents/slides/Adolescents_10.pdf, and www.cdc.gov/hiv/topics/surveillance/resources/slides/adolescents/slides/Adolescents_11.pdf.

22. The difference in means between blacks and Latinos and blacks and whites is statistically significant at the .001 level. The difference in means between Latinos and whites is not statistically significant.

23. Devah Pager, Bruce Western, and Bart Bonikowski, "Race at Work: A Field Experiment of Discrimination in Low-wage Labor Markets," paper presented at Princeton University workshop, January 2008, www.law.virginia.edu/pdf/workshops/0708/pager.pdf.

24. The difference in means between blacks and whites is significant at the .001 level. The mean difference between blacks and Latinos is significant at the .01 level. The difference in means between whites and Latinos is not statistically significant.

25. Chicago Public School Web site, http://research.cps.k12.il.us/export/sites/default/accountweb/Reports/Citywide/isat_msexcel_cps_categories_2007_mexc.xls, link to excel sheet with data.

26. The difference in means between the three groups is not statistically significant when analyzing weighted data.

27. The difference in means between blacks and whites and Latinos and whites is statistically significant at the .001 level. The mean difference between blacks and Latinos is not statistically significant.

28. The mean difference between black males and white males is significant at the .01 level. The mean difference between black males and Latinos is just outside the range of statistical significance at .078. The mean difference between Latinos and white males is not statistically significant.

29. In-depth interviews, Black Youth Project. It is important to note that none of the survey statements or quotations mentioned in this discussion are meant to lessen the tragedy that is black youth killing other black youth. Similarly, attention to the interactions that have been labeled black-on-black crime should not lessen our commitment to stop the harassment of black youth by the police.

30. Emile Durkheim, *Suicide: A Study in Sociology*, trans. John Spaulding and John Simpson (New York: Free Press, 1951).

31. Cedric Herring, "Acquiescence or Activism? Political Behavior among the Politically Alienated," *Political Psychology* 10, 1 (1989): 135–53.

32. James S. House and William M. Mason, "Political Alienation in America, 1952–1968," *American Sociological Review* 40, 2 (1975): 123–47.

33. S. Bowles and H. Gintis, "The Crisis of Liberal Democratic Capitalism: The Case of the United States," *Politics and Society* 11 (1982): 51–93.

34. David Easton, *A System Analysis of Political Life* (New York: Wiley, 1965).

35. Jack Citrin, "Comment: The Political Relevance of Trust in Government," *American Political Science Review* 68 (1974): 973–88.

36. House and Mason, "Political Alienation in America," 145.

37. David Easton, "A Re-assessment of the Concept of Political Support," *British Journal of Political Science* 5, 4 (1975): 437.

38. Ibid., 445.

39. See, e.g., Lyons, "Political Socialization of Ghetto Children"; Greenberg, "Black Children and the Political System"; and Abramson, "Political Efficacy and Political Trust."

40. A similar argument is made by Gibson and Caldeira regarding the diffuse support of black Americans for the Supreme Court in response to the fact that only limited advances in civil rights were made under the Warren Court; James L. Gibson and Gregory A. Caldeira, "Blacks and the United States Supreme Court: Models of Diffuse Support," *Journal of Politics* 54, 4 (1992): 1120–45.

41. David Easton has argued for a systems approach to the understanding and study of the political system. Such an approach would capture the multiple dimensions of political life that are structured around the processing of inputs into outputs through a number of functional organizational entities. A much more elaborate discussion of this approach can be found in Easton, *A System Analysis of Political Life.*

42. John S. Jackson, "Alienation and Black Political Participation," *Journal of Politics* 35, 4 (1973): 849–85.

43. The mean difference for blacks and whites is significant at the .01 level. The mean difference between blacks and Latinos is not statistically significant. The mean difference between Latinos and whites is significant at the .05 level.

44. The mean difference for blacks and whites is significant at the .001 level. The mean difference between blacks and Latinos is not statistically significant. The mean difference between Latinos and whites is significant at the .01 level.

45. The mean difference between blacks and whites and Latinos and whites is significant at the .001 level. The mean difference between blacks and Latinos is significant at the .01 level.

46. The mean difference among the three groups is not statistically significant.

47. Jamila Celestine-Michener, project manager of the Black Youth Project, and Claudia Sandoval, a graduate student researcher on the project, were both significantly involved in the statistical analysis presented in this part of the chapter. The statistical technique used for this set of analyses was the ordered probit. Ordered probit was used because the dependent variables under examination are ordinal scored as a Likert scale.

48. The reliability or consistency score (Cronbach alpha) for the government orientation dimension of my political alienation concept is .663 for blacks, .728 for whites, and .754 for Latinos.

49. Sidney Verba, Kay Lehman Scholzman, and Henry E. Brady, *Voice and Equality: Civic Voluntarism in American Politics* (Cambridge, MA: Harvard University Press, 1995).

50. For more on this term see note 16 of chapter 3.

51. Composite score from two questions asking whether the respondent or his or her parent(s) were born outside the United States.

52. Composite score from two questions assessing how often the respondent listens to rap music and watches rap music videos. This variable is a possible alternative or oppositional source of information about the government and the political system.

53. Composite score from four questions asking respondents how often they have experienced discrimination based on their race, sex, socioeconomic class, or age.

54. See, e.g., Verba et al., *Voice and Equality*; Robert D. Putnam, *Bowling Alone: The Collapse and Revival of American Community* (New York: Touchstone, 2000); and Steven J. Rosenstone and John Mark Hansen, *Mobilization, Participation and Democracy in America* (New York: Longman, 2002).

55. Composite score from two questions: "How often do you attend religious services?" and "How often do you engage in activities at your place of worship?"

56. Level of agreement with the statement "I believe that by participating in politics I can make a difference."

57. The degree to which black youth believe that what happens to most black people in this country affects them.

58. I assume everything else is at its mean.

59. Robert Samuels, "It's a Boxer Rebellion over Opa-locka's Saggy Pants Ban," *Miami Herald*, October 15, 2007; Niko Koppel, "Are Your Jeans Sagging? Go Directly to Jail," *New York Times*, August 30, 2007.

60. Bethany Thomas, "Memo to Britney: Lose the Low-Slungs: La. Lawmakers Weigh Banning Belly-baring, Bottom-peeking Pants," May 13, 2004, www.msnbc.msn.com/id/4963512/?GT1=3391.

61. City Room, "Students Settle with Bar Accused of Racial Discrimination, Chicago Public Radio, "News in Brief," October 29, 2009, http://www .wbez.org/Content.aspx?audioID=37763.

62. Chris Harris and Sway Calloway, "Barack Obama Weights in on Sagging-pants Ordinances: 'Brothers Should Pull Up Their Pants,'" November 3, 2008, www.mtv.com/news/articles/1598462/20081103/story.jhtml.

63. Clyde Haberman, "Can Obama Help Kill Baggy Pants Look?" *New York Times*, November 14, 2008.

64. Koppel, "Are Your Jeans Sagging?"

65. Entry on November 25, 2007, in *The Trail: A Daily Diary of Campaign 2008*, http://blog.washingtonpost.com/the-trail/2007/11/25/post_212.html.

66. For more information about the MCPCE Study and its findings see note 4 of chapter 1.

67. Approximately 370 of the respondents were aged 18–25: 91 whites, 76 blacks, 144 Latinos, and 59 Asians.

68. The reader should know that although respondents in the MCPCE Study were asked the same questions as were those who participated in the Black Youth Project, the answer structure was different for each study. The Black Youth Project provided for answers of "strongly agree," "agree," "disagree,"

or "strongly disagree." The MCPCE Study included the additional answer "neither agree nor disagree," and in fact a significant number of respondents choose that option: 42 percent of whites, 38 percent of blacks, 44 percent of Latinos, and 48 percent of Asians of our respondents aged 18–25.

69. When we reanalyze the Black Youth Project data using only the respondents aged 18–25, our original findings hardly change: 57 percent of blacks, 80 percent of whites, and 71 percent of Latinos feel like full and equal citizens.

70. When we compared these findings to an analysis of Black Youth Project data using only respondents aged 18–25, the contrast between the Mobilization study and the original Black Youth Project findings remain. Among those aged 18–25 in the Black Youth Project, 51 percent of blacks, 51 percent of whites, and 55 percent of Latinos agreed in 2005 that everyone has an equal chance to succeed.

71. Cornel West, *Race Matters* (Boston: Beacon Press, 1993), 12.

72. In-depth interviews, Black Youth Project.

Chapter 5

1. Howard Witt, "Racial Demons Rear Heads: After Months of Unrest Between Blacks and Whites in Louisiana Town, Some See Racism and Uneven Justice," *Chicago Tribune*, May 20, 2007, www.chicagotribune.com/news/nationworld/chi-elf2u1mmay20,0,5086697.story.

2. Wade Goodwyn, "Beating Charges Split La. Town along Racial Lines," *All Things Considered*, NPR, July 30, 2007, www.npr.org/templates/story/story.php?storyId=12353776.

3. Ibid.

4. Ibid.

5. Jesse Rae Beard was charged as a juvenile since he was 14 at the time of the attack.

6. "Victim in Jena Six Case Takes the Stand," Associated Press, July 2, 2007, www.katc.com/Global/story.asp?S=6719374.

7. Melissa Harris-Lacewell, *Barbershops, Bibles, and BET: Everyday Talk and Black Political Thought* (Princeton, NJ: Princeton University Press, 2006).

8. "Court Overturns Conviction in Jena Beating: Judge Rules Teen Should Not Have Been Tried as an Adult in Racially Tinged Case," Associated Press, September 15, 2007, www.msnbc.msn.com/id/20779755/. Prior to the decision by the Third Curcuit Court to overturn his conviction, Bell's conspiracy conviction was also vacated by Judge J. P. Mauffray, who heard Bell's case, on the grounds that conspiracy was not a charge on which a juvenile could be tried as an adult.

9. Talea Miller, "Jena Six Rally Highlights Racial Tensions," *Newshour Extra*, September 24, 2007, www-tc.pbs.org/newshour/extra/features/july-dec07/jena_9-24.pdf.

10. "Protestors March in Support of Jena Six," *Day to Day*, NPR, September 20, 2007, www.npr.org/templates/story/story.php?storyId=14556993.

11. See "Remaining 'Jena 6' Are FREE," www.blackpressusa.com/News/Article
.asp?SID=3&Title=National+News&NewsID=19148.
12. For more information about the MCPCE Study and its findings see note 4 of
chapter 1.
13. This Obama postelection focus group with ten black youth aged 18–24
from Chicago was conducted on the South Side of Chicago. Cathy J. Cohen
was principal investigator; Lisa Gaines McDonald of Research Explorers
facilitated the focus group.
14. U.S. Census Bureau, Population Division, Education and Social Stratification
Branch, "Voting and Registration in the Election of November 2004" (April
8, 2005), table 2, www.census.gov/population/www/socdemo/voting/cps2004.
html.
15. Martin Wattenberg, *Is Voting for Young People?* (New York: Pearson Longman,
2008), 99.
16. U.S. Census Bureau, Current Population Survey, November 2006 (and
earlier reports), table A-1, "Reported Voting and Registration by Race,
Hispanic Origin, Sex, and Age Groups: November 1964 to 2006"; data
reported in these tables have the total U.S. age and race population as
the denominator. This type of analysis allows for consistency in reporting
between data from the Black Youth Project and earlier data from Current
Population Survey but also leads to smaller percentages of turnout and
registration than data that use the citizen population, which is smaller than
the total group-specific population, in the denominator.
17. Ibid.
18. Mark Hugo Lopez and Emily Kirby, *Electoral Engagement among Minority
Youth* (Center for Information and Research on Civic Learning and
Engagement, 2005).
19. Katherine Tate, *"From Protest to Politics"* (Cambridge, MA: Harvard
University Press, 1993).
20. Palma J. Strand, "Forced to Bowl Alone," *Nation*, January 23, 2003,
www.thenation.com/doc/20030210/strand/2; Mark Hugo Lopez, Emily
Kirby, Jared Sagoff, and Chris Herbst, *The Youth Vote 2004 with a Historical
Look at Youth Voting Patterns 1972–2004*, working paper 35 (Center for
Information and Research on Civic Learning and Engagement, July 2005), 2.
Lopez and Kirby, *Electoral Engagement*.
21. Other sources, for example the Center for Information and Research on
Civic Learning and Engagement (CIRCLE), estimate the turnout among
young people slightly higher. They report that 47 percent of African-
American youth aged 18–24 voted in 2004, compared to 49.5 percent
of white youth and 33 percent of Latino youth. The increase in voting,
according to CIRCLE, was largest among African-American youth, who
showed an increase of 11 percent in those voting. One reason for the
discrepancy in numbers probably has to do with the fact that numbers
I report from the Census use U.S. residents to calculate voting turnout,
whereas the numbers that CIRCLE reports represent U.S. citizens. See
Lopez and Kirby, *Electoral Engagement*.

22. In 2006, the U.S. Census Bureau reported that 19 percent of black youth aged 18–24 voted, with a corresponding 24 percent of white, non-Hispanic youth going to the polls. Ten percent of both Asian and Latino youth voted in 2006. See U.S. Census Bureau, "Reported Voting and Registration by Race, Hispanic Origin, Sex, and Age Groups."

23. U.S. Census Bureau, "Voting and Registration in the Election of November 2004."

24. A significant number of Latino youth are not eligible to vote because of immigration issues and may face information barriers if political literature and mobilization efforts are not communicated in Spanish.

25. Timing may account for the lower rates of vote reporting among our black and Latino respondents. Our survey was fielded almost a year after the 2004 presidential election. It may be that during that time, some respondents did not remember whether they voted, although they were given the option to indicate that they did not know if they voted. Another possibility is that with the passage of time, respondents felt less pressured to report voting in the highly watched and contested presidential election of 2004. It may be that our numbers represent a more accurate representation of actual turnout. All of this is speculation and can be resolved only by validating turnout reports, something most surveys do not do.

26. Steven J. Rosenstone and John Mark Hansen, *Mobilization, Participation, and Democracy in America* (New York: Macmillan, 1993).

27. Frederick C. Harris, *Something Within: Religion in African-American Political Activism* (New York: Oxford University Press, 1999).

28. Cathy J. Cohen and Michael C. Dawson, "Neighborhood Poverty and African American Politics," *American Political Science Review* 87 (June 1993): 286–302.

29. Michael C. Dawson, *Behind the Mule: Race and Class in African-American Politics* (Princeton, NJ: Princeton University Press, 1994).

30. All the findings detailed below assume that all other factors included in our model, except for the one variable or characteristic being discussed, are the same for all respondents being compared; thus, we claim all other factors are constant.

31. U.S. Census Bureau, "Voter Turnout Increases by 5 Million in 2008 Presidential Election" (July 20, 2009), press release, in *U.S. Census Bureau Reports*, CB09-110, www.census.gov/Press-Release/www/releases/archives/voting/013995.html.

32. Emily Hoban Kirby and Kei Kawashima-Ginsberg, "The Youth Vote in 2008," fact sheet, Center for Information and Research on Civic Learning and Engagement, April 2009.

33. Again, numbers reporting the percentage of citizens who voted will be larger than those who report the percentage of the total population who voted, since some in the population are not citizens and therefore are generally not allowed to register and vote.

34. U.S. Census Bureau, Current Population Survey, November 2008, table 2, "Reported Voting and Registration by Race, Hispanic Origin, Sex, and Age for the United States: November 2008" (November 2008), www.census.gov/population/www/socdemo/voting/cps2008.html.

35. In studies of reported voting without validation of what is reported, it has been shown that a significant number of respondents misrepresent their voting, indicating that they voted when they did not.

36. See note 13. The quotations that follow in this section are all from this focus group.

37. Mark Hugo Lopez, Peter Levine, Deborah Both, Abby Kiesa, Emily Kirby, and Karlo Marcelo, *The 2006 Civic and Political Health of the Nation: A Detailed Look at How Youth Participate in Politics and Communities* (Center for Information and Research on Civic Learning and Engagement, October 2006).

38. See, for example, Robert D. Putnam, *Bowling Alone: The Collapse and Revival of American Community* (New York: Simon and Schuster, 2000).

39. See "William J. Jefferson," *New York Times*, August 5, 2009, http://topics .nytimes.com/top/reference/timestopics/people/j/william_j_jefferson/ index.html?inline=nyt-per.

40. Putnam, *Bowling Alone*.

41. Young people in the Black Youth Project survey who indicated they had no current or past religion with which they identified were not asked questions about attendance at religious service or civic activity through their place of worship. We lost no more than 5 percent of each sample group to this skip pattern.

42. I use the Black Youth Project data because it offers more respondents for my analysis here.

43. I have used here an ordered probit statistical analysis, as I have throughout the book, to gain some insight into the characteristics associated with those with little to no political voice.

44. All findings and tables with an (*) are based on a significance level of .1.

45. It is important to remember that very few young blacks are intensely aligned with the Republican party.

46. Mary Pattillo, *Black on the Block: The Politics of Race and Class in the City* (Chicago: University of Chicago Press, 2007).

Chapter 6

1. Matt Bai, "Is Obama the End of Black Politics?" *New York Times*, August 2, 2008, www.nytimes.com/2008/08/10/magazine/10politics-t .html?pagewanted=1&_r=1&ei=5070&en=92c1d43f9a7ce60f&ex=1218772800&emc=eta1.

2. Charles M. Blow, "No More Excuses?" *New York Times*, January 23, 2009, www.nytimes.com/2009/01/24/opinion/24blow.html?emc=tnt&tntemail1=y.

3. J. Phillip Thompson III, *Double Trouble: Black Mayors, Black Communities, and the Call for a Deep Democracy* (New York: Oxford University Press, 2006), 4.

4. U.S. Bureau of the Census, "Studies in Measurement of Voter Turnout," Current Population Reports Special Studies, ser. P-23, no. 168, November 1990, http://www.census.gov/hhes/www/socdemo/voting/publications/other/ p23/p23-168/index.html

5. Thompson, *Double Trouble*, 4.

6. Bai, "Is Obama the End of Black Politics?"

7. Thompson, *Double Trouble*, 4.

8. "Congressional Black Caucus," http://majoritywhip.house.gov/index .cfm?p=MemberCaucuses.

9. See "National Black Political Convention Collection 1972–73," *Indiana Historical Society*, May 29, 1998, www.indianahistory.org/library/manuscripts/ collection_guides/sc2643.html#BIOGRAPHICAL.

10. Adolph Reed, Jr., *Stirrings in the Jug: Black Politics in the Post-segregated Era* (Minneapolis: University of Minnesota Press, 1999).

11. Thompson, *Double Trouble*, 6.

12. Ibid., 11.

13. Benjamin Wallace-Wells, "The Great Black Hope: What's Riding on Barack Obama?" *Washington Monthly*, November 2004, http://findarticles.com/p/ articles/mi_m1316/is_11_36/ai_n7070004/?tag=content;col1.

14. Ben Wallace-Wells, "Obama's Narrator," *New York Times Magazine*, April 1, 2007, www.nyt.com/2007/04/01/magazine/01axelrod.t.html?pagewanted=print.

15. Wallace-Wells, "Great Black Hope."

16. Some readers may remember that Bill Clinton, in June 1992, while speaking at an Operation Push event, attacked rap artist, activist, and author Sista Souljah for her statements about racism, www.huffingtonpost.com/ catherine-crier/obamas-sister-souljah-mom_b_99138.html.

17. Ben Wallace-Wells, "Obama's Narrator," *New York Times*, April 1, 2007, http://query.nytimes.com/gst/fullpage.html?res=9A0CE6DA1230F932A3575 7C0A9619C8B63&sec=&spon=&pagewanted=3.

18. Ibid., 4.

19. "Barack Obama's Keynote Address at the 2004 Democratic National Convention," *Online NewsHour*, July 27, 2004, www.pbs.org/newshour/ vote2004/demconvention/speeches/obama.html.

20. Ibid.

21. Ibid.

22. Ibid.

23. Ibid.

24. Ibid.

25. Ibid.

26. Mark Shields, "Critique Immediately Following Obama's '04 Convention Speech," PBS, March 11, 2008, video, www.youtube.com/watch?v=QEzrJ-k9vHo.

27. Jeremiah Wright, "GOD DAMN AMERICA: Reverend Jeremiah Wright, Farrakhan & Obama" March 14, 2008, video, www.youtube.com/watch?v= 9hPR5jnjtLo&feature=related.

28. Jeremiah Wright, "BARACK OBAMA Pastor ANTI-AMERICAN Rev Jeremiah Wright Racism" March 16, 2008, video, www.youtube.com/ watch?v=hwQWuQVE6sw.

29. Jeremiah Wright, "GOD DAMN AMERICA: Reverend Jeremiah Wright, Farrakhan & Obama" March 14, 2008, video, www.youtube.com/ watch?v=9hPR5jnjtLo.

30. Barack H. Obama, "A More Perfect Union," repr. in *The Speech: Race and Barack Obama's "A More Perfect Union,"* ed. T. Denean Sharpley-Whiting (New York: Bloomsbury, 2009), 237.
31. Ibid., 238.
32. Ibid.
33. Ibid., 239.
34. Ibid., 240.
35. Ibid., 242.
36. Ibid., 244.
37. Ibid., 246.
38. Ibid., 247.
39. Ibid.
40. Ibid., 248.
41. Ibid., 249.
42. Ibid., 246–47.
43. john a. powell, "Symposium: The Needs of Members in a Legitimate Democratic State," *Santa Clara Law Review* 44 (2004): 969.
44. Ibid.

Epilogue

1. Tamara Draut, "Economic Statue of Young America," published by Demos: A Network for Ideas and Action (Spring 2008), www.demos.org/pubs/esya_web.pdf.
2. "Left Behind in America: The Nation's Dropout Crisis," published by The Center for Labor Market Studies at Northeastern University in Boston and the Alternative Schools Network in Chicago, May 5, 2009, www.clms.neu.edu/publication/documents/CLMS_2009_Dropout_Report.pdf.
3. Preeti Mangala Shekar and Tram Nguyen, "Who Gains from the Green Economy," *Colorlines*, March 29, 2008, http://news.newamericamedia.org/news/view_article.html?article_id=35f362176e74c7b6b1e98799f86444d6.
4. Center for Law and Social Policy. *CLASP's Workforce Education and Training Policy Recommendations to Promote Inclusive Economic Recovery,"* January 12, 2009, www.clasp.org/admin/site/publications/files/0451.pdf.
5. Jonathan F. Zaff, James Youniss, and Cynthia M. Gibson. *An Inequitable Invitation to Citizenship: Non-College Bound Youth and Civic Engagement*, PACE, October 2009.
6. Ibid.

Index